WILDFLOWER

WILDFLOWER

An "American Daughter"

A Chinese "Black Bastard"

Ann Lee Peebles

The stories in this book reflect the author's recollection of events. Some names, locations, and identifying characteristics have been changed to protect the privacy of those depicted. Dialogue has been re-created from memory.

Published by Amazon Publishing (APub)

www.apub.com

ISBN-13: 978-1-7347957-0-7 (paperback)

Cover design by William A Peebles

Printed in the United States of America

Dedicated to my grandmother; her unconditional love sustained me throughout my difficult life in China.

Most importantly this book is dedicated to my high school classmates. We were a group of bright, vigorous teenagers when we entered high school. We had exciting dreams of the future and were filled with youthful hope. When we left high school, our dreams had been shattered and our hopes destroyed. I hope I have done them justice.

Contents

Author's Note

The stories in this book reflect the author's recollection of events. Some names, locations, and identifying characteristics have been changed to protect the privacy of those depicted. Dialogue has been re-created from memory.

Some Chinese poems and phrases were retained in Chinese form with English translation. I hope this will allow a greater appreciation by those who read both Chinese and English.

Family Tree

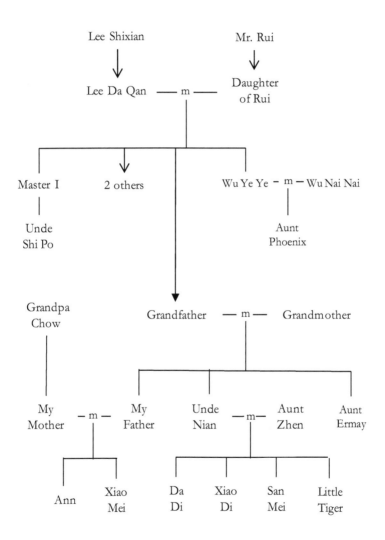

The Move to South Gate

It was a cloudy, early-summer day in 1952. The air was filled with humidity and drizzle. A thunderstorm threatened to soon arrive. I was only five years of age and was with Grandmother, my sister Xiao Mei, and cousin Da Di. We were walking along an unpaved road from West Gate to South Gate in the little Chinese town of Yiyang. I had been told that we were leaving our big house in West Gate and moving to a much smaller house in South Gate. My sister and cousin were both only 4 years of age. I often wondered whether they understood what was happening at that time.

As we walked, we were all complaining to Grandmother that we were very tired, that our feet hurt and we just couldn't walk anymore!

Grandmother comforted us by saying, "My sweethearts, don't worry. We are almost there!"

From West Gate to South Gate was about 1 mile, along a muddy road. Finally, we arrived at the South Gate Bridge.

Grandmother said, "Let's take a rest and sit on the riverbank until our boat passes."

The boat Grandmother mentioned had been borrowed from relatives in a small village, God Pond Valley, where her parental clan lived. The boat carried our furniture from West Gate to our new home in South Gate. We

1

were too young to understand the reason for the move. However, the sailboats in the river caught our attention, and we were happy and eager to sit down and rest for a while.

Yiyang was a small town in Jiangsu Province. A river called Hucheng River (护城河) encircled the inner-town. It was a typical Chinese town where a river moved around the inner-town and, next to the river, a town-wall had been built long ago to protect against enemy attack. There were four gates (North, East, West, and South) with four bridges that linked the inner town to the regions outside. The inner town was mostly occupied by the town hall and office buildings, and the majority of people lived in the outskirts of town. There were also vast rice fields surrounding the town. The town-wall was all but gone with only a few larger stones still lying around here and there. No new structures had been constructed to replace the damaged ancient wall. I was told later that, during the Japanese-Chinese war, the wall and most of the town itself were destroyed by Japanese bombs. Over the years the bridges had been periodically rebuilt and repaired. At this time, in 1952, the river still flowed and the four bridges still carried people and traffic between the inner-town and the regions outside.

Our original family home was located just outside the West Gate facing the river. The West Side was considered an affluent neighborhood, whereas the South Side was a neighborhood where poorer people lived.

My grandfather had owned a factory, Xin Yuan, which produced cooking oil and soybean products. We had occupied a large family complex on the West Side. I vaguely remember that there was a storefront at the entrance of the compound. Our clerks used to work there to greet customers and sell cooking oil, soybean products, wine, and the like. Behind the store, there was a courtyard paved with smooth gray bricks. To the left side of the yard were the offices. In these offices, my grandfather and his managers conducted their business. According to Grandmother, at the rear of the courtyard was a large two-story building. The downstairs was used for storage, where large ceramic containers were filled with oil and wine. The upstairs provided living quarters for the workers together with a small room, called the incense room, used by Grandfather for religious purposes.

The compound extended farther to the left, where there was another two-story building. This building was separated from the first by a small courtyard. Our family occupied the left wing of this building. In the rear were several storage rooms together with a large kitchen. Two chefs cooked and provided food for both the workers and our family. A large hallway separated the kitchen from the living quarters. Although our house would be considered primitive by today's standards, at that time, in this little town, it was considered a luxurious compound of a wealthy family. Even then, it was reasonably modern with hardwood floors and glass windows.

At the rear of the compound was a huge backyard that housed the processing factory. The backyard also contained a man-made pond and provided space to dry the soybeans that local farmers delivered to us. The soybeans were used to make cooking oil. The backyard always seemed a mysterious and sinister place to me — I seldom visited the backyard. The adults used to tell us there was a huge, ferocious monster there. In reality, they probably worried that, if we wandered into the backyard, we might fall into the pond and drown! The entire compound occupied approximately 2 acres.

Now we were moving from that large family compound! I was a 5-year-old innocent child. However, I had noticed that Grandmother, during that time, often cried. The riverbank where we rested was somewhat in ruins. We were sitting on a large rectangular stone near the bridge, patiently waiting for our boat. Across the river, houses lined the river's bank. Between the houses were stone staircases that allowed residents to use river water for washing clothes and cleaning vegetables. It was a typical ancient, shabby, water town.

As we looked out on the river, Grandmother suddenly shouted, "Here comes our boat!"

A small boat about 10 to 15 feet long without a sail suddenly appeared in the distance. At the front of the boat Grandmother's younger brother, Granduncle, pushed the boat forward using a long wooden pole, while, at the rear, one of her nephews used a similar pole to steer the boat.

On the boat were a couple of mattresses made of fiber from palm tree bark and a few pieces of old furniture in poor condition. There was also an old wooden door that Aunt Zhen had begged the Liberation Army to allow her to take. It would become Aunt Zhen's bedroom door — the only door in our new home. It was a very modest amount of furniture — all that was allowed by the new Communist regime. We waited and watched as the boat passed by under the bridge, then we started across the bridge and walked towards our future home.

Our new home was located in a small complex that branched off Dayin Lane, a small side street from the main South Gate Road. When we entered our new home, there was nothing but a single, empty room. Altogether, the room occupied less than 400 square feet. It consisted of a compacted dirt floor — no cement, no hardwood. Also, there was no ceiling. When you looked up, you simply saw the gray roof tiles. There were three sets of triangular wood beams supporting the roof. On the left side of the room, a wall was built up from the floor, which stopped near the base of one of the triangular beams. We were told that another family would soon occupy the space on the other side of this wall. On the right side of the room, there was a solid wall. A small opening in the wall allowed a single person to enter another small section of the house — an add-on room occupying roughly 60 square feet. It was clear that life would be very different in this new home.

During the months leading up to the move, our family had continuously been tormented by the new Communist regime. This was because Grandfather was a member of a religious group called Yi Guan Dao. He had joined for spiritual support during a business downturn. After the Communists took over, the Campaign to Suppress Counter-revolutionaries (镇压反革命) in 1951 led to Yi Guan Dao being condemned as an anti-revolutionary cult. Since then our household had come under siege.

The Lee Family

My grandfather was one of the five sons of my great-grandfather, Lee Da Qan, who started life as a lowly salesman. Lee Da Qan worked for a small business that made soybean curd. His job was to sell bean curd to the local village farmers.

It is said that my great-grandfather was actually the son of the Attendant King (King of Shi 侍王), Lee Shixian, of the Taiping Heavenly Kingdom, who died before my great-grandfather's birth.

Lee Shixian (李世贤) lived from 1834 to 1865. He was a distinguished military leader during the late years of the Taiping Rebellion. He was known as the cousin of military leader Lee Xiucheng, the Loyal King. Lee Shixian was a native of Guangxi Province and grew up in a poor peasant family. In 1851, at the age of only 17, he joined the Taiping Rebellion. During the middle of the Taiping Rebellion, he led Taiping forces to many military victories and was given the title, King of Shi (侍王).

In 1860, Lee Shixian and his army were stationed in Yiyang until it was overcome in 1864. During 1864, Nanjing, the capital of the Taiping Kingdom at that time, was besieged by the Qing Imperial force led by Li Hongzhang, and the elite Ever Victorious Army, led by European officers Frederick Townsend Ward and Charles Gordon. General Gordon, a British officer, decided to cut through the heart of the rebellion and capture Yiyang. After fierce fighting, the town of Yiyang eventually surrendered. After the fall of Yiyang, Lee Shixian and his remaining supporters escaped towards Fujian, where he was eventually assassinated by a traitor in Guangdong.

Meanwhile, Lee Shixian's pregnant wife remained in Yiyang and eventually wandered to An-Zhong village. This was the village of the Lee family clan and the birthplace of my great-grandfather, Lee Da Qan, who was raised in An-Zhong village by his widowed mother. His poor upbringing turned him into a hard-working young man. Every day, Lee Da Qan carried bean curd with a bamboo shoulder pole. Each end of the pole was loaded with heavy bean curd. He walked miles from village to village selling bean curd.

It is said one day he was in a village called God Pond Valley, where Mr. Rui, a landlord, lived. Mr. Rui saw Mr. Lee as a fine young man. My great-grandfather had a broad, handsome face and was filled with a bright spirit. Motivated by the boy's "rich" face, Mr. Rui was convinced the boy would be successful and have a prosperous future. After only a couple of conversations, Mr. Rui decided that his only daughter should marry the boy! Great-grandfather was delighted.

After the marriage, with Mr. Rui's financial help, my great-grandfather soon acquired his own bean curd business. As Mr. Rui predicted, the business soon became very successful and grew larger over time. With the money earned from the business, my great-grandfather accumulated large areas of land and subsequently became the biggest landlord in the county.

The happy couple produced five sons and two daughters. My grandfather was the fourth son. By the time my great-grandfather passed away, the Lee family not only owned a vast amount of land, but also had acquired silk, cooking oil, and soybean curd businesses. My grandfather inherited the cooking oil business, named Xin Yuan, located near the outskirts of Yiyang town. The first, second, and fifth sons inherited land, and the first and third sons were given the silk business.

Xin Yuan's business continued to boom even during World War II. During this wartime period, my father and my aunt and uncles all escaped to Sichuan with their schools. Sichuan was a province in southwest China. After the war, they all returned safely to Yiyang. My grandparents were blessed with good fortune and happiness.

In 1947, Grandfather decided to expand his business into wine production. However, there was already a wine business in town, named Zhen Chang Inc. As soon as Grandfather opened his wine business, Zhen Chang Inc. aggressively slashed their prices to try to squeeze Xin Yuan out of business. Under such fierce competition, Xin Yuan quickly started to lose money and accumulate a large debt. Under such tremendous stress, in 1948, my grandfather had a breakdown, and, in search of peace, joined a religious group named Yi Guan Dao. Very soon he experienced peace and so continued to focus all his time and energy on his religion. This forced Grandmother to take care of the daily business. She decided to end the wine production operation and concentrate on the inherited core business — the manufacture and sale of soybean products. Finally, in 1949, the business started to recover.

However, there is an old Chinese saying that goes, "Flowers do not always bloom, and the moon is not always round and bright" — that is, good things do not last forever. So it was in our family. The good days did not continue. In 1949, the Communist army crossed the Yangtze River and conquered the entire country. After the revolution, during land reform, my grandfather's oldest (Master I) and youngest (Master V) brothers were condemned as landlords by the newly established Communist government. My grandfather's second brother (Master II) also inherited land but died before the Communists took over. So, in his place, his wife was condemned since she was the landlord's wife. Master III was assassinated by bandits during the Japanese-Chinese war. After his death, the silk business soon became bankrupt. It was a really sad period for the Master III family; but fortune ebbs and flows, and on this occasion, Master III's family was spared from the Communist government purge. Unfortunately, our family would continue to be cursed with the scourge of the Yi Guan Dao.

My Maternal grandparents (Chow)

My parent's wedding picture

Aunt Ermay · Mother's first Stepmother

My paternal grandmother and children
front left, Da Di; front right, Da Mei (Ann);
back right, Xiao Di; back center, Xiao Mei; back
left, distant cousin

Mother and Ann   My nanny and Ann

My paternal grandmother and children
Front left, Xiao Mei; Front right, Da Mei(Ann)
Back left, Xiao Di; Back right, Da Di

Xiao Mei and Da Mei(Ann), first day school

Family picture
from left: Da Mei (Ann), Xiao Mei, Aunt
Zhen, San Mei, Uncle Nian, Xiao Di, Da Di

My Relatives

Grandfather was a leading member of the religious group called Yi Quan Dao. In early 1951, Grandfather suddenly disappeared for a couple of days without informing Grandmother, who thought he might have gone to stay with his concubine. Grandfather had a concubine who lived in a separate house together with their son, whom we called Uncle He-Shen. Grandmother was angry and jealous. When Grandfather returned, she kept nagging and complaining.

That night, Grandfather told Grandmother, "Ermay's Mom, please don't be mad with me!" Ermay was their oldest daughter and my aunt. He sighed. "One day, when I am gone, you will regret your words tonight. I have a doctor's appointment in Shanghai tomorrow. When I am away, take care of the family. You and the family are the most important things in my life."

These sudden, unexpected appeals to Grandmother immediately aroused her suspicion. She thought to herself, *He seemed so sentimental tonight. He's never this type of person. He's been to Shanghai many times, so what's the big deal this time?*

Next day Grandfather left home for good! Grandmother never saw Grandfather again. Then, a few days later, Yi Quan Dao was declared a counter-revolutionary religious cult by the Communist government. Two Yi Quan Dao leaders, Dr. Hsu and Mr. Chen, were condemned as counter-revolutionary and were immediately executed on the spot in the middle of town. Their homes were searched, and their entire family properties confiscated. Rumors circulated that Grandfather had received an early warning of the purge from their God. He was told danger was pressing and he must leave at once.

A year later, Grandmother received a letter from Hong Kong. The letter was written as if it had come from Aunt Ermay, who had been living in Shanghai when the Communists took power. She had many foreign connections and friends in Shanghai and realized the urgency to leave, as did many Shanghai residents at that time. My aunt evacuated to Hong Kong as a refugee.

Although the letter was signed as if from Aunt Ermay, Grandmother immediately recognized Grandfather's neat brush scripts. The letter indicated that "she" was in Hong Kong and was safe. "She" was sorry to leave home in such a hurry and asked Grandmother to take good care of herself and the family. Grandmother realized that Grandfather had escaped to Hong Kong. She was both relieved and sad. She mentioned many times that if she had known that night was the last one with Grandfather, she would have acted very differently. Grandmother buried her sadness and regret deep inside until her death.

After the purge of Dr. Hsu and Mr. Chen's households, Grandmother and Aunt Zhen realized that we would be next. Aunt Zhen was the wife of my father's younger brother, Uncle Nian. She had grown up in a business family. Her mother had died when she was only 9 years old. She had two older brothers and two sisters. Due to the early loss of her mother, she had become very independent with a shrewd business sense. She was astute, quick-witted, and somewhat selfish. Before she married into our household, as a teenage girl, she had already become quite wealthy. She traded cotton products for gain, and then loaned money at high interest rates to those in need. In response to the possibility of a purge, Aunt Zhen started to gather all her worldly possessions into two large trunks. There were also two trunks of fur coats and picture albums that were left by my mother.

My mother was born into the wealthy and influential Chow family in Hangzhou in 1920. Her father, Tsung Hua Chow (周宗华), graduated from Peiyang University, which is now known as Tianjin University, the first modern university in China. In 1906, he was then sent by the Qing government to America and enrolled at Brown University. Later he transferred to Yale University and graduated with a PhB in 1908. In 1909 he entered the University of Chicago Law School and received his JD in 1912. Upon graduation, he returned to China and was appointed Chinese

Assistant District Inspector at Shiherwei and later became the Director of Salt Administration. Before World War II, he had risen to Executive Officer of the China Central Bank in Shanghai.

After his return from America, he married my maternal biological grandmother. I was told that the young couple wanted to design and construct their own new home. Before the house was completed, my maternal grandmother became overly extended and died of pneumonia when Mother was only an infant. Mother was initially raised by housemaids and then a stepmother. She grew up with a wealthy and renowned father, but sadly with little love.

Mother's stepmother was college-educated and was also from a wealthy, but traditional, family. It was an arranged marriage. During the 1920s, Chinese society preferred girls to have little talent, but be virtuous (女子无才便是德), especially girls growing up in a traditional, high-class family. The stepmother had three children with Grandpa Chow. She focused her entire energy managing the household and taking care of the education of her children, including her two stepchildren.

At that time, due to his high position, many fellow workers flattered Grandpa Chow. One day Grandpa Chow was presented with a 16-year-old pretty girl to be his concubine. She was 24 years younger than Grandpa. Grandpa happily accepted the offer and purchased a house for the young girl without his wife's knowledge. For months, he hardly ever returned home for dinner. Eventually, his wife was informed that her husband was residing in a separate house with his young concubine.

In Chinese tradition of the time, a wife had no right to interfere with her husband's sexual life. A wife's duty was to serve her husband's needs! Of course, if things had been reversed, this would have been unacceptable. Mother's stepmother continued her duty and took care of all the children, but the disappointment and loneliness steadily took a toll on her. Her maids said that she often stayed alone in her room, bending and twisting her fingers constantly.

During the Japanese invasion of China, Grandpa Chow followed the government and retreated to Chongqing with his concubine and her children. My mother and her older sister also retreated to Chongqing with their school. Grandpa Chow left his wife and the younger children alone in Shanghai. Very soon afterwards she committed suicide and was found hanging inside a closet. In her will, she divided all her possessions into five equal shares. Each child inherited one share. Therefore, my mother, even though she was not her daughter, received a share equal to that of the younger blood siblings. As part of the inheritance, there was a large amount of gold for each child. Mother was always grateful to her stepmother for her kindness and fairness.

Prior to WWII, the Lee family had sent the children to pursue their higher education in Shanghai. Aunt Ermay, my father, and their older cousin Uncle Shi Po (Master I's son) attended college. The two younger ones, Uncle Nian and Uncle He-Shen, attended high school in Shanghai. After war broke out with Japan, Aunt Ermay and my father retreated with their colleges to Chengdu and took the two younger siblings with them. Uncle Shi Po was the oldest among them. He had secretly joined the Communist Party and went to Yan'an, which was a citadel of the Communist Party at the time.

During wartime, Grandpa Chow established a happy life in Chongqing. The young concubine was not only beautiful but also smart and attentive. They had five children together. Mother was never fond of the concubine and felt a strong resentment. She was longing for her father's affection, but seldom received it. She wandered around to different places and took her first job. The lonely young woman finally met Father in Chengdu, a major city in Sichuan Province.

Father was a charming and thoughtful young man. He was born November 11, 1917. During the war he was an instructor in the Chinese Air Force Technical School in Chengdu. In 1945, when the war ended with the defeat of Japan, Father was appointed as a liaison officer in The Advisory Team of the United States Air Force. Mother and Father fell in love, and Mother brought Father to meet Grandpa Chow. Grandpa Chow thought Father was a good-natured man and was very attentive toward Mother. Grandpa Chow thought Mother was a softie and needed some tender love. He told Mother that Father was the right one for her. My parents married on April 21, 1946, in Chengdu, and I was conceived while they were still in Chengdu.

The same year, they followed the KMT government and returned to Nanjing. Very soon Mother found a job in a savings bank in Nanjing. After their marriage, Mother continuously encouraged Father to study abroad — she wanted Father to follow in Grandpa Chow's footsteps.

After I was born, Grandmother sent a wet nanny and her niece to help the young couple. Her niece told Grandmother that Father loved to hold me and giggle with me. Mother kept shouting to Father, "Go back to study and prepare for the United States university entrance exam."

According to Grandmother, Mother felt she had a superior background to the Lee family. After she visited the Lee family for the first time, she found that her husband's family was only a low, business-class household in a small town. Mother was very disappointed. Mother was always proud of her elite family background.

When I was a couple of months old, nanny and Grandmother's niece complained to Grandmother that Mother had a very short temper and was very demanding. They could not take any more. Any small misfortune would lead to a totally disproportionate reaction from her. Young master, as they called my father, was always attentive to her, but in return she always responded that she should have never married into such a family. Mother had concluded that anyone from the Lee family would never be her equal.

Grandmother proposed to let nanny take me to Yiyang so that I could stay with the Lee family. Mother agreed. Maybe she thought I was a distraction from Father's studies. I prefer to think this way.

I was the long-awaited Lee family's first grandchild. When I was born, my father was 30 years old. At that time, marriage at 30 was considered to be very late. I was the precious princess of the family. My grandmother adored me. Later that year, Aunt Zhen also gave birth to a boy, my first cousin Da Di. In May 1948, my younger sister Xiao Mei was born. Grandmother sent a wet-nurse nanny to aid Mother a week before the birth of Xiao Mei. I heard from Grandmother and Aunt Zhen that Mother and Xiao Mei's nanny got along well. Father had obtained an acceptance letter to attend the University of Michigan in the USA. He left his family and sailed to the United States in 1948 when Xiao Mei was only 1 month old.

After the defeat of Japan, a full-scale civil war between the KMT (Kuomintang) and the Chinese Communist Party began. By the middle of 1948, many northern cities had fallen under Communist control. Fearing a Communist southward attack, Mother relocated her work to a branch of the bank located further south in the city of Hangzhou in Zhejiang Province. In fact, this was her family hometown where her father owned many mansions around West Lake. She had spent most of her childhood years in a lakeside mansion.

Before her job transfer to Hangzhou, Mother had sent Xiao Mei and her nanny to Yiyang. On October 1, 1949, when the Communist Party declared the birth of the People's Republic of China, Mother realized that Father's studies in Michigan would no longer be a temporary arrangement. Mother was desperate to get permission to leave China for the USA and reunite with Father. Eventually she received the permit to leave China and arrived in Hong Kong on April 1, 1950, where she had to apply for a visa to enter America.

In the meantime, the Lee family was expanding. In 1949, my second cousin Xiao Di was born. In addition to two chefs and a number of maids, there were also four nannies for the grandchildren. It was the happiest of times for Grandmother. After seeing the business take off successfully and gaining two grandsons and two granddaughters, she was able to spend time relaxing with the grandchildren and, of course, playing Mahjong. Aunt Zhen told me that Grandmother was very good at Mahjong! She would win most of the time. My nanny was crafty and took advantage of Grandmother's love for me. She often held me next to Grandmother and flattered her during the game. Once Grandmother had won the game, Grandmother would play with me and reward nanny with a portion of her winnings.

The Purge

There is no everlasting flower. The good times did not last long. The Suppression of Counter-Revolutionaries movement came to our hometown in 1951. All nannies were sent home. Fearing that a household search could occur at any time, Aunt Zhen tried to hide four trunks filled with valuables and personal effects, which she felt were important and worth saving. Two of these trunks, and their contents, belonged to Mother. Aunt Zhen immediately asked her relatives for help. Her older sister was too afraid to get involved and refused to help. Her second brother's wife was a member of Yi Quan Dao, so help from the second brother was out of the question.

For many years, her second brother and wife were unable to conceive a child. Grandfather suggested the wife join Yi Quan Dao so that their God could help. Very soon, they gave birth to two sons! After this blessed outcome, Aunt Zhen's sister-in-law became a faithful member of Yi Quan Dao. During the Suppression of Counter-Revolutionaries movement, she was classified as a counter-revolutionary and was placed under constant surveillance by the neighborhood committee. Throughout every Communist Party political movement, she would be singled out for public humiliation. In China this was known as a class struggle session (批斗大会)[1]. Insult and condemnation became part of her routine life. Even under these intolerable conditions, she never lost her faith in Yi Quan Dao.

Finally, Aunt Zhen begged her oldest brother for help. Her brother hesitated. Aunt Zhen cried out, "I have no mom and dad to help me. I am your sister! If you can't help me, who can?"

---

[1] 批斗大会 - class struggle session was a form of public humiliation and torture.

Finally, her brother agreed to take one of the trunks. Another trunk was hidden under a friendly worker's bed. The last two trunks, belonging to my mother, were carried into the house of Grandmother's niece.

The day we had feared was now upon us. The Liberation Army seized our house and removed all our belongings. We (my sister, my cousins, and I) were very young and did not understand what was going on around us. I vaguely remember being excited to see all the soldiers. We were singing the popular Korean War song: "holding our heads high with brave spirit, we cross the Yalu River" (雄赳赳，气昂昂，跨过鸭绿江).

During the purge, the Liberation Army found a bullet in Uncle and Aunt's dresser, and Uncle Nian was handcuffed and a gun placed to his head. He was immediately taken away by the soldiers. Uncle Nian had been arrested! Grandmother and Aunt Zhen were desperate and scared. The only thing they could do was cry. Although they had anticipated the raid, they could never have imagined the enormity of the impact. Tears filled their eyes. They felt hopeless and numb.

Next day, Grandmother was ordered to the Public Security Bureau to confess Grandfather's counter-revolutionary activity and reveal his connections. Grandmother sighed and claimed that she was never supportive of Yi Guan Dao. Grandfather had a concubine and seldom came home. She cried out, "I am only a neglected wife. I paid no attention to his activities and don't know any of his friends."

The officer smashed the desk with his fist and shouted at her, calling her a crafty, dishonest old woman. Grandmother was determined that she would not involve or hurt anyone else because of the chaos that was destroying her own family.

On the other hand, Uncle Nian's mind-set was desperate and he was completely out of control. Officers asked him, "We found a bullet in your dresser. Where is the gun?"

He claimed the bullet belonged to his father, and he didn't know what had happened to the gun. But the factory workers reported that they had never seen Grandfather carry a gun.

The officer said, "The bullet was found in your dresser. The gun must belong to you!"

Under all this pressure and threats, he told the officer that he had given the gun to one of his friends. Confused and desperate, he mentioned many names. All his friends denied the charge!

Aunt Zhen told me that Uncle Nian was a spoiled, rotten kid who never experienced any hardships. When he was a child, Grandfather arranged for a servant to carry him on his shoulders to ensure that he attended school. However, along the way, Uncle would jump off the servant's shoulders to escape school! During the Japanese invasion of China, my grandparents let Uncle Nian and Uncle He-Shen follow their older siblings to Chengdu for safety. Aunt Zhen said Father and Aunt Ermay were the only people Uncle Nian would listen to.

After the war, when he returned to Yiyang, Uncle Nian had grown up to be a 21-year-old young master, but showed no interest in the family business. He enjoyed Chinese opera and visited the theater often. He was a busy person — without a business! In 1946, with the Japanese war ended and back from Chengdu, he married Aunt Zhen. It was an arranged marriage. The marriage was well matched (门当户对). Both families were important, well-known business owners in Yiyang. Unfortunately, this innocent young man was destined to carry the family's guilty verdict on his shoulders for his entire life.

In fact, the gun belonged to Aunt Ermay's ex-husband who was an American. When Uncle Nian visited Aunt Ermay in Shanghai before the Communist takeover, he admired the gun so much that he asked Aunt Ermay if she would give it to him. Aunt Ermay gave the gun to Uncle Nian together with a bag of bullets. Prior to the Liberation Army search, Aunt Zhen had thrown the gun and the bag of bullets into the river on a dark night. Unfortunately, she missed one bullet.

Fearing for her husband's future and understanding that there were four children under her care, she thought the security officers would likely not want to harm her. Aunt Zhen was audacious and felt she had nothing left to lose, and so went to the security office. She cried, sniveling loudly, with tears flowing down her face. She explained that Uncle Nian was scared and was under tremendous pressure and so did not tell the truth. She claimed many KMT soldiers occupied the town as they were being defeated by the Communists and were retreating southwards. Some KMT rogues looted and stayed in our house. The bullet must have been left by them.

The officer told her it was a foreign gun. She refuted this argument, and asked why a KMT officer couldn't carry a foreign gun. She continued to scream and cry loudly. She repeated Communist policy — "Punish the guilty only." She said it was unfair to transfer the guilt of her father-in-law to her husband.

She cried out, "How can I take care of four young children and one older mother-in-law without my husband? I might as well die. I can't handle the situation anymore."

She refused to leave the security office. The officer was aware there were four toddlers, and Aunt Zhen was only a young woman without earning power. Finally, the officer told her they would look further into the matter. If no fault was attached to my uncle, they would release him.

To add insult to injury, someone had seen two trunks being carried out through the back gate before the purge. Unfortunately, after the purge, this was reported to the Public Security Bureau. The office immediately confiscated the trunks and condemned Aunt Zhen as dishonest and a bad element in society. Aunt Zhen argued that the trunks were not her property, but belonged to my mother. She contested that Mother was abroad and that she had responsibility to protect the trunks for the two young daughters.

During this early period of the People's Republic of China, the Public Security Bureau was run by young Communist Party members. Most of them were from reasonably wealthy families and were college educated, just like Uncle Shi Po. They became fed up with corruption at the KMT and years of foreign control of the motherland. In response they joined the Communist Party. They were somewhat softhearted and displayed some humanity.

They told Aunt Zhen, "If you can prove the trunks belong to your sister-in-law, then you can keep them."

Aunt wrote to Mother and asked her to declare that she owned the trunks. Mother wrote back, saying that she did not need the trunks as long as family members were safe. Mother did not understand the seriousness of the situation. She thought that if we gave up the property, we would be rewarded with peace! She was in Hong Kong and was anxiously waiting

21

for an American visa so that she could be reunited with Father. At this juncture in her life, these two trunks were unimportant to her. Aunt wrote again desperately urging her to admit ownership and indicating that without such action, Aunt would be severely punished for her dishonesty. Finally, Mother wrote to the Public Security Bureau and declared ownership.

Every year, during the summer, Grandmother and Aunt Zhen took these trunks out for airing. There were many fur coats. Aunt Zhen always said that someday she would alter them and make coats for the children and herself. Of course, at that time, Yiyang was under Communist control and nobody would ever dare to wear a fur coat.

One of the trunks contained many photo albums. Inside one of the albums, there was a wedding picture of Mother and Father. There were also pictures of Mother's relatives, including her father and birth mother. It was from these albums that I first came to know my father and mother. I always imagined that one day Mother and Father would suddenly appear in front of me and we would be happily reunited.

After confiscating our family property, we were formally denounced as an anti-revolutionary family. We were confined to our living quarters and were no longer able to walk around the family compound, including the kitchen. The chefs were no longer allowed to cook for us. A Workers' Union had formed under the Communist Party. Little Dragon, one of the workers, became the workers' leader. He was supposed to watch every movement of our family.

Our life had suddenly flipped from heaven to hell. Uncle Nian was still in jail. To support our family, Grandmother and Aunt Zhen started to wash clothes for the workers. Grandmother's nephew made a small stove to allow us to cook. The stove was made of mud. In the middle there was a pit that supported a wok. An opening along the side allowed fuel (wood or dried weeds) to be inserted under the wok. Every time, when we started cooking, smoke would spread all over the house.

Our factory produced soybean oil. The soybeans were poured into a cylindrical container, and a machine-driven cylinder would squeeze the oil out of the beans and leave a hard soybean residue cake. The soybean residue cake was about 1 foot in diameter and half an inch thick. These residue cakes would be sold to local farmers. Farmers would break down

22

the cake and cook it with water and other grain to feed their pigs. They were stacked in the hallway — golden in color and looking delicious, but very hard and dry to chew. We children started to nibble on them. The chefs felt so sorry for us. One evening, when the workers returned to their living quarters, one of the chefs snuck out a full wash basin of leftover cooked food.

He told Grandmother and Aunt, "Poor little kids, they are innocent. They did nothing wrong and should not be left to starve. Please empty the food into another container quickly and return the wash basin, so I can bring more food tomorrow. Don't let others see it."

Grandmother and Aunt Zhen were moved by his kindness. Tears welled up in their eyes, and sadness pressed their hearts. They never thought their lives would come to the point where they were pitied by their servants!

A female Communist comrade moved into Grandfather's worship room. The female comrade had started to organize a labor union and conducted meetings there every evening. In this room, Grandfather had conducted the Yi Quan Dao rituals.

Grandmother and Aunt Zhen worried about Uncle Nian who still remained in jail. Aunt Zhen was like a cornered dog, ready to jump the fence at any time. During many of the evening union meetings, Aunt Zhen would sneak close to the meeting room and listen to their conversations. She hoped she could gather some information about Uncle Nian.

Fallen from grace, Grandmother and Aunt Zhen washed clothes for workers to earn some money to support the family. We were always short of cooking fuel. Aunt Zhen started to sneak into the forbidden kitchen area to steal firewood during the night when the workers were sound asleep. Life was tough, but we managed to survive. Sadly, very soon, we were accused of listening to the workers' meetings, stealing state information, and causing a fire in the kitchen. We were ordered to move out of our own home and forced to relocate to South Gate.

We Settle in Dayin Lane

We settled in a side alley off Dayin Lane, South Gate. This alley continued toward the riverbank. Grandmother immediately put her brother, Granduncle, and her nephews to work. They separated the original rice storage unit (which was now to become our new home) into three sections. Simple weaved reeds were used to create two "walls" that were connected to pairs of wooden roof beams.

The left side of our new home became Aunt Zhen's room. Later, when we grew older, my sister, Xiao Mei, and I shared a small bed facing Aunt Zhen. Between the beds sat the famous dresser, where the bullet had been found. Aunt Zhen had asked the Liberation army to allow her to take the dresser with her. She argued that her parents had given her the dresser as dowry and so it didn't belong to her parents-in-law, therefore, it was not the property of an anti-revolutionary family.

A simple door had been erected for privacy. This was the only door inside our home, except for the main front door. No wonder Aunt Zhen begged for it as if her life was at stake. After all, a young woman needs a little privacy!

In the center of the house was the dining room/kitchen, where there was a wooden square table and four wooden benches. The benches were about 5 inches wide and 4 feet long and were arranged around the square table. This had previously been a dining set for workers at our old house that the Liberation army had allowed us to take to South Gate. Behind the dining set, there was a long, high, wooden console table that directly faced the front door. The paint had peeled off over time, and some wood had also been chipped away. We usually kept hot water thermos bottles on this table. In those days, hot water could be bought from a local hot water store. For 1 fen (=1/100 Yuan), you could fill your bottle with boiling hot water.

Granduncle and Grandmother's young nephews also built a double-wok cooking stove for us. The cooking stove was built with bricks and mud. There were two fuel pits, and two woks above the pits. In between the pits was a chimney to allow smoke to escape. The double-wok stove allowed us to cook rice in one wok and, at the same time, fry vegetables in the other.

Our next-door neighbors were Mrs. Shi and her two sons, who were a few years older than me. Mr. Shi was a Kuomintang army officer who escaped to Taiwan in a hurry, leaving his family behind. Only a 7-foot-high wall, open to the roof, separated us from the Shi family. We could hear each other's conversations without ever visiting next door.

Across the other side of the alley was Mr. Chang's family who had lived there a long time. He was an unlicensed doctor, who specialized in external medicine. He drank a lot and continuously scolded his wife. His stepmother lived with Mr. Chang, and, since she was an extra mouth to feed, she was also at his mercy and subject to his whims. His oldest son's large family also lived under the same roof. They had many children and were still growing their family. My friend Emerald was their oldest daughter, their third child. Emerald was a very faithful girl, who single-mindedly devoted herself to care for her siblings.

Mr. Wu's family also lived across the street from us, next to Mr. Chang. Mr. Wu had been classified as a big landlord. All his land and properties had been confiscated. In fact, the house we shared with Mrs. Shi was originally owned and used by Mr. Wu for rice storage. Between our house and the riverbank was a huge rice-processing complex that had also belonged to Mr. Wu before the Liberation. He, his wife, and two youngest daughters now occupied a very small section of the large house previously owned by Mr. Wu. That house was located on the corner of our alley and Dayin Lane. They had been assigned two rooms, one for a bedroom and another for cooking and eating. There was a separate side door to the alley for them to use. We directly faced Mr. Wu's large original home.

Adjacent to our house was a small, open yard. This was part of the now government-owned rice-processing factory, which was not accessible from the alley or from our house. Farther down the alley, next to the open yard,

25

was a two-story house right on the corner of our alley and Dayin Lane. There were two rooms upstairs and two downstairs, together with a kitchen for all the residents to use.

One upstairs room had been assigned to Mrs. Chen and her two children. Mr. Chen had been my grandfather's friend and a predominant member of Yi Quan Dao. Mr. Chen had been executed, while my grandfather managed to escape to Hong Kong. Mrs. Chen shared the upstairs with a widow and her son, a working-class family. She was a small vendor selling baked yams — everyone in the neighborhood called her Aunt Yam!

In the downstairs, one room was assigned to newly widowed Mrs. Hsu and her only daughter. Dr. Hsu had been executed at the same time as Mr. Chen, and was also a member of Yi Quan Dao. The other occupants were Mr. Yu and his wife with a small child.

Mr. Yu was also a small vendor, claiming to be part of the proletariat. Mr. Yu was a short, skinny man with a pair of suspicious, crafty eyes. He was always watching, watching over the hopeless widows and their innocent children. Who knows...they might do harm to Communist China! Mr. Yu could sometimes be a bully, and he made sure everybody was aware that he was in charge. It was only in front of his tall wife that Mr. Yu became humble and meek. We assumed Mr. Yu was a government eye.

Besides Mr. Chang's family, we were all newly-moved-in families. This little neighborhood was carefully planned by the local government. We were the condemned anti-revolutionary families under the watch of Mr. Yu and Aunt Yam, who were poor street vendors — part of the proletariat.

The widows were shedding tears during their lonely nights and thinking, *How can I survive and bring my children up?*

My grandmother and Aunt Zhen worried about my uncle who was still in jail. There was so much pain and agony in the grownups' lives. Yet for us, the children, we were simply too young to understand, though I did notice that the smiles had totally disappeared from the grownups' faces.

Most food was rationed by the government, but we had no money to buy our rations. In order to make money and survive, Grandmother and Aunt Zhen wanted to wash clothes for the local people. Sadly, there were no single men (like our factory workers) around us, and therefore no need for such a service. People living around us were either newly-moved-in, condemned anti-revolutionary families, or the so-called proletarian small vendors.

Later, Aunt Ermay in Hong Kong started to send us 30 Yuan every 3 months. She had finally got a job. Aunt Ermay escaped to Hong Kong in a hurry, leaving most of her property behind in Shanghai. She was now a refugee in Hong Kong. She never complained about the tough life there, but my grandmother was very worried — a single girl in a strange place. A mother's heart never leaves her daughter, regardless of how far she has flown away.

I often saw my grandmother lean against the front door and wait for the mailman.

She used to mumble, "How come I still haven't received Ermay's letter yet?"

It wasn't the money. It was the comfort of hearing from her daughter and, of course, to hear any news of her husband. In Aunt Ermay's letters there was always some hint about my grandfather.

In fact, Aunt Ermay could not find a decent job. She worked as a dancing girl in a night club. At that time, Hong Kong was flooded with refugees from the mainland, and job opportunities were scarce. Aunt Ermay and my step-uncle He-Shen, who accompanied Aunt Ermay to Hong Kong, shared a small rented room. When Mother left China and arrived in Hong Kong, she briefly stayed with Aunt Ermay too. Both my mother and Uncle He-Shen had no job at that time. Later on, my mother found a job as a live-in assistant for a family while waiting for a visa to America, and Uncle He-Shen worked as an airline attendant.

Aunt Zhen was a shrewd woman by nature and loved to save money. She wouldn't even spend all of the survival money she received from Aunt Ermay. After all, her husband was still in jail and she might need money for bail. Luckily, our nannies and some of our workers were very kind. Every time they came to the town shopping or selling their produce, they often brought us their seasonal home-grown food, such as sweet yams, potatoes, and vegetables. My grandmother was very grateful and thanked them with all her heart.

They always replied, "My lady, I am so grateful for your kindness when I worked for you. I am in debt to you forever. This little thing just shows how much my family appreciated your kindness. We feel ashamed that we do so little to help."

Aunt Zhen told us that Grandmother had always been very generous to anyone who needed help. Grandmother had a soft heart. When maids and workers complained to her about their family difficulties, she would reach out a helping hand without hesitation.

Grandmother was the opposite of Aunt Zhen. Saving money wasn't in her personality. Sometimes, her impulsive acts of generosity made Aunt Zhen mad. Grandmother recognized her own shortcomings. She had downgraded herself from being the household elder and allowed Aunt Zhen to take charge of the money. There wasn't any spare money to give anymore. In fact, her humble personality and natural generous heart spared her from the class struggle session[2] during every Communist movement. She always sought universal harmony and never held personal grudges against anyone. Therefore, she had no personal enemies, but she was the wife of an anti-revolutionary element.

During the same year we moved to South Gate, my cousin San Mei was born. She was Aunt Zhen's third child, her only daughter. With her birth, came extra income. Aunt Zhen became a wet nanny for a woman who did not have milk to breastfeed her own baby. She sent her baby twice a day to Aunt Zhen to be fed. Life was tough, but we learned to survive!

---

[2] "class struggle session" was a form of public humiliation and torture.

We Are All "Mat to Floor" —
Equally Low

In the new neighborhood, I suddenly had many new friends to play with. Besides Emerald, there were Xiao Qin and Mei Fang. Emerald was one year older than me. Xiao Qin and Mei Fang were both my age. Xiao Qin was the youngest daughter of Mr. and Mrs. Wu, and Mei Fang was the youngest daughter of Mrs. Chen.

Inside the house was crowded, so the alley was our playground. As we grew a little older, our playground extended to the lumber yard and neighboring farm fields. The grownups had lots on their minds. We were like a bunch of wild ducklings — only called upon at eating time. We had no toys. We played with anything we could find, such as a piece of stone lying on the ground, a block of wood; these were our toys. Only Mei Fang had a real toy. She had a big red bouncing ball that her college brother brought for her when he came home during the New Year holiday. Wow, so big, it was the size of our rice bowl! I envied her. She had a college-educated, nice brother. I loved to play with her big, red bouncing ball.

We also played hopscotch. We used a stone to draw squares on the alley mud floor, then we threw stones into the squares and we hopped and jumped. One day, Xiao Qin, Mei Fang, Emerald, and I were playing hopscotch and it was Xiao Qin's turn. She was aiming her stone into the far end square. Suddenly, Da Di, my younger cousin, stood in one of the squares right in front of Xiao Qin.

Xiao Qin shouted, "Da Di, what are you doing? Get out! Let me throw my stone."

Da Di said, "I want to play too."

"Da Di, please get out of the way. We are in the middle of our game," I said as the older sister.

Da Di insisted he wanted to play right now and refused to get out of the square. Xian Qin was mad. She shouted, "We girls are playing. Why don't you find a boy to play with!"

Da Di's face became red, and he was getting angry. He could see that Xiao Qin was hard to argue with. He was eager to find something to stop her and annoy her.

He shouted, "You're the big landlord's daughter!"

At first, Xiao Qin was angry and speechless. Then she suddenly burst into tears and ran home.

Da Di saw Xiao Qin crying and realized he had gone too far. He walked away. Even though she was only 5 years old, Xiao Qin understood that her father was classified as a landlord and had been pulled out for class struggle session many times. During these times, her family's life was often tormented and agonizing. Being called a "landlord's daughter" was a huge insult, and it hurt her tremendously. She was screaming to her mother and told her mother what Da Di had said.

Mrs. Wu lashed out and walked into our house asking for Grandmother. Every part of her body was in anger. We all lived quietly in the new neighborhood and were in harmony with Mrs. Shi, Mrs. Wu, Mrs. Chen, and Mrs. Hsu. Underneath, we knew each family's situation, but never mentioned it. It was painful for every one of the families. The adults were sympathetic toward each other, but never visited each other. Mrs. Wu's visit was alarming. Grandmother invited Mrs. Wu in. Mrs. Wu could not wait even to say hello.

She said to Grandmother bluntly in an unpleasant voice, "Your grandson called our Xiao Qin 'the landlord's daughter.' We are all 'mat to floor,' equally low. People who live in glass houses shouldn't throw stones! We don't need to smear ash on each other's faces."

Grandmother was dumbfounded. How could her grandson be so hurtful? She was ashamed of her grandson's behavior. She apologized to Mrs. Wu and told her that it was very regrettable that Da Di had said such a nasty word. She argued that Da Di was only a 4-year-old child and did not know what he was talking about. She would punish him heavily — spank him when he got home. She promised Mrs. Wu that it would never happen again. At the same time, she also acknowledged we were in the same situation and shouldn't insult each other.

Since then, the phrase "mat to floor, equally low" has been imprinted on my mind. We were all a condemned class, and I was a child from a condemned family.

When Da Di came back, Grandmother talked with him and asked him to never, ever again use such a hurtful phrase. Da Di didn't get spanked. Grandmother never spanked us. To her we were precious with no limits.

Joint Public-Private Ownership

The new Communist government had adopted the Soviet economic model based on state ownership of industry, large collective units in agriculture, and centralized economic planning. This was revealed in the first five-year Communist manifesto. In the preface of the first five-year plan, it called for joint public-private ownership (劳资合作).

The Public Security Bureau finally released Uncle Nian. They could not find any anti-revolutionary activities connected to Uncle Nian, other than the bullet they found in the dresser during the family raid. My uncle could now potentially represent Xin Yuan as part of this planned public-private ownership, since my grandfather was a counter-revolutionary element and had escaped to Hong Kong and my father was in the United States.

Mr. Chen was our business manager. During our family purge, Mr. Chen remained in charge of Xin Yuan's business and hadn't talked to us for quite a while. Any further connection with us might threaten his own job, so he had to draw a clear and firm "class line" between us.

Suddenly Mr. Chen paid us a visit. "Hi, my lady, I have heard the young master has come home."

Mr. Chen still used the old title to address Grandmother. He greeted her with his usual flattering smile, but displayed a little awkwardness.

"Mr. Chen, we haven't seen you for a long time. What wind blows you here? You are now in charge of Xin Yuan. I am so surprised you even come to visit us." My grandmother spoke sarcastically with a smile.

"My lady, you should understand the situation I am in. I really hope you forgive me. From my heart, I have wanted to show respect to you for a long time, especially since you have been so nice to me over the years. But the political wind prevented me from doing so. I have come today to tell you some good news. The workers' union informed me that the government now promotes joint public-private ownership. Young master now has a possibility to rejoin Xin Yuan."

Grandmother became very excited. After his release from jail, Uncle Nian could not find a job. Rejoining Xin Yuan would be a dream come true!

"Really, how is this so?" Grandmother asked anxiously.

"It is real. Little Dragon [the workers' union leader for Xin Yuan] told me so. The only thing you need to do is contribute money. In fact, I contributed quite a sum myself. The workers are all excited. They have also contributed their own savings to become part of Xin Yuan. Since the company belonged to the old master, Xin Yuan's entire worth was confiscated and now belongs to the government. If the young master wants to be a partner in the new company, he must buy back some company shares," Mr. Chen answered.

"How much?" Grandmother asked.

"At least five thousand Yuan!" said Mr. Chen.

"How can we find that kind of money? You know our situation. We basically try to survive and not let the kids starve." Grandmother was disappointed.

"My lady," Mr. Chen responded softly. "Young master is now staying at home with no job and no career. If you could borrow the money to get young master into the company, I could train young master to manage the business. Your family would then be part of the company business again, and young master would have a job. I was your loyal servant before and will not betray you." Mr. Chen declared his loyalty.

Grandmother told him, "We have to think about it. We don't know if we will be able to borrow such a large sum of money."

Mr. Chen acknowledged that it was a large sum. However, he encouraged Grandmother to think about it and let him know her decision in the near future.

Grandmother discussed the matter with Uncle Nian and Aunt Zhen. Uncle Nian was so bored and felt hopeless, and Aunt Zhen worried about his future. He had no skill of any sort. Letting her husband stay home and do nothing was not a solution. The Communist government promotion of joint public-private ownership was a mass movement. It made people believe that being part-owner of a company would lead to prosperity.

Grandmother, Uncle, and Aunt dreamed that things would return to normal and that they might even again recover ownership of Xin Yuan. They thought that the purge and the confiscation of their property were purely a result of Grandfather's involvement in Yi Quan Dao. Finally, they decided to borrow as much money as they could within their means.

Aunt Zhen started with her relatives. Her older sister-in-law was reluctant, but Aunt's brother and older sister joined together to provide some money. It was difficult to refuse their sister's request. Also, a well-known Chinese proverb says, "Ten years east of the river, ten years west of the river — fortunes come in cycles." Her relatives hoped that Aunt Zhen's prosperity would return again.

Grandmother came from a farmer's family, and her relatives were either landlords or farmers. The landlords' fortunes had been stripped away during the earlier land reform movement. They were lucky to be alive. The poor farmers never had much from the beginning, and things were no better now.

So, Grandmother started to visit her close friends, friends with whom she used to play Mahjong. At this critical moment, she knew it was not the time for saving face. She received a cold reception from all her friends. Not only did Mrs. Song not loan money to Grandmother; in fact, she asked Grandmother to hide behind her stove to make sure her neighbors couldn't see Grandmother visiting. Grandmother remained tolerant through all these insults. Grandmother realized, for the first time, that human feelings are very shallow. It was easier to ask for help than to actually receive it. Rather than beg from her friends, Grandmother decided to negotiate with a local business owner. She offered to borrow money at a high interest rate and too-good-to-refuse terms. The owner eventually agreed to provide some money to Grandmother.

So far, the money they had gathered was still far from enough to satisfy their needs. Aunt Zhen had a few *liang* of gold, which she had carried with her in her inner clothes during the house raid. They decided to sell the gold to raise the required funding. We were a condemned family. Our house had been raided, and we were not supposed to own anything. Aunt Zhen sent Uncle Nian to Wuxi with 5 *liang* of gold. Uncle sold the 5 *liang* of gold on the black market. He also pawned his Swiss watch, a gift from his older sister, Ermay, that he had managed to keep during the raid. They exhausted all possibilities, but were still only able to raise less than one-fifth of the required amount. They were quickly running out of ideas.

Grandmother and Me in Shanghai

As they pondered over all the possible options to resolve their desperate financial need, Grandmother suddenly remembered that there were a few close friends of Aunt Ermay still living in Shanghai. When Aunt Ermay left Shanghai in a hurry, she gave her house to one of her close friends. In fact, Grandmother met the friend when she visited her daughter in Shanghai many years ago when Aunt Ermay and the young girl were college schoolmates.

Now the young girl had married Mr. Pan and was living in my aunt's house. Grandmother remembered that the girl seemed a straightforward person who was very easy to get along with. Even though she had been brought up in a wealthy family, she was not all high and mighty. Grandmother also had stayed in the house for a short time when she visited her daughter. It was a European-style, two-story, single-family home surrounded by a garden. Grandmother thought the house was worth a lot of money. The lady, Ermay's friend, came from a wealthy family and both her husband and she were well educated. Grandmother convinced herself that it would not be a problem to ask for some money under our current situation. After all, "Man proposes, God disposes." It was up to God, whether they would help us or not.

Next day, Grandmother was up before dawn. She washed and did her hair. She packed her best clothes and some ready-to-eat pancakes for the journey. Grandmother decided to take me with her for company. After all, I had never been out of her sight since I had been brought to Yiyang by my wet nanny.

Grandmother sailed to Shanghai with great hope. Although Shanghai was less than 150 miles away, it took one day and one night to get to

Shanghai. In those days, steamboats were the only transportation for people in Yiyang. Grandmother only bought a boat ticket for herself. I was 7 years old — in China, you are 1 year old on the day you are born and it goes up from there. Any child older than 5 should pay for the ride, but because I was so petite, Grandmother carried me on the boat and claimed I was still 5 years old. After all, the ticket money came from our lifeline for food and fuel.

I was so excited to have an outing to the big city. On the boat, Grandmother taught me a few greeting words to say when I met the ladies and gentlemen in Shanghai. The long boat ride was very boring. People started talking to each other. I was the only child on the boat. Aunts, uncles, Nai Nai, and Yi Yi played with me and asked me how old I was and whether I was able to count. I answered smartly. Grandmother was pleased and proud. One of the middle-aged women even shared a boiled egg with me. The egg yolk was so delicious that I gulped it down in no time.

Grandmother was an uneducated, country woman. She didn't want her modest upbringing to become a laughing stock and ruin her planned proposition. It would be a wasted journey. Grandmother decided to first stay with an old friend in Shanghai. Her friend lived in the Hongkou district, which used to be Japanese territory during WWII. We faced a long bus ride to reach Hongkou.

On the bus looking through the window, I saw rivers of people, shoulder to shoulder flowing down the road. The buses, taxis, and rickshaws were bustling back and forth. I was absolutely a country girl; I had never even seen a bus before. The only thing I knew, besides the boat, was that water buffaloes could also carry people around. As the common Chinese saying goes, "The frog in the well knows nothing of the great ocean."

On the bus, Grandmother told me where we were going, the address of the household where we would stay, and what roads we would be taking. As a young girl, I always had a good memory. I squeezed and swallowed all the information into my little head. Grandmother tested me several times and called me the smartest girl she ever knew. Grandmother also exhorted me never to trot off by myself. There were lots of bad people in Shanghai, who would snatch little girls and sell them for money. I promised I would never walk alone. That night, we stayed in the little apartment of my grandmother's friend.

Early morning on the second day Grandmother dressed up. She wore a clean, ironed, traditional Chinese blouse — cotton, light blue in color, with a mandarin collar and frog button, right side opening. On the bottom, she wore a pair of black silk pants cut just above her small, fragile, bound feet. She wore a pair of silk, dark blue shoes with flower-patterned embroidery. Grandmother combed her hair toward the back and neatly formed a bun secured to her head with a hairnet and pin. Although it was plain and tidy, an old woman's simplicity can sometimes be seen by others as elegant. Mr. and Mrs. Pan lived in the old French territory. Grandmother had to take several buses to get there. She decided to leave me with her friend since it was easier to discuss important problems without children around.

Grandmother finally arrived at the garden house in the afternoon. She pushed the doorbell. A woman in her early fifties answered the door. Grandmother guessed that she must be the young Mrs. Pan's nanny. The woman had been Mrs. Pan's wet nanny when she was an infant. Afterwards, the nanny stayed with the family to take care of the young lady she had previously nursed. It was a Chinese tradition that when a girl from a wealthy family married, one of her close maids would follow her into her husband's family as one of her dowries. At first glance, the nanny seemed very gentle with kindness in her eye.

The nanny scrutinized Grandmother up and down and asked, "May I help you? Who are you looking for?"

She was certain, due to Grandmother's clothes, that Grandmother was not a local Shanghainese.

Grandmother advanced a smile, mustered up her courage, and answered, "I am Ermay's mom."

After hearing Ermay's name, the nanny invited Grandmother in with great enthusiasm. She let Grandmother sit in the living room and told her that Mrs. Pan was upstairs. She would report to her at once.

Grandmother glanced around the living room. The decorations had been altered, but the fireplace was still the same. Grandmother was remembering the last time she visited her daughter in the same house. There used to be a huge bowl full of apples, oranges, and pears on the living room table. Fruits are never seen in Yiyang. Grandmother told us many times in later years, with glory in her eye, that Aunt Ermay always bought bananas in bunches. Aunt Ermay used to encourage Grandmother to taste all kinds of fruits when she visited. Aunt Ermay said these fruits had been shipped from many different parts of the world and were not locally grown. She wanted Grandmother to take the opportunity to experience different foods. She also took Grandmother to department stores to purchase all kinds of clothes, including a fur coat. Grandmother often showed off her daughter's gifts to her Mahjong friends. The house was still here, but the circumstances had totally changed. Tears welled up in Grandmother's eye. Grandmother calmed herself and reminded herself that this was not the time to cry.

Mrs. Pan came downstairs and greeted Grandmother as "Ma Ma," the same way Aunt Ermay called Grandmother. Grandmother hadn't seen her for many years. The little girl had grown up to be a young lady. She wore a light green Qipao. It was made of silk with a blooming plum flower pattern. Her hair was professionally done with curls. She was gentle and soft and behaved with grace and ease.

You could not say the same for my grandmother. After all the struggles during the last few years, Grandmother had become much older. Many streaks of gray hair were visible. The wrinkles on her forehead and around her eyes had deepened. Mrs. Pan could almost not recognize Grandmother.

Grandmother got off the chair, adjusted her clothes, and replied with full respect. "Mrs. Pan, I haven't seen you in such a long time. You are so beautiful. You are blessed with fortune."

"Thank you, Ma Ma. How are you doing? How is Ermay doing? I haven't heard from her for a while. Is she okay in Hong Kong?"

After a few general inquiries, she asked about Grandmother's visit. "Were you just passing by, or did you have a special reason for visiting?"

Grandmother's sudden appearance gave Mrs. Pan a good idea as to the real purpose of the visit. A blush of shame spread across Grandmother's face. Grandmother briefly described what had happened to our family over the last few years since Ermay had left for Hong Kong. She described Grandfather's escape to Hong Kong, the house purge, the forced move to South Gate, and now the need to raise funds to buy back a share in the family business. However, she didn't mention that Uncle Nian had been in jail. Instead, she emphasized that Ermay's youngest brother Nian was at home without a job. If we could raise the required amount of money, Nian had been promised by the government that he could become part-owner of the business again.

It was abundantly clear to Mrs. Pan that Grandmother came here for help, but had been too embarrassed to speak up. "I am so sorry that all these things have happened to your family."

Mrs. Pan was horrified by our family's misfortune and was very sympathetic. "I practically saw young brother Nian grow up when he was with Ermay during the war. I always regarded Nian as my own little brother. We are very lucky at the moment. My husband is a highly skilled senior engineer and is under government protection. Ermay's family is my family. It is our duty to help. How much do you need in order get Nian back to the company?" She put Grandmother out of her misery with a gracious smile.

A wisp of light flashed through Grandmother's head. Grandmother answered with hesitation, "Four thousand Yuan!"

I hope I'm not being "a lion opening his big mouth" and scaring people away, Grandmother thought to herself.

"It is a large amount," Mrs. Pan said candidly. "What if we wait until my husband comes home. I will discuss this matter with him and see how much we can gather. Meanwhile, you stay with us for a few days. Let's work out a solution together." She ordered the nanny to prepare a welcome dinner for Grandmother.

With many expressions of gratitude, Grandmother said she could not stay for dinner. Her granddaughter was staying with her friend and she was very worried. Mrs. Pan invited Grandmother to come the next day and to bring me with her, so she could stay in Shanghai for a few more days. Grandmother happily accepted her invitation.

Meanwhile, I was waiting anxiously for Grandmother to return. Grandmother had left early in the morning, and by dusk she was still not back. I was bored and worried about Grandmother. No one paid attention to me. I wandered outside. I had forgotten what Grandmother told me and had broken my promise. I wanted to look for Grandmother.

I made my way out of the Hutong (small lane) and trotted off to the main street. At twilight, the street glowed with neon lights. Small vendors were selling freshly baked yams, freshly toasted chestnuts, and sweets for children in front of the Hutongs. I was fascinated by this new world.

I started to run along the sidewalk and was excited by the strange, exotic scenery. There were mannequins inside big glass windows, all dressed in fancy clothes. There were many refined ladies and gentlemen stepping in and out of taxis. There were also many beggars sitting on the street corners.

Suddenly I didn't know where I was. I was lost! I was scared and desperately wanted my grandmother. I cried loudly, calling out, "Nai Nai!"

A nice policeman came and asked me, "Are you lost?"

I didn't answer and kept crying.

"Where do you live?" the policeman asked.

Finally, I remembered the address — the name of the Hutong that Grandmother mentioned on the bus as we entered Shanghai. The policeman took me to the Hutong. Nobody had missed me. I came home before Grandmother arrived. Nobody would ever know my secret!

The next day, Grandmother revisited Mr. and Mrs. Pan. This time Grandmother brought me with her. After we stepped out from the bus, we walked a long distance and entered a quiet, Sycamore-lined residential neighborhood. We went through a big iron gate. There was a paved path leading into a housing complex. Two-story houses stood along both sides of the paved path, and every house had a manicured front yard. All the houses had previously been occupied by foreigners prior to the Communist Party takeover.

Mr. Pan's house had a living room with a large dining room connected to a kitchen. There was also a study downstairs. The bedrooms were all located upstairs. Aunt Ermay's former husband was an American and had purchased the house for her.

Mr. Pan was a kind and sincere person and felt obligated to Ermay. Mr. Pan was also a practical man. He knew that today his family could live in this fantastic house because of Ermay. Mr. Pan handed Grandmother 4,000 Yuan without an ounce of hesitation. Grandmother was so relieved. She thanked them profusely. Words could not express her appreciation.

Mrs. Pan ordered the nanny to take good care of me. Mr. and Mrs. Pan's youngest daughter was nicknamed by her family Little Dragon because she was born in the year of the dragon. She was a few years older than me. The nanny got us together and sang her hometown folk songs to us. She was kind and extremely easygoing. I felt safe and relaxed. Little Dragon was obviously spoiled, from the expression in her mother's eye when she looked at her daughter and from the way Little Dragon talked to her mother. She was the princess of the family. But she behaved well towards me and let me play with her toys. I was fond of her and envied her.

She had many toys. There was one in particular that I loved so much. I named it "Jade Bird." It was carved and made of marble, approximately 2 inches long and 1 inch wide, white with a touch of pink — you could hold it in your hand. When it came time to say good-bye, Little Dragon handed me Jade Bird and let me have it.

I treasured it for a long time, until Xiao Di broke it! One day Xiao Di put Jade Bird in a teapot and shook the teapot hard. He enjoyed the sound of the stone hitting the porcelain. Finally, he smashed the teapot into pieces and Jade Bird fell to the ground where it broke into two pieces. I was so sad, like I had lost a dear friend. I screamed and cried for hours.

The nanny also gave Grandmother a package. Inside were clothes that Little Dragon had outgrown. There were shirts and skirts for little girls. My sister Xiao Mei and I only wore them during special occasions, such as when we took family pictures or on our first day of school. In Yiyang, we were countryside girls, playing all the time with mud or in the dust. It would have been such a shame to ruin such delicate clothes.

Grandmother returned in triumph and rejoiced with pride. She said to Aunt Zhen, "I never thought I, as an old woman, would still have some influence."

Uncle Nian returned to Xin Yuan and started work with Mr. Chen.

Uncle Nian to Shanghai

After Uncle Nian rejoined Xin Yuan, he became increasingly mature and dedicated himself to the business. It was a second chance for him, and he realized he had to work hard to establish a career for himself.

Very soon, Zhen Chang Inc., a competitor of Xin Yuan, merged with Xin Yuan. This was driven single-handedly by the government without any shareholder involvement or consensus. It turned out that joint public-private ownership had been a total hoax orchestrated by the Communist regime.

Initially, the Communist Party coaxed factory owners and merchants to empty their pockets and contribute to the companies. Then the Five-anti Campaign harassed these "capitalists" until they relinquished "ownership" in their companies. The five antis were anti: bribery, tax evasion, cheating on government contracts, theft of state property, and stealing state economic information. One way or another, the factory owners and merchants would be accused of one or more of these offenses. By the end of the Five-anti Campaign, the government acquired ownership of all companies in every business sector regardless of whether they were small or large.

After the merger between the two companies, a staff layoff followed. Mr. Chen told Uncle Nian, "Everyone is on the chopping block. You are much younger than me. There are many roads ahead for you. You should be prepared."

It was a dog-eat-dog world. Uncle Nian was devastated and came home extremely distressed. He told Grandmother and Aunt Zhen the bad news.

Grandmother sighed. "It's hard to see into another person's heart. We always treated Chang-Sheng (Mr. Chen's first name) well. When he came to our company, his family was very poor. They begged your father to take

43

on their teenage boy, so they could save the extra mouth to feed. Chang-Sheng was a respectful and polite boy. We took care of him as if he was our own child. We promoted him from an odd-job boy all the way to manager. Our kindness in those early days has been forgotten. What has this world come to?" Grandmother was in disbelief.

The possibility of Uncle Nian being laid off consumed the family's brain. Uncle Nian was not a strong, persuasive person. Grandmother recognized that Aunt Zhen had far more business sense than Uncle Nian and could be more diplomatic.

Grandmother told Aunt Zhen, "Chang-Sheng owes us many favors, and we don't know any government officials at the factory. You may have to pay Chang-Sheng a visit. Nian is too shy to beg for help."

So, the next day, Aunt Zhen went to see Mr. Chen. Mr. Chen immediately gave Aunt Zhen a solemn look when Aunt entered his office. Aunt Zhen, seeing such an unpleasant face, felt a chill come over her.

She squeezed out a smile and said, "Hi, Chang-Sheng, I am sorry for coming here to bother you. Yesterday, Nian told us that the company is going to lay off people. You know our situation. Nian's job is the only hope for our family, and we have so many mouths to feed. In order for Nian to return to Xin Yuan, we followed your advice and raised money for Xin Yuan. We are now burdened with a mountain of debt. Mother asked me to discuss with you how we can save Nian's job. Mother told me that our families have always had a very good relationship."

Before Aunt could continue, Mr. Chen firmly interrupted and no longer addressed Aunt Zhen as the Second Young Mistress (二少奶奶). He said, "Zhen, the dynasty has changed. Nian is the son of an anti-revolutionary element. Even if Xin Yuan decided not to lay off Nian, in the middle of the Five-anti Campaign, he should leave voluntarily." Mr. Chen spoke coldly.

For a moment Aunt Zhen stared at Mr. Chen in disbelief, and then began shaking in anger. "This is a huge shock to me. A few months ago, you came to us asking us to raise money for Xin Yuan. At that time, you didn't mention that Nian was the son of an anti-revolutionary element and should stay away from Xin Yuan. In fact, at that time, you pledged loyalty to us and promised to help Nian. In the blink of an eye, you now tell us that Nian must go."

Aunt Zhen became more and more distressed. She continued, "Mother told me that you had been with us since you were a little boy. She always considered you a loyal and respectful person. All we are asking is that you put in some good words for Nian and save his job."

Mr. Chen gazed at Aunt with the hint of a wicked smile on his face. "Sorry, the final decision has been made by the board, and Nian will be the first to go."

Aunt Zhen was devastated and cried out, "How can you be so heartless? We treated you well. Is this the way you return our kindness? You are a wolf in sheep's clothing. We thought you were a good friend of our family, but it turns out you are a brutal, cold-blooded, evil man. You have sold Nian down the river to save your own skin. Evil for evil, no one can escape retribution. You will see — you bastard!" Aunt Zhen had now lost all control.

In the twinkling of an eye, all their efforts were suddenly in vain and they were left with a mountain of debt. Our family had been driven to the wall again!

The fear, the anxiety, the anger, and the sadness overwhelmed the three adults during the following days. Finally, judgment day came, and Uncle Nian was kicked out of Xin Yuan. The storm-sweeping Five-anti Campaign cast a dark shadow over everybody's mind, especially those who were factory owners or relatives of factory owners. Uncle Nian and Aunt Zhen worried about their future. The fact that Uncle Nian had sold five *liang* of gold on the black market also made him a target for one of the five antis.

Aunt Zhen was a very alert and resourceful person. She felt that Yiyang was no longer a safe place for Uncle. If Uncle were arrested again, he would not only suffer in jail, but it would also affect the entire family's future. It would be best if Uncle Nian left town. Shanghai was a huge city. In Shanghai, nobody knew who you were or where you had come from. Aunt Zhen discussed the situation with Uncle Nian and Grandmother.

Grandmother remembered her niece Phoenix who lived in Shanghai. Grandmother suggested, "Your cousin Phoenix lives in Shanghai, and her husband is a member of the Communist Party. I heard he is some sort of official. Nian, why don't you write to her?"

Phoenix was the daughter of my grandfather's youngest brother. We called him Wu Ye Ye — the fifth grandfather. During the period of land reform, Wu Ye Ye was classified and condemned as a landlord. At that time, Phoenix had just graduated from a school of education and had earned her teaching credentials. Faced with this sudden calamity in the family, she realized that the burden of taking care of her aging parents and her younger brother had fallen to her. So, when a matchmaker came to the door, Phoenix immediately accepted the marriage proposal. Her husband was 12 years her senior and was the Principal of a middle school in Shanghai. After her marriage, she was hired as a teacher in one of the middle schools.

Uncle Nian wrote to Phoenix, and the response was positive. She thought that Uncle Nian could get a clerk position in their school since Uncle Nian had a couple years of college education. Finally, a ray of hope had dawned on us. Uncle Nian immediately rushed to Shanghai. Unfortunately, the clerk position wasn't approved by the school's superiors. Aunt Zhen always claimed that Phoenix's husband was too gentle and didn't scratch his superior's back enough.

There were a number of young men from Yiyang in a similar situation. They told Uncle Nian that Huangpu port was looking for dock workers. Together, these pampered young dandies (少爷), all from formerly wealthy families, now had to start a tough life in Shanghai. They found a tea house close to the port and negotiated with the owner to let them stay there overnight in return for rent. The owner saw that these young men were well behaved and didn't look like gangsters. So, he showed them pity and let them sleep on the tables in the tea house. He told them that they had to get up and pack up their belongings before 5 o'clock each morning so that the tea house could open on time.

In those days, there was no modern equipment, and so work at the docks was very physically demanding. Every day they loaded and unloaded cargo from ship to port and port to ship. Soon, life in Shanghai became unbearable. Many decided to return to Yiyang. Uncle wrote to Aunt and expressed his desire to come home. A young woman would normally love to have her husband next to her, but Aunt's analytical thinking convinced her that Yiyang was a very dangerous place for her husband at that time.

She wrote back encouraging him to stay in Shanghai. She persuaded him that, although she understood the tough and lonely life he was experiencing, he should realize that our family background was very different from his friends. Now that the Five-anti Campaign was at its peak, it was unwise to come back to Yiyang. She also included 20 Yuan in the letter to Uncle. We had just received money from Aunt Ermay in Hong Kong for family living expenses. Aunt Zhen said the 20 Yuan would give Uncle an occasional break from the heavy work at the docks. Uncle had been in jail for months and so fully grasped his wife's point of view. Being called in and interrogated by the security officers every couple of days wasn't a life he wanted to live. Uncle Nian decided to continue his lonely life in Shanghai, although all his friends returned to Yiyang.

Uncle Nian grew up in a pampered and spoiled environment as a young master. He spent most of his time in the opera house practicing Beijing opera and never got his hands dirty. Now he had to endure humiliation and insults in silence. He claimed that the 8-year war with Japan, where he followed his elder siblings to Sichuan Province, made him tougher than others.

In Shanghai he was just a port worker — the same as all other port workers. He never revealed that he was the son of a counter-revolutionary until it was uncovered later during the infamous Cultural Revolution. He had a good nature and never argued with others. He always followed the crowd, especially those superior to him. Most port workers were migrant peasants who came from the northern part of the Yangzi River, a very poor area that suffered yearly floods. He was the only educated worker, and so his accounting and writing skills allowed him to be promoted to perform clerical work.

Although he had a strong desire to move back to Yiyang, all jobs were assigned by local governments and exchanging jobs was almost impossible. Very soon, all the residents had to be registered with a specific Hukou (registered residence). In fact, a Shanghai Hukou was superior to a Yiyang Hukou. Shanghai residents received more rations such as clothes, soap, and food.

Uncle and Aunt got together about twice a year. Uncle came home during the Chinese New Year holiday, and Aunt visited him during the summer. Every time when Uncle returned home, Aunt cooked special food for him: egg fried rice, salty duck, and pig ears. We, the children, watched him devour all the good food with our mouths watering. He never offered anything to us, not even to Grandmother. He always seemed so remote. There was very little interaction between him and us children. I used to resent him eating our rations and not taking responsibility for our family. He never sent a penny home and was a selfish man. He was a lonely man in Shanghai, and he must have felt that he deserved to be pampered at least once a year.

Uncle Nian, by staying in Shanghai and working at the port, avoided the Anti-rightist Campaign and the Great Leap Forward. The Great Leap Forward failed and was followed by a huge famine across China.

In the summer of 1959, a special conference was held in the mountain resort of Lushan. The majority of the population was not aware of the details of the conference, but there were rumors that Marshal Peng Dehuai had openly criticized Mao's Three Red Flags policy. He was then placed under house arrest at Yuantouzhu resort next to Tai Lake. After the Lushan Conference, Liu Shaoqi became the State Chairman. For most people, the only thing they needed was enough food to fill their stomachs and enough clothes to keep them warm during cold weather. All these political maneuvers didn't register with them. They were irrelevant to their daily lives.

After these failures, there were less political campaigns such as the Great Leap Forward. Chairman Mao had crawled away into a political cave to calculate his next move, and the people finally had some peace in their lives. The class war was softening, and the line between proletariat and other classes became murkier over time. Uncle Nian was able to make many friends who were Communist Party members. Grandmother used to tease him and say, "You are a white duck sneaking into a gaggle of geese."

Uncle Nian was slowly brainwashed and became a loyal follower and supporter of the Communist Party. He told his friends that he would like to persuade my parents, his brother, and sister-in-law, to return home to China. He knew my father was a Senior Staff Engineer working for a major aerospace company in America. Uncle Nian admired Qian Xuesen, a leading Chinese pioneer in nuclear and space science. Qian Xuesen was educated at MIT, a US university, and worked for the California Institute of Technology. He eventually returned to China to develop China's nuclear and space industries. Uncle Nian thought my father should follow in Qian Xuesen's footsteps and return to China to contribute to his motherland.

God Pond Valley Village

While Uncle Nian lived a lonely life in Shanghai, Grandmother and Aunt Zhen raised five children and struggled to maintain their existence in Yiyang. Debtors, one after the other, visited daily. We lived on the scant money sent by Aunt Ermay and my mother in Hong Kong. There was no spare money to pay the debts. Grandmother and Aunt Zhen had to have elephant-thick skins and act deaf-and-dumb in order to tolerate the daily insults.

Food was in short supply. Grandmother once in a while visited her parents' village — God Pond Valley Village — and I used to accompany her. We normally stayed with her younger brother, Granduncle. He was classified as a landlord, but certainly was not treated as a landlord by the villagers. He didn't have much land, but did have more than the other villagers. The government confiscated his land, and he now had to share his house with another family, one of his cousin's families. He was an easygoing and honest man. In addition, almost the entire village shared the same clan name, Rui. The families that lived in the village were all related via their ancestry. They were cousins or distant cousins. So, for all these reasons, he didn't receive the harsh treatment experienced by other landlords. The villagers in God Pond Valley lived in peace and harmony.

Everyone in the village called my grandmother Grand Aunt or Great Grand Aunt. I always felt that my grandmother's homecoming visits generated great excitement among the villagers. Families lined up to invite Grandmother for lunch or dinner. They saved their best food for Grandmother — fresh eggs and pork, all the delicacies that seldom appeared on their daily dinner tables. Luckily, I was also the beneficiary of these feasts! Aunt Zhen told me that when we were prosperous Grandmother had been exceptionally generous to the God Pond Valley villagers. Whenever there were requests for help, Grandmother would be there. Village people were poor and simple, but were kind and believed that "what goes around comes around."

Most villagers lived in houses made of bricks with tile roofs. There were also a few houses made with mud bricks and thatch roofs. Usually, the thatched cottages were occupied by outsiders who had emigrated there from other parts of the country during natural disasters, such as flood or drought in their home villages. These cottages were located at the outskirts of the village.

There was a wooden bridge over a creek, which separated the village residents into two sections. The bridge was only 3 feet wide, and there were no rails. One or two pieces of wood had shown their age and rattled in the wind. I was so scared to cross it; I could hear the wood creak as I walked on it. The village was surrounded by vast rice fields networked throughout with water channels. There was no electricity in the village. An entire home was lit by a small lamp using an oil-soaked, straw-thread wick. During the evening, the villagers would gather around tables chatting and joking to pass their time.

Grandmother's visit was an opportunity for them to show their appreciation for Grandmother's previous kindness. Those who didn't have a chance to invite Grandmother for a meal prepared a gift. They would watch their hens carefully and hoped they would drop more eggs, so that they could give Grandmother more to take home when we returned.

In front of Granduncle's house was a pond, overgrown with water lilies and water chestnut plants. During our summer visit, my distant cousins would go down to the pond to gather water chestnuts for us. They would sit in floating, wooden basins that were about 3 feet in diameter and less than a foot high. The basin was sealed and waterproofed with palm oil and only had enough room for one person. The water chestnuts hung underneath the plants. They could be eaten raw when shelled and could also be cooked with meat. Water chestnuts cooked with meat was one of our hometown delicacies.

I enjoyed watching my older distant cousin pick water chestnuts in the pond. Her agile maneuvering of the wood basin excited me. I screamed, begging her to let me try. Grandmother told me it was dangerous, saying, "It looks easy but is difficult to do. You can't even swim!"

By the time we returned home, there were lots of gifts from all the relatives. There were eggs, water chestnuts, fresh vegetables, and also homemade bamboo baskets and floor sweepers made of rice straw.

The village relatives used a small boat to carry our goodies back home. I had traveled on the small village boat many times. There was no direct steamboat from Yiyang to God Pond Valley village. We had to take a steamboat from Yiyang to a little town called Qiantang. It was about 3 miles from Qiantang to God Pond Valley. Most of the time the village relatives took us to Qiantang, and then we would take the steamboat home. Sometimes they also took us all the way to Yiyang in this small boat. My village uncles would paddle the boat, and my grandmother and I, and sometimes Da Di and Xiao Mei, would sit on the wooden benches in the center of the boat.

Along the waterway we would pass vast marshlands. Patches of green reeds rose from the water, flocks of birds perched among the reeds, and wild ducks chased each other, splashing water as they went. On the horizon, migrating birds formed a "人" display against a boundless blue sky. We were surrounded by vast, calm waters, and for miles around there was nobody — only us. I was a young child; I didn't have the poetic soul of spring flower, autumn moon (春花秋月), or blue mountain and green water (青山绿水). Thinking back to those peaceful, tranquil scenes, I so much wish I could visit again.

I have really fond memories of my time at God Pond Valley. I liked the simple, plain, and kind village people. They didn't distance themselves from us when we became poor. I enjoyed their hearty welcome and the mouth-watering food they provided. At the time I didn't realize they were sacrificing their own food for us! I was simply too young to comprehend.

We Were the Wild Ducklings

Since we lived on the outskirts of Yiyang, there was a huge, natural playground all around. We played in the neighboring lumberyard. We loved hiding in the piles of wood. We were innocent. We didn't know the immensity of heaven and earth and certainly didn't know how dangerous it was to play underneath the wood pile. We used to run along a path that led to the river behind the rice-processing complex. We would roll up our trousers to stand next to the river and catch fish using tin cans.

One day Mrs. Hsu came to the river to wash her clothes, and she screamed at us and chased us home. She told my grandmother we were at the river. Grandmother was cooking dinner while at the same time taking care of San Mei, Aunt Zhen's baby daughter. Aunt Zhen was taking sewing lessons, and so most of the household chores fell onto Grandmother's shoulders. Grandmother was scared and feared she would lose control of us.

During hot summer days, the river swelled as the snow melted in the mountains above the Yangtze River. When the river was high, there were lots of fish pulled along by the fast-moving upstream current. Local farmers would use a huge net many feet in diameter to catch the fish. It was very exciting and thrilling to see the big fish jumping around inside the net after they were caught. Every year, when the unruly river tumbled through our town, children drowned. Grandmother ordered us to kneel on the floor for 10 minutes as punishment for playing near the river. We hated Mrs. Hsu and her big mouth!

As children we didn't understand why we didn't have enough food to eat. We were always craving for food. There were patches of cultivated land only a few blocks away from our house. We often wandered to the farmland and picked up soybeans from the soil dropped by farmers as they harvested their crop. Then we put the soybeans on a metal spatula and cooked them over a firepit. We often burned the soybeans so they weren't very tasty, but the adventure was really exciting.

Summertime was the season for fruits and vegetables. It was also the time of the year when days lasted longer. The boys had so much energy, yet they had no place to exhaust it. My cousins Da Di and Xiao Di often ran around in the neighboring vegetable gardens. In one of the gardens there were young, tender cucumbers hanging on the vine that were tempting and enticing the boys. Da Di and Xiao Di picked and ate the watery, crunchy cucumbers.

While they sat under the cucumber plants and enjoyed their treasure trove, a rough and raspy voice came from the farmer's house. "Who's there?"

Da Di and Xiao Di were so scared, they threw away their uneaten cucumbers and ran for their lives. Xiao Di was only a 3-year-old toddler and had a big baby head. When he ran, he couldn't balance himself and fell.

He started crying for his older brother, "Wait for me!"

The farmer saw they were only two little boys, and so stopped chasing.

One morning, Grandmother was sorting and binding the dry grass for cooking fuel in the alley outside our house and we were all "helping." The farmer walked toward the rice-processing complex and happened to pass our house. He recognized the two boys who "stole" his cucumbers.

He smiled to Grandmother. "Are these two boys yours?"

"Yes, they are our Hua Da and Hua Er (华大，华二)," replied Grandmother with a smile.

Hua Da and Hua Er were two characters in a folk drama. Hua Da and Hua Er were two brothers growing up in the Hua mansion. They were kind of stupid and always getting into trouble. Grandmother was mocking.

The farmer said, "I caught them stealing my cucumbers, and if I catch them again, I plan to keep them with me!" He winked at Grandmother to show he was joking.

Xiao Di was terrified and immediately ran behind Grandmother. That was the last time they ran into the farmer's garden. We girls were never brave enough to "steal."

Yiyang has four distinct seasons. Spring is the best, Goldilocks time — not too hot, not too cold. Wild green grass and vegetation start sprouting everywhere in the neighboring fields. There is a wild vegetable, known as Qi Cai, which grows among the green grass on the edge of the footpaths separating the rice paddies. Qi Cai dumpling is one of our hometown delicacies. Chopped Qi Cai with ground pork makes delicious dumpling filling. We sometimes would go out to search for Qi Cai in the rice fields so that Grandmother could make dumplings. We seldom were able to harvest young, tender Qi Cai. Usually, by the time we got there, the majority of the Qi Cai was gone. It had been dug up by the farmer's children. We had to use our sharp, eagle eyes to search for leftovers.

One bright, warm, and pleasant spring morning, I was playing in our alley with friends. Wu Mei came to me and asked if I would like to accompany her to her aunt's school. She said there were lots of tender Qi Cai near the school. If I wanted to go, I should bring a basket and she would help me dig up lots of tender Qi Cai.

Wu Mei's family had just moved to Yiyang from Shanghai. Her father was a capitalist, a factory owner who had passed away during the Five-anti Campaign. Nobody knew if it was suicide or if he had died of natural causes. After her father passed away, her mother, Mrs. Fang, brought the entire family to Yiyang to stay with her younger brother's family. Mrs. Fang had seven girls, and Wu Mei was the fifth born. Wu means fifth or five. People in Shanghai or near the Shanghai region would nickname their girls Mei (younger sister or girl) and their boys Di (younger brother or boy). The first-born boy would be nicknamed Da Di, and the second-born boy Er Di. Therefore, everybody at my home and in the neighborhood called me Da Mei — I was the first-born girl in our household.

Wu Mei was a teenager, and more than twice my age. Wu Mei's mother asked her to take a package of spring clothes to her aunt, who taught at an elementary school in the nearby countryside. Wu Mei needed a companion for the journey. The possibility of tender Qi Cai excited me, and I said "yes" enthusiastically. I immediately ran home, gathered a large bamboo basket, and headed off with Wu Mei, full of excitement.

We left Dayin Lane and turned onto South Gate Road walking away from town. After walking several blocks, the paved section of South Gate Road came to an end. The road continued but became a smooth stone-laid footpath. On both sides of the path were rice fields as far as the eye could see. Yiyang was located within the Yangtze River Delta, which had very fertile soil with rice as the dominant crop.

We passed many ponds with water reeds that housed lots of wild ducklings. Yiyang was crisscrossed by numerous bodies of water adjacent to Tai Lake. There were lots of rivers and ponds densely scattered all over the place. As we walked, we enjoyed the warm spring day. I was anticipating a huge crop of Qi Cai! We had walked quite a while, but the village we were heading for was still nowhere in sight.

"How far away is your aunt's school?" I impatiently asked Wu Mei.

"Not far," she answered.

I didn't realize the school was so far away. It took us more than an hour to get there. When we arrived, as Wu Mei promised, we found lots of young, tender, green Qi Cai behind the school wall. They were all about 4 to 5 inches long. I had never seen such huge Qi Cai! I was so excited, thinking how happy Grandmother would be when she saw me arrive home with so much fresh, tender Qi Cai. I started to dig out the Qi Cai. Wu Mei, as she promised, also helped. We gathered a whole basketful, and then started our long trek home. Wu Mei carried the basket for me all the way until we separated, so she could return to her home. When I arrived, it was way past lunch hour.

As I ran and bounced to my home, eager to show my harvest to Grandmother, Aunt Zhen suddenly rushed out of our home and shouted at me in an angry, stern tone, "Where have you been? You worried us to death!"

Before I could answer, Grandmother walked out with a smile of relief on her face, saying, "Thank God you are home. Have some lunch, you must be hungry."

This made Aunt Zhen indignant, and she suddenly slapped my face in anger. "You made Grandmother so worried, and had me running around all over the place looking for you. How could you do this to me?"

It turned out that at the time when Grandmother called all the children home for lunch, I was the only one who didn't show up. Grandmother searched everywhere and asked all the neighbors. Nobody knew where I had gone. Grandmother was really worried and was continually nagging Aunt Zhen to start a search. Aunt was a young woman in her twenties. In the beginning, she felt Grandmother was overreacting. Grandmother became more anxious and started to blame Aunt Zhen for neglecting her responsibility. Aunt argued that I should have let them know where I was going and should be punished as soon as I returned. Grandmother agreed. However, the longer they searched and waited, the more anxious and restless they both became.

Once I appeared, Aunt's anxiety turned into anger. Grandmother was simply relieved and grateful that I was safe. Aunt Zhen was upset that Grandmother didn't punish me as she had promised but instead immediately offered me lunch. She couldn't argue with Grandmother, so all her rage was directed at me. I was too young to fully understand, but was frightened. *Why were they so worried and angry?* After being slapped by Aunt, I felt wronged. Tears swirled in my eyes. I stared at Aunt with my tearful eyes.

Aunt fiercely slapped me again. "You dare to stare at me with your two big watering eyes. I will continue to smack you until you know you were wrong."

Aunt Zhen was so wrathful, not only because I didn't bend, but also because she was challenging Grandmother's authority. Grandmother was afraid to say anything. After venting her anger, Aunt walked out. Tears continued running down my face. I sobbed bitterly for a long time.

Grandmother comforted me. "Next time you should let us know where you are going. It was Wu Mei's fault. She should have understood that we would worry when she took you out for such a long time without telling us. My sweetheart, it is so nice to have such a wonderful basketful of Qi Cai! I will make dumplings tomorrow. Meanwhile, have some lunch and don't let yourself go hungry."

Later Mrs. Fang (Wu Mei's mother) apologized for this episode in my life. She let Wu Mei take the blame. Wu Mei didn't tell her mother that she invited me to go with her. As far as I can remember, this was the first and last time I was physically punished.

However, Grandmother did tell me a story many years later that I had been smacked by my mother when I was very young — a little over 1 year old. When I was only a couple of months old, Grandmother brought me and my wet nanny back to Yiyang. Only a few months later, my mother became pregnant with my sister, Xiao Mei. After Xiao Mei was born, Mother took Xiao Mei together with her wet nanny to Yiyang for a visit.

My grandparents were so fond of their first-born grandchild they often let me sleep with them during the night. When my mother came home, I didn't recognize her. Mother thought it would be a good idea to let me sleep with her so that there could be time for mother-child bonding. But I would not let her touch me and refused to sleep with her. When she carried me to her bed, I kicked and screamed loudly, asking for Grandmother. It was terribly disappointing and upsetting for my mother. She slapped me hard. "You are a spoiled rotten child!" The harder she slapped, the louder I cried. Finally, Grandmother had to take me with her, so that everyone could have some peace.

I had slept with Grandmother even after we moved to South Gate. By that time, we all had to share beds anyway. I was never close to Aunt Zhen, but I never feared her either. I remember, sometimes she would sit at Grandmother's bedside and chat about our family problems, such as all our debts. I would stay quietly beneath the cotton quilt to make sure she didn't notice me. Grandmother was always there for me. I remember once when I was sick with high fever, I vomited on the bed. Grandmother quietly changed my bedding and constantly put her hand on my forehead to feel whether my fever had passed.

Winter was the worst season for us, especially during our childhood years. After a snow storm, the icicles were more than a foot long, hanging from the roof rim. It would take days for the snow to melt. The icicles kept dripping freezing water, and the alley turned into mud mixed with melting snow. It always seemed colder when the snow was melting than during the snowstorm itself.

Our house was originally converted from a rice storage facility. There were no windows. After we moved in, Granduncle together with the God Pond Valley villagers made an open window for us. The window was covered with two pieces of wood that closed as a crude shutter during the night. Cold air would still channel in around the shutter. On sunny days, outside was warmer than inside, so we used to stand against the southeast-facing wall in the sun to get warm.

During winter, we all wore cotton padded jackets made by Aunt Zhen. Since we were growing, Aunt had to make sure they would last for many years, so she made the jackets big enough. The cotton padded jacket couldn't be washed. If washed, the cotton inside would harden and the insulating air would be squeezed out. Aunt Zhen also made us overalls that were washable and protected the jacket from wear.

During the Chinese New Year holiday, it is Chinese tradition to wear new clothes. We didn't have new clothes, so Grandmother and Aunt ordered us to take off our overalls so they could be washed. In this way at least we could wear clean clothes on New Year's Day. Since we only had one overall, Grandmother let me wear her overall and Xiao Mei would wear Aunt's overall. Their overalls were so big they would hang over our little bodies all the way down to our feet. We were too embarrassed to go outside, but Grandmother insisted. She understood it was cold in the house, but outside, under the sun, it was much warmer.

My childhood memories are fading, but I remember that I never expected much besides craving for food. I can't imagine how difficult it was for Grandmother and Aunt Zhen to see the children starving for food. Their life had changed so drastically, for the worse. Primarily for the sake of the children, or perhaps simply to survive, they fought hard each and every day. They suffered tremendous political and social downfalls, but still managed to hold the household together. The years fully tested their limits to survive in a rapidly changing world.

A Mediocre Student,
An "American Daughter"

When the Communist Party founded the People's Republic of China in 1949, the majority of the population was illiterate. Almost the entire peasant population never entered school. This was especially true for women — even those born into a wealthy household. Women, in traditional Chinese, feudal, patriarchal society, were considered the lowest class or status. In many cases, they were viewed as the property of men. An old Chinese proverb says, "an uneducated girl is a virtuous one" (女人无才便是德). My grandmother never went to school and was never able to read or write. Two good things emerged from the Communist takeover: the liberation of women, and the Anti-illiteracy Movement. During the early 1950s, the government promoted equal rights for men and women, monogamous marriage, prohibition of adultery and prostitution, and free education for all. All children, when they reached 7 years of age, were required to enroll in elementary school.

In the autumn of 1954, when I turned 7 years of age, Da Di, Xiao Mei, and I started school. Da Di and I were first graders, and Xiao Mei a kindergartner. Because we lived in the South Gate neighborhood, we should have enrolled in the South Gate School. However, West Gate was known to have the better school, and Aunt Zhen's older sister, we called her Da Yi (大姨), taught kindergarten there. Luckily, Da Yi managed to get us into West Gate School where she could keep an eye on us.

Grandmother and Aunt Zhen dressed Xiao Mei and me for the first day of school. Xiao Mei and I normally wore identical clothes — the same style and the same fabric. Xiao Mei was one year younger than me, and we grew up wearing Aunt Zhen's homemade clothes. We were practically twins. However, on this special, first day of school, Xiao Mei and I wore special clothes. On the top, we both wore identical shirts newly made by Aunt Zhen with a checkered fabric pattern. Xiao Mei wore a pink butterfly-style dress, and I wore a colorful patterned skirt. These were pieces from the clothes that Little Dragon had outgrown and we had brought home when Grandmother and I visited Shanghai. Grandmother also put red ribbons on our braids.

This made Da Di very jealous. He wondered why he also didn't get special clothes for school. He hid under the dinner table and refused to go to school. He demanded that he should also be given a dress to wear!

Grandmother had to explain to him, "Boys wear pants. Dresses are only for girls. It's a tradition."

Da Di didn't understand, but, after Grandmother's persuasion, we finally started school.

West Gate School had been converted from an ancestral temple associated with the Peng clan — a place where the Peng clan offered sacrifices to their ancestors. It was a walled compound with a large yard located on the left side of the temple that was very well suited for use as a children's playground. The Chinese Communist Party had declared itself to be atheist, and so almost all ancestral temples were converted into schools or local government offices.

The worship hall of the Peng clan became the teachers' office. In front of the worship hall was a small courtyard where two large Ginkgo trees marked the entrance. I vividly remember these two old trees because I had seldom been in a courtyard with such beautiful trees. I grew up in a ramshackle alley with no plants, no flowers — only mud. Our classrooms were scattered around the compound outside this central courtyard. In the classroom, there were many rows of long benches. Each row had two benches, four pupils for each bench. Each classroom allowed seating for 40 to 50 pupils.

Only Chinese, math, and handicraft were studied in first grade. Pupils stayed in the same classroom every school day until the semester ended. Different teachers came to the classroom to teach the subject in which they specialized. The homeroom teacher was normally assigned to be the teacher who taught Chinese. My homeroom teacher was Miss Wu, a nice young lady.

West Gate School was located outside the West Gate. The gate itself was no longer there, but there was a bridge (West Gate Bridge) that connected the inner town to the outside residential communities. The school was at the outskirts of this west-side residential neighborhood. In China, school was six days per week with only Sunday free.

Walking from our home in South Gate to school took us more than half an hour. There were two possible routes that could be used to go back and forth to school. Both routes passed along the river known as the Hucheng River, which encircled the inner-town.

From home, we crossed the South Gate Bridge and walked along the riverbank on what was called Up-Riverside Road, until we reached the West Gate Bridge. After passing over the West Gate Bridge, we then walked away from the inner town towards West Gate School. There were very few homes along Up-Riverside Road. Up-Riverside Road followed the remnants of the original town wall that enclosed the town. The town wall had been destroyed and dismantled during WWII. All that was left were a few large granite stones scattered along the riverbank. Up-Riverside Road was unpaved and desolate. We sometimes used this route to return home on sunny, warm days. We had fun jumping between the stones when they lined up one after the other.

However, most of the time, we walked home along Down-Riverside Road, which followed the other side of the riverbank — across from Up-Riverside Road. Down-Riverside Road was densely populated. On both sides of the road were rows of terraced houses. The road was narrow and paved with large, long granite stones. The sidewalk was elevated from the road and aligned with the wood façade of the houses. It was similar to roads seen in Roman ruins such as at Pompeii. Most of the houses along the river had direct access to the river. There were occasional gaps between the houses with stone staircases leading down to the river that provided neighborhood access for washing.

Grandmother never attended school, and Aunt Zhen only spent a couple of years in elementary school. She could read and write a simple letter, that's all. For them, school was a place that confined and restrained us. They never tried to motivate us to learn — no inspiration or enlightenment. However, they made sure we got up early and would not be late for school.

Walking to school always seemed to take such a very long time. In early summer on stormy days, torrential rains made the road very slippery. I was often afraid that the strong wind and heavy rain would push me toward the river. I held my oiled, paper-made umbrella tight in the wind to prevent it from flying away, but it still pulled me to and fro and made me stumble in the storm. Often, when we crossed a small stone bridge over a water channel that branched from the Hucheng River, the water rose to almost the same level as the bridge. When we crossed the bridge on these stormy days, I was always so scared I might be blown into the water. Most days we came home for lunch. Sometimes, on stormy days with heavy rain or on cold, snowy days, Aunt Zhen would bring our food to school to save us from having to return home for lunch. We were always excited when Aunt visited the school.

At West Gate School, I was a mediocre, meek student. Nobody pushed me to learn or supervised me to complete homework. I did just enough to avoid punishment from the teachers. My grades weren't great either — equivalent to Bs or Cs in America. At the end of the schoolyear, many of my classmates received awards. Some were given new pencils. Some got new notebooks. I got nothing. I admired them. It would have been nice if I could have been rewarded with some new pencils and notebooks to use, but being without an award didn't really bother me. I was too innocent to be jealous; too young to be vain.

I was very petite and thin and so appeared very fragile. Grandmother told me I was born prematurely and had stayed in a hospital incubator for a week after I was born. I was a good target for the unruly boys, the bullies, and even the big girls. I tried to avoid the playground and always got out of school before other pupils, but sometimes, before leaving, I needed to visit the toilet.

The toilet was on the other side of the adjacent courtyard next to the kindergarten room. I had to cross the courtyard to get there. The toilet wasn't a place anyone would want to visit; only if you were desperate. The girls' toilet was a big manure-pit, and there were four large, long granite stones across the pit, allowing two girls to use the toilet at the same time. We would squat on the stones across the pit. The stones were wet and scattered with human feces. You had to choose your footholds carefully to avoid the feces. In the warm spring and summer, you could see white maggots swarming in the pit. I avoided looking down when I had to visit. The smell was horrible.

One day, after passing water, I rushed out. As I left the toilet shack, there were three unfriendly boys waiting for me. They blocked my way and roared at me, "Money for the pass!"

They must have watched gangster movies or read stories about gangsters who blocked the mountain passes to harass and bribe people.

"I have no money," I answered quietly and began to tremble.

They closed in on me and started shouting, "Tolls, tolls!"

I was terrified and tried to squeeze between them. One of the boys pointed his finger at me and demanded: "You, American daughter! If you don't give us money, I'll hit you hard!"

Calling me "American daughter" hurt me tremendously. I suddenly burst into tears. "Overthrow American Imperialism" was a popular slogan. I knew my parents lived in the US — the American imperialist country. I knew anything associated with the word "American" was bad. At the age of 7, I didn't know my parents at all. I didn't even know what they looked like. I had no images of them. Grandmother and Aunt Zhen hardly mentioned them, and I did not miss them, but I knew "American daughter" was a huge insult. I summoned up my courage and was no longer afraid. I screamed at the top of my lungs and pushed them out of my way. The boys were astonished, stunned, in shock. They let me go.

After school, I wept and told my grandmother what had happened at school. Grandmother comforted me. "Don't cry. They are just a bunch of stampeding wild horses."

She mumbled, "They lack good parenting!"

Grandmother never dared challenge the boys' families regarding their parenting. They might have come from Red class families. Xiao Qin's mother scolded my grandmother for her parenting when Da Di called Xian Qin "landlord's daughter," because she knew we belonged to the same undesirable class. I had no choice, but had been born into a Black class family.

All the people in China were categorized into Red (紅五類), Gray, and Black (黑五类) classes according to their family background (阶级成分). Those children whose parents were high officials or army generals were honored as the supremely Red class — the newly established aristocracy. They were arrogant and often flaunted their privileges. The original (pre-founding of the People's Republic of China) poor factory workers and peasants were also classified as Red. A person's education and job assignment were all based on one's family class background rather than on professional merit. The children that came from Red families received the best treatment of all, a good college education that led to good jobs and high salaries.

There was an undefined class, the Gray class. It consisted of highly educated intellectuals (artists, writers, teachers, doctors, engineers), as well as factory clerks. However, later, after the anti-rightist campaign, millions of intellectuals were condemned as rightists and became part of the category known as the Black (黑五类) class. The anti-rightist campaign attacked those who dared to speak up during the Hundred Flowers Movement — a movement that supposedly promoted pluralism of expression and open criticism of the government.

Families that had a member with an anti-revolutionary element, families that had foreign connections where their relatives lived in foreign lands, families whose relatives had escaped to Taiwan or Hong Kong and had worked for the Kuomintang were all sadly part of the Black class. Of course, the Blacks also included landlords. The Blacks were the scapegoats during all the Communist Party campaigns. They were always attacked as the "class struggle" targets. Children from Black families were continuously discriminated against. They often became the victims of political purges. The vast majority of condemned rightists came from Black families.

My grandfather was an anti-revolutionary religious leader who had escaped to Hong Kong. Just that fact alone condemned us as a Black Family. My parents resided in America, Aunt Ermay and Uncle He-shen were both in Hong Kong — it could be said we were an extremely complicated, foreign-connected family! We were Black to the core as far as the Communist government was concerned. I was a Black, undesirable child — an American daughter!

My Childhood Friend Juan

Before the start of the anti-rightist and Great Leap Forward campaigns, there was a short period of peace. It was a recovery period for the people after the Five-anti Campaign. During this period, people in general had a more peaceful life, including our family — a Black family. Nobody knew that during this peaceful period the anti-rightist campaign was in its period of gestation.

The Communist Party galvanized middle and high school students to form propaganda teams that focused on promoting the "sweep out illiteracy" and "liberation of women" policies. Juan, a teenage girl in our neighborhood, was enrolled in the local middle school, Jiangsu Yiyang School. Juan was medium height and slightly chubby, as most girls are during puberty. She had two big, clever, moving eyes. She was sweet and polite. To look at her was to love her. Her birth parents had eight children, and she was the fifth. When she was a toddler, her parents lived in Yiyang next to Mrs. Xia.

Mr. Xia was a clerk for a coffin store who originally came from the countryside well outside Yiyang. He had an arranged marriage with his wife who was a few years older. It was common practice in Chinese feudal society for a family to "buy" a girl or arrange to raise a girl from a very poor family while at the same time treating her as a servant. At the proper age, they would then arrange for her to marry and take care of their son. The girl was usually called a "raised daughter-in-law" (童养媳, *Tong Yang Xi*). It was rumored that Chairman Mao had a Tong Yang Xi, whom he never acknowledged as his wife. Mr. Xia had a son with his Tong Yang Xi, but he never had feelings for her. After he came to Yiyang to work at the coffin store, he fell in love with the girl next door and they got married. Even though his Tong Yang Xi occasionally brought his son to visit,

66

everybody in the neighborhood recognized that the second wife was Mrs. Xia.

Unfortunately, Mrs. Xia could not produce any children and was longing for a child of her own. Juan was a cute, beautiful toddler. Mrs. Xia fell in love with Juan once she set eyes on her. With Juan's large number of siblings, Juan was always neglected. Mrs. Xia offered to babysit Juan, and Juan's parents gladly accepted. Soon, Juan ate with Mrs. Xia and slept with Mrs. Xia. Juan practically became Mrs. Xia's daughter. When Juan's family was ready to move to Shanghai, Mrs. Xia asked whether Juan could stay with them in Yiyang. Juan's family said "yes" without any hesitation. They had eight children already. Juan wouldn't be missed.

Juan was actively involved in the propaganda team at her middle school. For some reason, wherever she went she would take me with her. I was her follower. In fact, her friends called me "the little follower." The young student team marched toward the countryside singing various songs.

"Walking on the road toward socialism!"
"Sweep away illiteracy!"
"Liberation of women!"
"Peoples' collective farming for our socialist country!"

Loud drums and gongs accompanied all these songs to intensify their impact. The students were enthusiastically engaged in all of their propaganda activities. They taught peasants to read and write. They offered slideshows to promote equal rights for men and women. However, "walking toward socialism" was a little vague and "collective farming" was too far-fetched. They didn't know that the Chinese Communist Party planned to nationalize everything as the Soviets had done in their country. The songs were all simply slogans at that time.

Juan became my mentor. Although we were about 5 to 6 years apart, I followed Juan everywhere she went. I enjoyed going out with her and often played at her house. At the beginning of the summer in 1960, Juan graduated from high school. Unfortunately, she failed the university entrance exam and so wasn't accepted at any university.

The exam was held each year during the summer after the spring semester had ended. All the high school graduates would take their exams at the same time across the entire country. The exams took place over three days and covered the subjects studied during their senior high school years, which included Chinese essay, Math, Physics, Chemistry, Biology, and a foreign language. These exam days were "holy days" for all the high school graduates and their families. These days were so important because they determined a student's entire future. If you failed to get accepted by a university, you would be forced to work in the countryside as a hard laborer among the peasants.

In Communist China, the peasants were the poorest class, even though they had been liberated from exploitation by the landlords. Unlike city residents, peasants in the countryside received no food rations. They often faced shortages during the period after the food from the previous harvest had all been consumed, and prior to the next crop being harvested. They worked hard all year long so that they might have enough food for their family. The government land redistribution, land nationalization and collective farming policies ruined the landlords, but also didn't help the peasants put food on their tables! Everybody became equally poor!

The recent "down to the countryside" high school graduates were not used to physically demanding heavy labor work and so couldn't generate enough food for themselves. They became a burden to the local village. In most cases their parents had to share their own food rations with their "down to the countryside" sons or daughters. Following all the hard work and study necessary during their high school years, being sent to the countryside was an enormous mental punishment for these former students. They often ended up losing all hope and lived one day at a time. There were very few universities in China. For the majority of high school graduates, the only road ahead was to be a young peasant. It was a most unpleasant and grim future, one the graduates wanted to avoid at all cost.

After being rejected by the university, Juan was in agony — depressed and desperate to avoid being sent to the countryside. She no longer called on me, and I absolutely understood. Grandmother told me, the "residence committee" had started visiting Juan's mother daily to persuade Mrs. Xia to allow Juan "down to the countryside."

They said to Mrs. Xia, "The order came directly from Chairman Mao. Everyone should obey. There are no jobs here in town. You should not allow Juan to stay at home with nothing to do. Letting Juan stay at home is not good for her or our Communist society."

Mrs. Xia was determined to not let her daughter go. She argued, "You can kill me, I don't care. Juan is my only daughter, and I need her help at home. I am a seamstress making clothes for our community. I need Juan's extra helping hands!"

Finally, the residence committee went after Mr. Xia. They talked to Mr. Xia's boss. They needed his boss to cooperate with them so that if Mr. Xia didn't agree to let Juan "down to the countryside," they could hint that he would be sacked. The job was his entire livelihood, or as expressed in a Chinese saying, the job was his "rice bowl (*fan wan*)." Without a job the entire family would starve. Juan had to go.

Juan was finally assigned to a countryside village and worked as a peasant. She sometimes came back to visit her parents and often stayed home a long time, consuming her parents' food rations. Once you became a "down to the countryside" person, your registration of residency (Hukou) would follow you to your assigned village and you would lose all your rations. Most "down to the countryside" young people would stay home longer than allowed. They needed to recover from the physical and mental pain. This placed an extra burden on the rest of the family as food rations had to be shared.

When Juan came home, I would visit her. She was no longer cheerful and wasn't quite herself. She kept busy helping her mother with sewing and household chores. I was often left out in the cold. Juan and I finally separated and no longer saw each other.

Yiyang was a small town, and gossip spread very quickly. In the beginning, people thought Juan to be a likable girl. She had managed to obtain a teaching job in the countryside at the local village elementary school. Then rumors started to spread that Juan had fallen in love and married a local village teacher in the countryside without the consent of her parents. In Yiyang, the majority of people still held the traditional feudal view that marriage should be arranged by parents and a matchmaker.

Local housewives were whispering that the young girl hadn't respected tradition and lacked their perceived moral values. There were many legendary stories, folk operas of tragedies befalling young lovers. People were sympathetic towards young lovers when they read such stories. They shed tears for the young couple when they were forced to part during an opera. However, in real-life situations involving young lovers, sharp tongues were dominant. Once you stepped outside traditional boundaries, your life became everybody's business.

Juan's marriage was a devastating blow to her parents. Marriage to a local village teacher in the countryside destroyed any hope that their daughter might return to the city. Mrs. Xia cried day and night. She refused to accept her daughter's marriage. Juan and her new husband tried to earn her mother's heart, but all their efforts were in vain. The door was held tightly shut by Mrs. Xia: divorce or I disown you!

Meanwhile, Mr. and Mrs. Xia discussed Juan's situation with her birth parents. Juan's birth father belonged to the Red workers' class. He was a middle-ranking manager in a Shanghai factory. They suggested that, if they persuaded Juan to come alone and visit them in Shanghai, the resulting separation between Juan and her husband might change the situation. Mr. and Mrs. Xia agreed. Juan's birth mother wrote to Juan and invited her to visit them in Shanghai.

Juan had lost the affection of her adopted mother and felt she had been deserted. Under these circumstances she was, of course, delighted to accept the invitation to visit her birth parents, although her husband had unspoken reservations. As it turned out, this would be the last time they would see each other.

The sweet invitation to visit was followed by daily, intense discussions between Juan and her birth mother, full of persuasion, threats, and temptation.

"Being a village teacher in the countryside isn't the life your adopted mom wanted for you. She's heartbroken; she loves you so much. You are her entire life, her hope. How can you do this to your mom! Since you and your husband's Hukou are in the countryside, you will be poor your entire life. Your future children will also be poor villagers and will never obtain a city Hukou. Prospects for a village kid are very dim." — Persuasion.

"Your mom will never accept you until you divorce." — Threat.

"After your divorce, we can help you find a job in the city." — Temptation.

"There will be a team in your Abo's factory (Juan called her birth father Abo) that will be transferring to Chengdu in Sichuan Province. Your Abo could submit your name as our daughter. Chengdu is a big city, and you would have a much better life there instead of being a village teacher. But they only allow unmarried children of factory workers to apply. If you don't divorce your husband, you will have no chance to go." — Another threat!

Village life was miserable. Juan was longing for a comfortable city life where the government provided rations and there was the possibility of larger earning power. Being a "down to the countryside" youth meant heavy labor work, meager food provided by the village for her teaching contribution, and a grim future as a peasant. All these problems depressed Juan, who slowly became more amenable to the suggestions of her birth mother. The hopelessness and emptiness Juan had experienced over the past year had pushed her to fall in love and escape the pain. Now, she began to think that their love was maybe not so strong. Juan was confused, and the love for her husband was weakening. During this same period, Juan had discovered that she was pregnant. The depression, the anxiety, the confusion, the temptation all weakened Juan's beliefs. It seemed a lost battle. Juan finally gave in and agreed to divorce her husband.

While Juan's birth parents had been working to change her mind, Mr. and Mrs. Xia were already preparing her divorce proceedings. Divorce was scarce and uncommon. It was the first time I had ever heard the word "divorce." It was the first time such a thing had happened in our town. Following the new rules, divorce needed to be agreed upon by both parties — husband and wife. In addition, the local government had a final say to "seal the deal." Local rumors were that Mr. and Mrs. Xia were bribing government officials and were doing all they could to prevent any attempt to stop the divorce.

Juan's husband rejected the divorce proposal and demanded to see Juan. Mr. and Mrs. Xia said, "Juan is in Shanghai, and she will write to you."

Juan wrote to her husband. She cried out that she could not bear the hardship of village life in the countryside. She told her husband she was sorry. While she was writing, there were tears in her eyes. She went on to say she thought it would be best for both of them if they separated. Finally, she also told her husband she was pregnant with his child.

Her husband's heart was broken, but he was a sensible man. His own mother had warned him not to climb up to the top branch of a tree and marry a city girl.

He wrote back to Juan saying, "Your heart for me is gone. It is no use for me to hold on to you. The child you are carrying belongs to both of us. I want to raise the child after he or she is born. It will be a memory of our love. I hope you really loved me when we first met, married, and lived together."

The divorce was approved, and the divorce paper affixed with many official seals. Juan's husband reluctantly signed the paper. Months later, Juan gave birth to a little boy. She reluctantly gave up the boy that she had carried for nine months. She finally said good-bye to Yiyang and left for Chengdu. As Mr. and Mrs. Xia had hoped, Juan remarried and had two more children. Juan's new family had a Chengdu Hukou. The little boy she gave up was never mentioned again.

People in Yiyang were angry with Mr. and Mrs. Xia. They said Mr. and Mrs. Xia had bullied the poor and favored the rich. People's lips can flip back and forth so easily. What a peculiar, ill-conceived society! Thousands of years of feudally constrained minds had suddenly been interleaved with new Communist rules to create a complicated and conflicted society. Since that time, I have never seen or spoken to Juan.

The Execution of a Korean War Hero

In the summer after I had finished second grade in the West Gate School, Miss Chen visited our house and asked whether I would like to be part of the summer students' dance group. Miss Chen was the third-grade teacher. She was in her early twenties with a slender figure, oval face, and phoenix eyes under crescent eyebrows. She had ancient beauty and a seductive grace. Many young teachers in my school were not local people. Young teachers had usually newly graduated from educational universities and were then assigned to schools all over the country. They would not take the summer off. Often, they organized summer activities with local students. "The Buffalo Boy and the Weaver Fairy" was one of the dances that Miss Chen was organizing for her pupils.

"The Buffalo Boy and the Weaver Fairy" is based on a legendary Chinese fable. The weaver fairy was the seventh daughter of the Goddess of Heaven. She had become bored and escaped from heaven to have some fun. The buffalo boy and the weaver fairy fell in love and became happily married with two children on Earth. Once the Goddess of Heaven found out the weaver fairy had married an Earth boy, the Goddess became furious and immediately ordered the fairy to return to heaven to continue her weaving duties.

However, with the help of the boy's buffalo, they secretly met again in heaven. The Goddess discovered this and was very angry. Taking out her hairpin, the Goddess scratched a wide river in the sky between the stars Altair and Vega to separate the two lovers forever, thus forming the Milky Way (银河). Their love was so strong it moved the magpies. Once a year all the magpies in the world would fly up into heaven to form a bridge (鹊桥, the bridge of magpies) over the Milky Way so that the lovers could be together for a single night — the seventh night of the seventh month in the Chinese calendar. It is referred to as the Qixi Festival.

During summer nights, it would become very hot inside the house, so we often stayed out late into the evening. We would set up our bamboo folding bed in front of our house. All our neighbors did the same. On hot summer nights, our alley was always very crowded. We would lie on the cool bamboo bed and look up at the dark summer night sky, densely studded with thousands of bright, twinkling stars. There was the Milky Way we called the Silver River (银河) with Altair and Vega on either side. Grandmother repeated the story of the buffalo boy and the weaver fairy again and again on those nights. She used a fan made of a palm leaf to chase away the mosquitoes for us until eventually we fell fast asleep. When the house became cool enough, she carried us in one by one and laid us down inside the mosquito nets.

Miss Chen wanted me to play the part of the buffalo boy, since I had a loud, boyish voice. "The Buffalo Boy and the Weaver Fairy" dance was performed each summer by young students on the town streets. The dance was a small portion of the story itself. The dance was happy and comic, recounting the time when the weaver fairy came down from heaven to be with the buffalo boy. She openly flirted with the boy, but the slow-to-respond, dim-witted boy didn't take the hint from the weaver fairy. I was not an outgoing student and was very shy. When Miss Chen asked me to play the part of the buffalo boy, I said no. Miss Chen was very disappointed and went looking for another candidate. Afterward, I was a little disappointed in myself too. I felt I had been rude to her.

Two days later, shocking news came that Miss Chen had been found dead in her living quarters located inside the West Gate School compound. Soon after, people said she had been murdered. Her face was covered with blood from her mouth, eyes, and ears. She had been strangled. The entire town was in disbelief, and everyone was terrified. The Communist Party had declared the eye for an eye (一命抵一命) policy. If you killed someone, your punishment was a bullet to the head. Murder hadn't happened for many years in our little town. It was earth-shattering.

Everybody was talking about it. She was such a nice, pretty teacher; a beautiful young life so tragically shortened. I was sad and remorseful. I should have said "yes" to Miss Chen when she asked me to play the buffalo boy.

About two or three weeks later, the Public Security Bureau caught the murderer, a Korean War hero, who had killed many Americans and injured himself during the war. After the war he had been assigned a job in the movie theater working at the ticket window. Miss Chen had gone to the movie theater a couple times and bought tickets from him. Each time he saw Miss Chen, his wolfish nature became aroused.

On the night in question, he went to West Gate School and entered Miss Chen's living quarters, which was basically a small room sectioned off from the third-grade classroom. According to the Public Security Bureau, Miss Chen had awakened from her sleep and found the man on top of her. She started screaming loudly, and so he strangled her. After her death, he raped her.

Rumors spread that the war hero was confident he wouldn't be executed. He was, after all, a hero of our Communist country. However, the Communist Party never valued human life highly, even if you were a hero. The death penalty was handed down quickly, and his execution would be carried out immediately!

The execution and public condemnation would be held in the town stadium, which was located at the end of Dayin Lane, near the outskirts of the residential neighborhood. That afternoon, people from all over town started gathering at Dayin Lane and began walking toward the stadium. People said the condemned killer would come down along South Gate Road from the downtown jail and then turn into Dayin Lane. Grandmother, Aunt Zhen, and our neighbors were all on the street waiting to see the condemned man pass by toward the stadium. People were seemingly excited, but were mostly curious.

I was in the crowd behind the grownups. I didn't want to be at the front. A little before 2 o'clock, the crowd started moving, pushing, shouting.

"They are here!" someone cried.

A bunch of security officers, more than five, surrounded a cart carrying the convicted man to his death. The cart was made of wood with two large wheels on each side. The man was laid on wooden planks inside the cart and was covered with a padded cotton quilt secured with flax rope. They rushed down from South Gate Road and passed us quickly, in the blink of an eye. People immediately ran after the cart toward the town stadium. I didn't follow.

People said the man had already lost his soul, and he had to be carried onto the stage. He couldn't stand up, so two security officers had to hold him. Thousands gathered at the stadium; the public condemnation meeting was short.

The head of the Public Security Bureau announced, "This man has raped Miss Chen and strangled her to death. The government policy is an eye for an eye."

The Korean War hero had been sentenced to death and was to be executed immediately. The security officers dragged him down from the stage to the countryside field and shot him in the head.

That night was eerily quiet. I couldn't sleep. My imagination was running wild. Images kept entering my mind: Miss Chen's gory face, the cart carrying the killer, the shot in his head. I couldn't help but feel ghostly scared. I crawled into Grandmother's bed. The light was still on. Grandmother couldn't sleep either.

Soon after, I was happy and relieved to learn that I wouldn't have to return to West Gate School. The local government announced that all children would be enrolled in their local district school. My school would now be the South Gate School. I had been so scared about returning to West Gate School as I imagined sitting in the third-grade classroom right next to Miss Chen's living quarters.

My "Rightist" Teacher

My third-grade homeroom teacher in South Gate School was Mr. Wong. He was a tall, dark-skinned, middle-aged man. Coming from West Gate to the South Gate School, I suddenly found I had become a swan among the ducks, a phoenix among the chickens. West Gate School was a far better school than South Gate. I, a mediocre student in West Gate School, had now become a top student after transfer to South Gate. Mr. Wong often praised me in front of other pupils, which made me feel so good about myself! I worked harder and became a top student. It was my turning point academically.

Unfortunately, near the end of the second semester of third grade, Mr. Wong suddenly disappeared. We had a substitute named Miss Lee. Miss Lee didn't tell us what had happened to Mr. Wong. Nobody asked about him either, but I always wondered. Later we learned that Mr. Wong came from a Black family. His father had been a landlord. During the anti-rightist campaign, he became classified as a rightist. He was sent to the countryside to do hard labor under surveillance. Nobody knew what he had said or what he had done to become labeled a rightist.

During that same summer in 1957, the older son, Fu, of our next-door neighbor, Mrs. Shi, failed to return home from university. The elder Mr. Shi was a Kuomintang army officer who had escaped to Taiwan before the Communist Party took over China. Fu had been attending a technology university in Nanjing during the anti-rightist campaign. He had been classed as a Black family student because of his father. Aunt Zhen told Grandmother that Mrs. Shi was crying because Fu had been persecuted as a rightist in the university and so would be sent to a gulag camp in Xinjiang — an autonomous region in the far northwest of China.

Before he was sent to Xinjiang, Aunt Zhen accompanied Mrs. Shi to visit Fu in Nanjing. Witnessing the scene of mother and son parting forever — a tragic Swan Song (生死离别) — gave Aunt Zhen a sharp pang of sorrow and sympathy for them. Fu was eventually released and reunited with his family in 1980; 23 years of a productive young life totally wasted. Through the mercy of God, he was still alive.

The first crop of rightists in the Communist quota system came from the Black class families. They were the scapegoats in all the Communist movements and campaigns. Black family members could be persecuted for doing nothing, saying nothing; we were simply part of the Black class. In such circumstances, how could we ever be happy? We had to be resentful. The addition of yet another rightist made the family even "blacker." Very soon, Mrs. Shi and her second son, Yun, had also been forced "down to the countryside," a Communist movement called "whole family down to the countryside" (*quan jia xia fang*, 全家下放). Their city Hukou was stripped from them, and their government rations were removed. Our new neighbor was a Red class family — a vendor, a widow with an adopted teenage son.

Great Leap Forward and the Famine

I only stayed at South Gate School for one year. By the summer, the Three Red Flags and the Great Leap Forward campaigns were in full force. Chairman Mao wanted to industrialize China and "overtake the British and compete with the Americans," but he had no patience. He wanted to speed things up, which led to the Great Leap Forward. He encouraged the entire country, including the peasants, to produce steel (大炼钢铁). He wanted more rice crops from each acre of land. He also initiated collective farming or "The People's Commune" where the peasants ate together in a canteen, lived close to each other, and worked together on the land. Within this community, everyone had food to eat, work to do. Mao believed that when the land was combined in this fashion, farming would become more efficient — a cult system. Sadly, as is human nature, no one was motivated to work hard, and three years of famine quickly followed! The Great Leap Forward turned out to be a Great Leap Backward for China!

In Yiyang, South Gate School became the steel production center. All South Gate students were merged into Peace School on Peace Street in the northern outskirts of town. It was an exciting summer for us, the kids, but was a headache for the adults. The residence committee galvanized all residents to work at South Gate School and "Make Steel" (大炼钢铁). A tall steel-making furnace was built in the school courtyard. It was made entirely from mud even though nobody actually knew how to make steel.

Fuel was needed for producing steel, so people searched all over town for wood. There was no wood to spare, so wooden doors came down and wooden tools were chopped up for fuel. What was needed to make steel? People initially searched for scrap iron. When they couldn't find any more scrap iron, they contributed their spare cooking woks and spatulas. All woks, spatulas, door knobs were melted down together and became useless odd-shaped lumps of iron. This was Yiyang town's contribution to the Great Leap Forward — Make Steel. I didn't know how much steel was reported to Chairman Mao by our town's government, but afterward we heard nothing about it. Chairman Mao must have been very satisfied with our contribution!

During each Communist Party campaign, Chairman Mao would use the idea of a mass movement (群众运动) to get everyone involved. When he heard that the birds were eating the crops, he ordered all the peasants to bring out gongs, pans, and anything that could make a loud noise to scare away the birds. When someone told him that rats were stealing the food, he ordered us to kill the rats. Our school principal told each pupil to bring in rat tails to prove how many rats he or she had killed. We had rats at our home, but our cat and our neighbor's cats took care of them and I couldn't compete. We went to the local farms to catch rats, but couldn't get any! We didn't know how, and we were afraid of rats. Grandmother was our savior again. She asked her nephews in God Pond Valley to help out. Each one of us got a rat tail to bring to school.

During this period, it seemed that basic common sense had disappeared from society. We did what we were told to do. No one dared say no. Even the birds were scared! During these three disastrous years, I never heard the birds sing; never saw magpies or even the small sparrows.

After the Great Leap Forward, our townspeople became restless and worried. The worst famine in China's history was spreading across the entire country. The Communist government blamed the famine on natural disasters.

One morning, Grandmother sent me to South Gate Road to buy some soy sauce. While I was waiting for the store clerk to fill my soy sauce bottle, there was suddenly a rush of people running outside the store. They were chasing a skinny man — a skeletal peasant. As he ran, the man was stuffing a bun into his mouth, gobbling the bun as fast as he could. Finally, they caught him, but, by that time, the bun had been eaten. People said the man grabbed the bun from a street vendor, and then ran as fast as he could. Most people felt sorry for the man. A cornered dog would jump over a wall; only a desperate person would resort to such desperate measures. They said let him go.

For the townspeople, there were government-provided rations: 24 *jin* (one *jin* equals 1.1 lb) rice and 0.25 *jin* cooking oil per person, per month. The townspeople went to the government-operated stores to buy the rice and oil with cash, accompanied with the government-provided rice and oil ration tickets. We called them: *liang piao* (粮票), and *you piao* (油票). No one in the town or city had starved to death yet, but daily news came from friends and relatives in the countryside that people were starving and dying every day.

One of the neighborhood teenagers, Wei Wei, who was a couple years older than me, had become creative. He called on us, a few neighborhood teenagers/preteens, to form a "defense group" to prevent bad people from coming into our neighborhood to steal. It was an exciting and challenging prospect, but it was just talk, there was no action. We were so young and simply couldn't comprehend starving to death. In our minds, we always thought that stealing was bad.

The 1959 winter was extremely cold. Two feet of snow piled up in our alley. Foot-long icicles hung from the rim of our roof. On one of these cold nights while we were in a deep sleep, a sudden loud noise awakened us.

Grandmother said, "What was that?"

It seemed as if the sound had come from the kitchen. Before Grandmother had finished her sentence, we heard someone running outside. Aunt Zhen and Grandmother immediately got up to check it out. There was a big hole in the kitchen wall, large enough to allow a person to enter our house. Luckily, inside our house right below the hole there was a metal pan. The thief had carefully removed the bricks from the outside and then, as his last action, tried to push in the inner clay plaster wall. As he pushed, a chunk of plaster dropped onto the metal pan and made a noise. This noise was not deafening, but in the quiet hours during the middle of the night, it woke all of us up. Although it was unlucky for the thief, who had unfortunately opened the hole just above the metal pan, it was very lucky for us!

Grandmother and Aunt Zhen were discussing what they should do other than seal the hole. Aunt said that we should report the incident to the Public Security Bureau, but we didn't want the Public Security Bureau "chasing the wind and clutching at shadows (捕风捉影)" and then make groundless accusations on us! At the same time, we had foreign connections, so we should report anything that might cause suspicion. Aunt ordered me to get out of my warm bed, put on my cotton padded jacket, and go with her to the Public Security Bureau.

It had stopped snowing, but the ground was covered with white, soft snow. It was so quiet; we could hear our own footsteps. Every step I took made a deep imprint in the snow. The town was in a deep sleep. There was only a single light hanging high on the street pole near the intersection of Dayin Lane and South Gate Road. The white snow illuminated the dark winter night. The light rays from the street pole made the snow seem yellowish and patchy. I saw large footprints leading away from the hole in our wall. There was no wind, but it was still frigid. I tucked my head into my jacket collar and crossed my arms, keeping my hands under my armpit. I was shivering and running behind Aunt.

The Public Security Bureau was located in the town center, which was quite a distance from our house. When we reached South Gate Bridge, Aunt re-thought the situation: it was too far to go in the middle of the night. On such a cold night, there might be nobody in the office when we arrived. She decided to cancel the trip and return home. She was probably scared herself. I was so glad that Aunt decided to go back home.

Next day, Aunt reported the incident to the Public Security Bureau. Nobody put any importance on the incident. Nothing was done! Aunt Zhen paid someone to fix the wall. Grandmother said the thief had known the layout of our house, as he seemed to know where our kitchen was. During the last few days while the sun had been shining, we had been hanging our preserved salty duck and chicken outside for airing and drying. In the evening, we would bring them back to our kitchen. Tempted, after seeing these salty chicken and duck during the day, he must have decided to come during the night to snatch them.

We raised our own chickens. Besides making clothes for our family, Aunt Zhen also started making clothes for others. In exchange, they gave us ducks or vegetables. During the summer, Aunt would kill the chickens and ducks. She and Grandmother would pull off the bird feathers, clean out the insides, salt the poultry, and place them into a sealed jar. Then when the cold winter came, the jar was opened and the poultry hung outside to allow them to air dry.

After experiencing so much family hardship, Aunt Zhen became very handy and daring. She killed the birds without hesitation, even though before the Communist Party takeover, she was the second young lady (二少奶奶) in our household, served by maids and nannies. She would hold the bird's head back, remove the feathers on the neck, and then slit the throat. Then she would drain the blood into a bowl as she held the bird's neck backward. The bird struggled to escape during the entire time she was doing these things.

We would not consume these delicacies until Chinese New Year after offering sacrifices to our ancestors. Grandmother said, every year in the past when she hung the poultry out, nobody paid any attention, but now people had become desperate for food.

Starting in 1956 our financial situation improved. My father had already graduated from the University of Michigan with a master's degree in Engineering. He had started to work for the General Motors Company. After many years of waiting for an American visa in Hong Kong, my mother was finally reunited with my father in the US, and they established a new, well-deserved family. My parents started sending money to us to help support the living expenses of my grandmother and their two daughters — me and Xiao Mei. At that time, there was no diplomatic relationship between the US and China. The money was first sent to Aunt Ermay in Hong Kong, and then Aunt Ermay would transfer it to us.

Although the money was only meant for the three of us, the entire family relied on it to exist, and there were also debts to be paid. However, we had enough food to fill our stomachs and occasionally "new" Aunt Zhen homemade clothes to wear. There were no luxuries. A piece of toasty rice crumpet bought from a street vendor for breakfast was an absolutely luxurious treat. Our normal daily breakfast was rice porridge with pickled vegetables. Candy for the children was out of the question. Once, Grandmother got a piece of candy from her friend. She didn't allow herself to enjoy the candy. She brought it home and cut the candy into four small pieces for my two cousins, my sister, and me to share.

By 1959, although famine was spreading across the country, our financial situation became much improved. We paid off our debts, and my parents sent more money regularly. There was an unbridgeable personality gap between Grandmother and Aunt Zhen. Aunt was cunning and witty. She was manipulative and extremely social. Grandmother came from the countryside and was plain-spoken. She never held grudges and would not take advantage of anyone. Her friends described her as magnanimous and tolerant. In terms of money, there was also a huge chasm between them. Aunt Zhen loved to save money. Money was very important to her, and she never felt she had enough. She was shrewd and grasping. She would like to take petty advantage of others. Grandmother was infinitely merciful. If there was money in her pocket, she would like to spend it on us, the children.

She said, "Money is for people to use, not to be stacked inside a dresser."

She loved to help. She gave our leftover food to beggars who came to our door and reached out to her friends who had difficulty.

There were constant quarrels. Aunt Zhen complained Grandmother was wasteful and extravagant. Grandmother admitted she had loose hands with money. She agreed to let Aunt control all the money sent from my parents. Grandmother asked that money sent by her daughter Ermay be her pocket money. Aunt Ermay didn't do well in Hong Kong. She only sent small amounts of money, about 15 Yuan, every 2 months. Grandmother tried her best to control her spending habits.

The starvation in God Pond Valley drove relatives to come ask for help. Grandmother always tried to help them. She gave them money but didn't have enough. She gave our rice to them when Aunt wasn't home. Aunt was mad when she found out.

She shouted, "You seem to have no regard for your own grandchildren! You give out our rations and let your own children starve. These boys will carry your family name and continue the Lee generation."

Aunt was proud she had given birth to two boys. She told Grandmother to save some money for their future, instead of spending money like there was no tomorrow. "You want to be nice to everybody! How about being nice to your own children?"

Grandmother became angry and shouted back, "You are so heartless. People are dying in the villages. These people treated us well and helped us when we were down and starving. You are so ungrateful. Since when do I not love my grandchildren?"

Grandmother wept. We all loved our grandmother, including Da Di and Xiao Di (Aunt's two sons). She was always there for us.

Aunt Zhen did her sewing at home. The rest of the time she would often visit her friends or neighbors. Grandmother, with her bound feet, worked in and out doing all the household chores. Her bound feet were a curse for her. If she ran, she would stumble. Every time, I went to the riverbank with Grandmother to wash clothes and clean vegetables, I worried that Grandmother might fall.

She told me that her feet were actually larger than most girls of her age. The feet-binding years started when she was only about 2 years of age. The process was awful. She was in agony. Her mother felt sorry for her even though her mother had bound feet herself. During the night, when Grandmother cried out in pain, her mother would loosen the cloth around her feet.

When her grandmother found out, her grandmother would scold her mother. "You are ruining your own daughter's future. Who will marry a girl with big feet?"

I was especially close to my grandmother. She raised me. Her unselfishness toward me was far more than you would expect even from a birth mother. It made me sad when Aunt Zhen and Grandmother fought. When I was a young child, I didn't pay much attention, but later, when I saw Grandmother crying, I would say to Grandmother quietly, "Nai Nai, Grandma, please don't cry."

I didn't understand why Aunt Zhen set such a watchful eye on Grandmother's pocket money. It was her money. She should be able to spend it as she wished.

I had become more sensible as I grew older and started to enter my teens. Aunt Zhen had tried her best to let me and my sister know that she treated us fairly. She also made sure all her friends and neighbors knew that she was treating us far better than her own children.

During the Chinese New Year holidays, there were treats for the children: rice crackers, caramelized peanuts, and candies. Aunt would divide treats equally into four glass jars for Da Di, Xiao Di, Xiao Mei, and me. She said, normally boys should have more because boys have a much bigger stomach and they would usually eat more. But she wanted to give equal amounts to me and my sister, Xiao Mei. She wanted us to know she was being fair and not favoring her own children.

During those days, I always appreciated Aunt's fairness. She seldom shouted at me or punished me, but there was no love. Love should be an unspoken feeling, not hanging on the mouth. I had always sensed a wall between Aunt and me. When I was a young, innocent child, I used to open Aunt's dresser and take out Aunt's fake jewelry to play with. However, lately, Aunt had become very defensive of her dresser.

A couple of times when I opened her dresser looking for my sweater, she would ask, "What are you looking for? I will get it for you."

I had become more sensitive and mature, and so never opened the dresser again. I had the feeling that Aunt stored her cash there and that it wasn't a place for me to poke around. I knew my place in the household and never stepped outside my boundary. I was expected to be sensible and not upset anyone, especially Aunt Zhen. Although Aunt was never suspicious of me stealing, she didn't want me to know that she had money hidden away. In later years, when her own daughter, San Mei, became a teenager, she didn't mind if San Mei opened the dresser and took things in and out.

Grandmother also complained that Aunt was a penny pincher. She said Aunt didn't buy enough food for the children. Grandmother thought that growing children needed nutrition and so often used her own pocket money to bring pork home for us.

Aunt said, "You don't know how to manage money. You don't realize how expensive things are!"

In 1959, the residential committee encouraged residents to join the local canteen. They said, "This is the socialist road we shall walk." Forced to follow the rules, Aunt sent Xiao Mei, Da Di, and me to join the canteen and represent our household. Very soon, Da Di withdrew from the canteen. Aunt said the two girls were more sensible than the boy and would manage their rations better. We young teenagers never second-guessed Aunt's argument. We never wondered what they were eating at home during the "eat in canteen" period.

We joined the canteen willingly and, in the beginning, were excited. Every month Aunt gave each of us 24 *jin* rice tickets (our monthly ration) and some money to purchase cooked or pickled vegetables at the canteen. Aunt was right. Xiao Mei and I managed our rations very carefully and never overspent.

In the morning, we would buy 2 *liang* (3.53 oz) of rice porridge and 2 *feng* (Chinese penny) of pickled vegetables. Sadly, there was little rice in the bowl. Most of it was water. In the morning, I was always so hungry. In the middle of my classes, my stomach started grunting and groaning. If you cooked at home, 2 *liang* of raw rice would yield a full bowl of cooked rice.

For lunch and dinner, we would buy 3 *liang* of cooked rice and some cooked vegetables. For us in the canteen, 3 *liang* of rice turned out to be only half a bowl. It was up to the canteen worker. If you were their friends, they would give you a full bowl of rice. The vegetables were boiled, and there was hardly any cooking oil used. Sometimes they even sold water weeds to us, and they tasted awful.

The canteen was run by the residence committee who hired their own relatives and friends to work in the canteen. They stole the rice and cooking oil and sold them to the black market. During the "eat in canteen" years, the residence committee's family and friends got fatter as Xiao Mei and I starved!

When I was 12 years old, I entered puberty and had my first period. I was skinny and petite. I sensed that Grandmother worried about my growth. One day, when nobody was around, she called me into the kitchen and offered me a bowl of rice. I was so hungry; I quickly devoured the rice in mouthfuls. As my chopsticks dug into the rice, I discovered a whole boiled egg! I was so excited, my eyes brightened up.

I exclaimed, "Egg!"

Grandmother hushed at me. "Shush! Hurry up and finish it."

I noticed sadness in Grandmother's eyes. I was too young to fully comprehend the reason for Grandmother's feelings. Grandmother tried her best to help me, given her limited power.

Grandmother was getting older each day and became more and more fragile. Xiao Mei and I started carrying out more of the household chores. Following traditional feudal social customs, household chores were not for boys. In contrast, girls had to learn to cook, to sew, and to do embroidery in their early teens. Grandmother became more irrelevant in managing the household, and Aunt Zhen climbed up, showing her dominance. There was a love-hate relationship between Grandmother and Aunt Zhen.

Aunt Zhen married into our family when she was only 17 years old. As a new daughter-in-law, she was obedient and respectful and knew how to please her parents-in-law. Knowing that Aunt Zhen had lost her mother when she was only 9 years old, Grandmother had a soft spot for her new daughter-in-law. Yet Grandmother had reservations regarding my mother who was college-educated, arrogant, and born of aristocracy. Grandmother was afraid to get close to my mother.

After the Communist Party took over China, unceasing mishaps and misfortunes fell upon us, one after the other. Grandmother and Aunt relied on each other for comfort and strength. In fact, they complemented one another. Grandmother was a kind, gentle, good-natured person, who lived in harmony with our neighbors. Aunt Zhen was audacious, yet smooth and diplomatic. She would not let anyone take advantage of her or her family. She made friends with the residence committee members and offered to do sewing for their families for free. She started volunteer work for our South Gate residential neighborhood.

Grandmother always praised her behind her back. "My daughter-in-law is very able and smart." When Aunt got sick, Grandmother cried: "She is an important person for our family. We cannot live without her."

Aunt also acknowledged that Grandmother had a kind heart and was a generous person. She said, "Such a good heart will receive good returns. Grandmother's charity will be rewarded with good fortune for our children." These were all in the good days.

Mr. Zong

When I became a fourth grader, I transferred from South Gate School to Peace School where I studied hard. I wanted to maintain my top student status. During the second semester of my sixth grade, there were countywide tests for all students. The sixth graders were only tested in Math and Chinese Essay. A few weeks after the tests, we were all called to the schoolyard, and the principal announced the scores of the top-performing students in our school. To my surprise, I was number one in Yiyang county in both the Math and Essay tests. The school principal was very proud of my achievements, as I had made a name for our school. It also roused my self-confidence and gave me the driving force to excel. I started to develop some childhood pride and self-esteem.

After the finals, we had entrance exams for middle school admission. I felt good and confident on the entrance exams. I was excited and relaxed when summer recess started. On one of the hot, quiet summer afternoons when most people take naps, I decided to visit a girl in our neighborhood named Little Spring. Little Spring loved opera and intended one day to join the local opera troupe, which she later did. I was also a fan of local opera — Yue opera. Grandmother used to take me with her when she went to the local opera. One block from Peace School was our town's opera house, and it was on the way home. After school, I often entered the opera house to watch them rehearse.

That afternoon, Little Spring and I decided to practice the Yue opera "Butterfly Lovers." We called it "Liang Shanbo (梁山伯) and Zhu Yingtai (祝英台)." The opera is similar to Romeo and Juliet — a tragic love story. Yue opera originated in Zhejiang Province, and most of the people in my hometown loved Yue opera. My ears had been tuned to Yue opera since I was a little girl. I remembered that my friend Juan played Liang Shanbo (梁山伯) in one of the high-school operas. I had been invited to the show.

Her mother, Mrs. Xia, was so proud of her and kept saying, "Look at our Juan! She is so good. She sings so well."

While I was humming with Little Spring during the "Meeting at the Chamber" part of "Butterfly Lovers," San Mei came up and said, "Grandmother is asking you to go home at once."

Grandmother had been told by a Xinhua Middle School clerk that I had been accepted by their school. During those days, before the formal announcement, news of admitted students usually spread through word of mouth.

Xinhua Middle School was the third-ranked school in our county and was run by Yiyang town itself. There were three middle schools in our town. One was Jiangsu Yiyang School, affiliated with the Provincial Educational Department; it was ranked number one. The second was Yiyang County Middle School, and, by its name, it was run by Yiyang County. Jiangsu Yiyang School would first choose their preferred students from all the elementary school graduates in the county. Then the remaining students' files would be passed to the Yiyang County Middle School. After the selections were made by the Jiangsu Yiyang and Yiyang County schools, then it would be the turn of Xinhua Middle School and other equivalent local schools. Only unselected Yiyang local town resident students would be referred to Xinhua for selection.

I was utterly disappointed: Xinhua Middle School? It was like a bucket of cold water had been poured on me. I had been so confident I would enter Jiangsu Yiyang School, but I couldn't even get into Yiyang County Middle School! I always dreamed that someday I would be a student at Jiangsu Yiyang School. The school combined both middle and senior high schools together. It taught students from 7th grade all the way to 12th grade.

I had visited Jiangsu Yiyang School many times. Juan used to take me there when she visited her schoolmates at the girls' dormitory. It was a beautiful campus. There was an island surrounded by a running stream. There were two arched wooden bridges connecting the island to the rest of campus. Along both sides of the stream, neatly planted willow trees swung in the breeze and the tips of the branches kissed the water of the creek. Only the teachers' offices were located on the island. There were many rows of single-story buildings for classrooms on the west side of campus, and the dormitories were located on the southeast side of campus. From the outset it was designed to be a school campus; not like my elementary schools, which had all been converted from clan temples. During the visits to Juan's friends, I was teased as Juan's "little follower." It was my greatest desire to study there when I grew older.

After I received the news, I didn't scream, although I wanted to! I took it quietly. I held onto my tears.

Grandmother tried to pacify me. "Emerald, across the street, only got into the Sand River School. She has to live in the school, and you get to stay home."

The Sand River School was a newly established school. It was located about 7 miles from Yiyang town near the Sand River Dam. All unselected Yiyang town students were sent to Sand River School. A year later, the Sand River School was dismantled. Emerald was sent back home, where she spent most of her time taking care of her younger siblings. Later, after she reached 18 years of age, she was forced "down to the countryside" and became a poor peasant.

Not getting into Jiangsu Yiyang School was an unexpected disappointment. My dreams had been shattered. However, after a few days of unhappiness, it was forgotten. Nothing bothers a 13-year-old for very long, and besides, Da Di, my cousin, was also admitted to Xinhua Middle School. It was a long, boring summer. Juan had been rejected for university admission and was hiding at home in no mood to do anything else.

On the first day of middle school, the admission officer, Mr. Zong, called me into his office. He said, "You did extremely well on the entrance exams. Jiangsu Yiyang and Yiyang County Middle School rejected you solely because of your family background. According to government policy, admission should be based, not only on exam results, but also, more importantly, on family background."

He paused, and then continued. "Since your parents moved to America, your exam papers were automatically overlooked. Your file was thrown out even before taking a look at your results. When I chose our students, at first, I did the same thing as the other schools and immediately put your file in the rejected pile. Later, I became curious and wanted to know how you did on the exam. Once I opened your file, I had second thoughts. It was a tough decision — whether to follow the rule or not — but finally I accepted your file."

He looked at me with a kind smile on his face and said, "I think you have great potential for success. 'Where there's a will, there's a way (有志者 事竟成).' Everything depends on a person's effort. I want you to work hard in our school and be proud of yourself."

I didn't say anything. I was very quiet. I was too young to comprehend the logic of Communist policies. At that time, I didn't appreciate that Mr. Zong had done me a tremendous favor. He saved me. Without him, I would have been like Emerald. I would have been sent to Sand River School. After being dismissed as a student, I would have been forced "down to the countryside."

Xinhua Middle School

Xinhua Middle School campus wasn't as attractive as Jiangsu Yiyang School. Instead, it was more like an army barracks. There were three one-story buildings, each with two classrooms and a classroom size of normally 50 to 60 students. The teachers' office was located at the center of campus. In front of the office were two sweet-olive trees. In the autumn, their sweet, delightful fragrance would spread across the entire campus. Behind the office and classrooms was a large lawn. Across from the lawn was a small hill with trees and a babbling brook. It formed a natural boundary between the school and adjacent farms. Before finals, I often studied in these woods.

It turned out that the three years of Xinhua Middle School were the best school years of my life in China. China had been suffering through a terrible famine with tens of millions starving to death. Mao had gone into hibernation. He had left Liu Shaoqi and Deng Xiaoping to clean up his mess. There were no more political movements, and class distinctions had become murky. The Communist Party was no longer indoctrinating class warfare. Deng Xiaoping said publicly: "It doesn't matter if a cat is black or white, so long as it catches mice." In 1962, the moderate Lu Dingyi was promoted to vice premier and minister for culture and propaganda. He advocated strongly for academic excellence. Countywide tests were continually being held, and schools were competing for academic performance.

My test results always scored at the very top of the list. Da Di and Xiao Mei also did very well. Xiao Mei was admitted by Xinhua in 1961, one year after me. The Xinhua Middle School was glad to have three high performers from our Black family. By 1962, things had definitely changed for the better. Xiao Di, a Black family born child, was admitted into Jiangsu Yiyang Middle School, the very best school in our county.

I had been so focused on my schoolwork that I hadn't realized the school admission policy had changed. It no longer discriminated against students from Black families. I had grown more confident in myself. During the tests, since I was petite, I always sat in the front row. The examination teacher would stand right next to my desk and monitor how I was doing. This never bothered me; I was so focused on the exam.

By the time I started middle school, I had become a bookworm. I studied hard in all environments. In 1961, the community canteens were dissolved. Xiao Mei and I had to return home to eat. By that time, our household had become moderately well off. With my parents' money, we could buy pork in the black market and so had sufficient food to eat. However, specialty foods, such as bean curd, bean sprouts, and other processed foods, were made by government-controlled businesses and so were in short supply and rationed. In order to purchase these food items, you had to line up for a long time. Unfortunately, each item was sold by a different government shop, and often, when you eventually reached the shop window, all the supplies were gone. The shop clerk would say, "All gone! Come back tomorrow!" The bean curd products were important items for the New Year celebration and the New Year's Eve ancestor ritual.

During New Year school recess, I was often sent to stand in line at a local shop. To make sure we would be able to make a purchase, Aunt Zhen would wake me up before dawn to secure a place in line. I would line up in front of the shop around 6 o'clock, although the shop wouldn't open until 7. A few minutes before the shop opened, Aunt would arrive with the money and ration ticket to replace me. During these times I would always bring a school textbook with me. I would memorize historical events or the various terminologies of biology while I was in line. The winter in Yiyang was cold, especially in the very early morning hours. People in line would chat loudly, while I jumped up and down for warmth and at the same time recited my textbook in my head.

During the summer, when inside the house was too hot, I would sit outside and study in a shady area. The alley was busy. People passed me all the time going back and forth to the riverbank or to the adjacent rice-processing factory. The dust from the factory was choking me, but all the noise and dust couldn't prevent me from studying!

By the third year in middle school, I became very interested in physics. While I was studying preliminary circuit theory that described series and parallel circuits, I decided to try an experiment myself. There was only one lightbulb in our home. At the center of our kitchen and above the dinner table dangled a twisted wire to which was attached a single, naked lightbulb. I could use the theory of parallel circuits to add a second lightbulb in Aunt Zhen's room above a table where Aunt did her sewing on a cutting board. While I was working to set up the electrical circuit, I felt a sudden shock strike my legs, as if someone had hit me with a heavy baseball bat. Luckily, I was standing on a wooden table, otherwise things might have been much worse – I could have died. After wearing my rubber rain boots for safety, I finally managed to get an additional lightbulb working in our home, although exactly how I succeeded I still do not know today!

While we studied Newton's law of universal gravitation, the Physics book included a short biography of Newton; also, when we were introduced to the periodic table of elements, there was a short biography of Marie Curie. These famous scientists fascinated me. I admired their devotion to science. I dreamed of growing up to be a devoted scientist just like them!

I had become a favorite among my schoolteachers, including even members of the Communist Party. Mr. Zhu, our history teacher, was also a leader of the Communist Youth League, an organization of older teenagers that was controlled and supported by the Communist Party. At the end of my second year in middle school, Mr. Zhu asked me to give a speech that described achievement of the three virtues (三德): "Moral Integrity, Academic Excellence, and Physical Fitness." The speech was to be given at the end of the school year assembly. I had never given a speech in front of people and was afraid. Mr. Zhu smiled and told me not to worry. He would write the speech for me, and the only thing I would have to do was read it out loud in front of the school assembly. That day I stood up and felt somewhat lost at the beginning, but then I began reading loudly in front of all my schoolmates. Although my voice was shaking and my lips were trembling, afterwards Mr. Zhu said I did a great job. However, I doubted that.

One day, Mr. Zhu called me into his office and said, "We are recruiting outstanding students who possess the three virtues for our Communist Youth League. I think you are a good candidate, and I am inviting you to apply."

He handed me the application form. I remembered I had been a Young Pioneer of the Communist Party when I first started primary school. All schoolchildren became Young Pioneers as soon as they enrolled in school. The Young Pioneer of the Communist Party was run by the Communist Youth League. Every school day we wore a red scarf around our necks and pledged:

> 我是中国少年先锋队队员。我在队旗下宣誓：我
> 热爱中国共产党，热爱祖国，热爱人民，好好学
> 习，好好锻炼，准备着：为共产主义事业贡献力
> 量.

I am a member of the Young Pioneers of China. Under the Flag of the Young Pioneers I promise that: I will love the Communist Party of China, the motherland, and the people; I will study hard and toughen myself, and prepare for my contributing effort to support the cause of Communism.

Joining the Communist Youth League would be glorious and one step closer to membership in the Communist Party. Only the best could join the Communist Youth League. I was excited and glad to be invited to join. I took the form and ran home to fill out the application.

As I read the form I became more and more discouraged. The form asked for three generations of family history. I asked Grandmother to help me. Our family history had problems: from my great grandfather to my parents' generation, they were all big landlords, capitalists, anti-revolutionaries (my grandfather), and my parents had become "American Imperialists"! There wasn't one bright spot. It was embarrassing.

Grandmother was wise and told me, "You don't have a chance. Your teacher isn't aware of your grandfather and our other relatives' history. He probably only knows that your parents moved to America."

Should I tell the entire true story? I had never lied before. Should I tell the truth? Lying on the application would be a punishable offence. Perhaps I should not turn in the application. If I turned in the application, Mr. Zhu would disdain my family history; it would be very intimidating. If I didn't turn in my application, he might think I didn't want to join the Communist Youth League. It would be anti-Communist. Besides who wouldn't want to be a member of the Communist Youth League?

After days of agonizing over the decision, I turned in my application. As anticipated, it was immediately rejected. I was glad it was over. I never again thought of the importance of joining the Communist Youth League. My name, together with Da Di and Xiao Mei, was always posted on the school honor roll board without being listed as a member of the Communist Youth League.

Spring had passed, and summer had started. My teacher handed out the high school admission applications for senior students. This year there was one more school to choose from — Jiangsu Zhongzhou Senior High School. We were told that it was the best high school in the entire Jiangsu Province, and it had started to recruit the best students from all the counties in the province. My teacher suggested I put Jiangsu Zhongzhou High as my first choice, which I did, although I had never previously heard of it. Jiangsu Yiyang School was my second choice, followed by the Qandu High School. Qandu High was located in Qandu, a smaller town in Yiyang county.

That summer, after we had finished our finals, Da Di and I were preparing for the high school entrance exam. The entrance exam was held a few weeks after finals. We studied day and night. We knew if we could not get into a high school, we would become "Society Youth (社会青年) — jobless urban teenagers." Just like my friend Emerald, we would have no school to attend and no job to perform. Just like Juan, after we reached adult age of 18 years, we would be sent "up to the mountains and down to the countryside" (上山下乡, shangshan xiaxiang).

It was miserable studying during the hot summer nights. Most people stayed outside to cool down until 11 o'clock, but since we needed light we studied inside. In Yiyang, summers were always hot and humid. Sweat continually ran from my forehead down my face. My shirt was soaking wet. The worst thing of all was the mosquitoes that were always flying around me. Grandmother said I had "sweet skin" that attracted mosquitoes. My skin was so sensitive; each bite from a mosquito became a huge red lump; it itched like hell.

Every evening, I would spread DDT all over the house. At that time nobody mentioned, or perhaps knew, that DDT was harmful to humans. We never asked: "If DDT kills mosquitoes, how could it not harm human beings?" We were ignorant. No matter what I did, I was entangled and harassed by the mosquitoes. They seemed not to mind the stinking smell of DDT and were always attracted by the light. By exam day, my arms and legs were covered with red lumps. You could hardly see any clear skin.

Grandmother was very sympathetic and mumbled, "I never went to school. I don't know what the word 'one' looks like, and yet I still live happily. Please don't mistreat yourself."

I was glad the entrance exam was over and I patiently waited for the result. I was calm and relaxed.

The Glory of Our Family

After taking the high school entrance exam, most of my days were occupied with household chores. Early morning, Xiao Mei and I would immediately start cleaning the house. We swept the floor and wiped the furniture. Dust was everywhere because of the adjacent rice-processing complex. Every day the tables were covered with a thick layer of dust. After finishing the dusting, we, together with Grandmother, would sit in the alley to sort out the vegetables. We got rid of yellow leaves and cut off any tough roots. Then we would go to the river to wash the vegetables and rice so that we could start cooking lunch. After completing the morning shopping, Aunt Zhen was busy with her sewing.

Lunch was the big meal of the day. After 3 years of famine, the food situation had vastly improved. For lunch we normally cooked a soup together with two dishes, which were shared among the family. This year, we often had some pork in one of the dishes; a small amount of pork mixed with vegetables. Grandmother used to say, "Adds some flavor to the dish and puts some fat in our stomach." Sometimes, Aunt Zhen also brought home some small fish. Smaller fish were much cheaper.

After lunch we would usually have some spare time. I would help Aunt do some sewing: stitching buttonholes and putting buttons on clothes. I also started reading novels. While I looked after the slow-to-cook simmering porridge for our dinner, I often read stories of the underground Communists fighting the Japanese, such as *Night Escape to Changbai Mountain* and *Stormy Years*.

Summer recess was coming to an end. After dinner everyone had a turn taking a bath to wash away the day's sweat. In search of coolness we set our bamboo beds outside in the alley. After I had taken my bath, I sat on a small stool in the alley washing clothes in a large wooden basin. A man in his fifties walked up and approached me, seemingly very excited. He called out my name. I was puzzled initially, but then recognized him as the man who did odd jobs at Xinhua Middle School.

He said to me, "Principal Gao wanted me to let you know early that you have been admitted to Jiangsu Zhongzhou High!" Then he added, "Only two students from our entire county have been accepted into Jiangsu Zhongzhou High, and the other student was from Jiangsu Yiyang School."

He also let Aunt know that Da Di had been accepted by Jiangsu Yiyang School.

It was a hot summer evening. All our neighbors were enjoying the outside cool air and came up to congratulate me. Grandmother and Aunt were delighted and were all smiles. Of course, I was also very happy. Jiangsu Zhongzhou High had been my first choice. I finished the washing and went to the river to rinse the clothes. All the way to the river and back I hummed Liang Shanbo (梁山伯) and Zhu Yingtai (祝英台), *Butterfly Lovers*.

There were about 20 to 30 families in Dayin Lane. However, since our arrival our immediate neighborhood had totally changed. When we moved to Dayin Lane, there were five condemned families, including our own.

Mrs. Shi was our next-door neighbor. Her husband, a Kuomintang army officer, had escaped to Taiwan. Then, in 1957, her older son was persecuted as a rightist during the anti-rightist movement and was sent to a gulag camp in Xinjiang. This resulted in Mrs. Shi and her teenage son being forced "whole family down to the countryside." Luckily, she had sewing skills and made clothes for the village people, which spared her from heavy labor work.

Mrs. Chen's husband was an important member of Yi Quan Dao who was executed during the Suppression of Counter-Revolutionaries movement. Mrs. Chen and her daughter, my childhood friend Mei Fang, were also forced "down to the countryside." Mrs. Chen died before reaching 60 years of age from poor nutrition and the overwhelming heavy labor demands. My friend, Mei Fang, later married a village peasant.

Mrs. Hsu was spared, even though her husband was also a significant member of Yi Quan Dao and was executed by the Communist government. Her daughter had married into a Red class family and became a nurse in Suzhou. Mrs. Hsu went to Suzhou to take care of her grandchild.

Mr. Wu, who lived across the street, was the "big landlord." He was a very pleasant man and always had a nice smile on his face when he greeted you, regardless of whether you were a child or an adult. In 1958, he was sent for "reform through labor" at the Sand River Dam. During one of many class-struggle sessions, he fainted and never recovered. He passed away from a brain hemorrhage. Mrs. Wu and her youngest daughter, my childhood friend Xiao Qin, went to Beijing and took shelter with her oldest daughter.

Her oldest daughter was a beautiful young girl who had married a Communist Party member during the Korean War. She then worked as a member of the Communist propaganda team during the war. Later, during the Cultural Revolution, Mrs. Wu and Xiao Qin were forced out of Beijing to a village near Yiyang town. Xiao Qin married a "down to the countryside" young man.

According to Aunt Zhen, both Mei Fang and Xiao Qin endured untold suffering. Looking back, I really feel I must have been born under a lucky star to have survived this period in history.

Things had changed dramatically since those early days. Now we stood alone as a condemned family surrounded entirely by working class, Red or Gray families. Aunt Zhen always said that, after all the Communist movements, if Uncle Nian hadn't moved to Shanghai, we would probably also have been forced "whole family down to the countryside." Aunt Zhen also claimed that her clever maneuvers and volunteer work in the neighborhood had saved us, and I agreed with her.

There were only three students admitted to high school in Dayin Lane. In addition to Da Di and me, there was a boy from Jiangsu Yiyang School who was accepted by Qandu High School. As the boy's mother was preparing the bedding for her son's boarding school, she became jealous and complained to my aunt, "You are happily preparing the bedding for your niece. She is going to the best school in a big city, while my boy has been downgraded to a countryside school."

Her jealousy made Aunt Zhen feel very proud and happy, not only because I was going to the best high school, but also because Da Di was accepted into Jiangsu Yiyang School. She told Grandmother that she had never felt so proud of our family, since the dark days that had befallen us after the Liberation of China.

She also told Mrs. Xia, my friend Juan's adopted mother, "Our Da Mei (my nickname) will have a good future. I expect she will take care of me in my old age."

I had occasionally visited Mrs. Xia to ask about Juan. During one conversation, Mrs. Xia let me know that while I was in elementary school, my parents had asked Aunt Zhen to apply for a visa, so that Xiao Mei and I could go to America and be reunited with my parents.

Aunt had told Mrs. Xia, "They are my two money trees. You are kidding that I would let them go."

Mrs. Xia and Aunt Zhen were "friends." Aunt Zhen often visited Mrs. Xia to chat. At the time, I was young and with all the Communist propaganda, I assumed that visiting the American Imperialist country was like visiting hell, and so I had no desire to go. At the time, I didn't pay much attention to Mrs. Xia's words.

Starting My High School Away from Home

As the start of school approached, Aunt was busy making a new shirt for me. Grandmother had taken out the homemade loom to weave me a belt using her trembling hands. She told me that a strong belt could fasten my bedding when I traveled to school and afterward could be used to hang up my wash towel.

Grandmother also started using her own pocket money to buy pork and fish at the street black market. She felt the dormitory food would be much worse than the food at home. She wanted me to enjoy some good home-cooked meals before my journey to school.

She kept exhorting and cautioning me, "When you get to school, you will be on your own with no one to lean on."

She continued giving me lots of advice. "You should be careful and never believe what people tell you; use your own head; remember to put your cotton padded jacket on when the weather turns cold; take care of yourself so you don't get sick." On and on she went. Grandmother was getting old. She was now 67 years of age.

We also had a number of surprise visitors. In those days there were no phones, so every visitor was an uninvited guest. One day a student from Jiangsu Yiyang School, named Cheng He, showed up at our front door together with his parents. Cheng He had also been accepted by Jiangsu Zhongzhou High. He was from a nearby countryside village, and his parents were worried since their son had never traveled a long distance from home. They asked us if he and I could travel together so that we could help each other. Aunt and Grandmother thought it was a great idea.

Soon, on a clear, late-summer morning, we were on our way to Jiangsu Zhongzhou High. Aunt Zhen took me to the bus station, which was at the outskirts of the west side of Yiyang town, quite a walking distance from our home. I carried a big roll of bedding consisting of a bamboo bed-mat, a quilt with cotton wadding, and a cotton base pad. The bedding was all rolled together and fastened with the Grandmother-made belt. I also had a medium-sized wooden trunk that held my four seasons' clothes: i.e., cotton padded jacket, a wool sweater, and my washing stuff (wash basin, cup). Without Aunt's help, it would have been too much for me to carry.

The bus station was very primitive. A small ticket office and a few benches for people to sit on while waiting for their buses. Cheng He and his parents were already there. Very soon Cheng He and I said good-bye to Cheng He's parents and my aunt. We placed our luggage on the top of the bus and quickly got inside. It was so crowded that even after everyone had squeezed next to each other no one could move.

The bus left Yiyang town, which slowly faded from sight, and we were soon surrounded by vast green rice fields. I had started my high school life away from home. I was 16 years old. The road was bumpy. The bus jolted around, and the sweat and heat from the passengers filled the air, suffocating me. I felt sick and wanted to vomit, but tried hard to hold on. It took more than two hours, but we finally reached Zhongzhou.

Zhongzhou is a Prefecture city about 50 miles northeast of Yiyang town. It is situated on the main Shanghai-Beijing rail line and is one of the main stops on the busy route. It is a major center for the textile and weaving industry. Cheng He and I arrived in Zhongzhou during the afternoon. We asked people how far it was to Jiangsu Zhongzhou High. It was less than two miles and on the same road as the bus station — Xinghe Road. We had too much luggage to carry and decided to call a three-wheel rickshaw. It was the first time I had ridden a rickshaw.

Along Xinghe Road, there were lots of buses and trucks speeding along on the broad, smoothly paved road. Terraced stores and restaurants lined both sides of the road. Most of the people were dressed in Mao-style clothes. They were clean, neat, and you might say stylish for that era. They were not dressed like the peasants and local residents in Yiyang. Most of the people in our little town dressed poorly with simple, traditionally styled clothes.

Zhongzhou was another level of sophistication. I was, as described in the Chinese fable, "a frog at the bottom of the well" that only sees a small portion of the sky with a limited horizon. Growing up in a small town and seldom traveling outside of Yiyang, Zhongzhou was certainly a very different and strange place at first glance.

After passing this busy commercial region, we entered a quiet section of Xinghe Road. On one side of the road were high-walled compounds containing various government institutions, including Jiangsu Zhongzhou High School. On the other side were mainly traditional residential courtyards.

We were dropped off at the front gates of Jiangsu Zhongzhou High. Standing in front of my new school, I felt very proud. The iron gates were grand: the tall, big center gate was closed, as was the right gate, which left only the left gate open. Separating the gates were two concrete pillars. Large golden characters were inscribed vertically on the left pillar announcing "Jiangsu Zhongzhou Senior High School."

Behind the left gate, there was a gatehouse. A man in his fifties at the gatehouse greeted us. He told us that the boys' dormitory was inside the school grounds, whereas the girls' dormitory was across the street in a walled complex, called Xindeli. Cheng He and I said good-bye to each other. After that farewell, we never spoke again because we were assigned to a different classroom. Although the government policy was Liberation of Women, society still followed the traditional feudal system, where young men and women should not be seen alone together.

Xindeli was likely a former residence of a rich family prior to the Liberation of China. The gatekeeper was a lady in her thirties, and the gatehouse was her home. She lived there with her young boy. There were two large two-story buildings within the complex. Between the two buildings was a courtyard. In the center of the courtyard was a small, one-story apartment which I later discovered was the home of Mrs. Wong, our dormitory counselor. At the rear of Mrs. Wong's apartment was a shed that housed the water well where we pumped water for washing.

The gatekeeper directed me to a large building on the right side and told me that my dormitory was upstairs. There were three big rooms upstairs, and each class grade occupied one room. Downstairs, there was a hallway that cut through the middle of the building. On the right side of this hallway was the residence of our principal, Mr. Xi. The left side had been divided into three sections for three teachers and their families.

Following the given directions, I passed through the hallway and reached the staircases. The right staircase led to the dormitory for the seniors, the left staircase led to the dormitory for the first and second graders. The gatekeeper told me that the two-story building on the left side of the complex was for single female teachers.

I shared a room with 27 other first-grade girls. There were two rows of four bunk beds on opposite sides of the room set against the walls. In the middle of the room there were two rows of three bunk beds back-to-back to each other. There was plenty of room to walk between the different rows. Between the windows were two tables for our cups. Our wash basins and luggage were kept underneath the lower bunk beds.

I was assigned a top bunk next to one of the windows. My bottom bunk roommate, YuYu, was a nice, good-natured girl who came from a village near the outskirts of Zhongzhou. I had a habit of not wanting to disturb anyone. I always tried to make less movement, as I was in the top bunk. Unfortunately, I was petite and, with my two short legs, found it very difficult to climb up, so I had to spring up. It seems that the bunk beds came originally from army barracks. They were made of heavy metal and were very tall. I managed to get up there using all my might.

It was early September and very hot. I laid down my bamboo bed-mat and pushed the cotton-padded beddings to the far end of the bed as they were for the winter. I secured the two ends of the belt that Grandmother made to the two vertical end rods of the bunk bed and hung my wash towel on it. I already started missing Grandmother.

Most of my roommates were from the countryside. They were daughters of commune officials, members of the Communist Party. I noticed that two of them, YingYing and Ling, were noticeably different from the rest. Both were from Wenjiang, a major city also situated on the Shanghai-Beijing rail line next to the Yangzi River.

YingYing was a medium-height, slightly chubby girl with two big round lively eyes that radiated smartness and confidence. When she walked, her two short braids swayed like a child's hand-swinging tambourine. She talked a lot. She told us her mother was a schoolteacher, but never mentioned her father. She often told stories where she imitated the voices of the characters and made us laugh. We were fascinated by her stories, and everyone was immediately attracted to her.

In contrast to YingYing, Ling was a slender, clean-cut girl. Her frail body made it appear that the wind could easily blow her over. Her face was pale, so pale you believed she must be suffering from some deficiency. Her two small slit eyes displayed gentleness and softness. She was quiet and well-mannered, but, at the same time, made you feel she was from the aristocracy and was untouchable. Later we learned she was a privileged, high official's daughter.

We came to school three days before the start of the term. We needed to get to know each other and get familiar with our new environment. Mrs. Wong, our girl dormitory counselor, called a meeting and provided us all the necessary information regarding the school history and, of course, the rules. She was proud that Jiangsu Zhongzhou High always had a high percentage of students admitted to university and that the school's academic excellence was always ranked at the top in our nation. She told us that we, as newcomers, should be proud that we had been chosen to be part of this great high school. We should work hard to continue our school's excellence and maintain the school's great reputation. She was a Communist Party member, but she didn't use any Communist propaganda or bureaucratic jargon. She seemed a very nice person, easygoing and unassuming. She told us she had arranged a local tour for the next day: a tour to Plum Flower Park and a visit to Tianyun Temple.

Next day, Saturday, was a bright, windless day. After waking in the early morning, the first thing we did was wash. We pumped water from the well into our washbasin. The water was so clean and cool. People told us that we could drink the well water. Students from small towns (like Yiyang) or from the countryside used river water all the time. We had to boil the water before drinking. The well water made us feel privileged and special. We gathered in the center courtyard at 9 o'clock. Then we followed Mrs. Wong out from Xindeli to visit Plum Flower Park and Tianyun Temple, which were located on the southeastern side of our school. Plum Flower Park was originally the property of Tianyun Temple, but now the Communist government had confiscated the park for public use.

We headed off along Plum Flower Road. Our school's eastern boundary wall was on one side of the road, while a canal ran along the other. Huge trees, which must have been planted a long time ago, lined both sides of the road. The dense green foliage shaded the road with occasional rays of sunlight piercing the leaves. On this hot summer day, this gave us a very pleasant feeling.

Soon, we passed over a stone bridge and entered Plum Flower Park. Mrs. Wong immediately pointed out lots of well-trimmed, nicely shaped trees spread all over a vast field. Mrs. Wong told us that these were Plum Flower trees. During the winter, the flowering plum tree blossoms would appear like pink and red clouds set against the white snow.

"It will be a fantastic winter scene that we should return to see," she added.

We continued to stroll until we reached a lake where boat rowing was a scheduled activity. Four of us were assigned to each boat. Two girls from the countryside eagerly took charge of the two paddles. Boat rowing was recreation for city people. It was foreign to me, but I was happy to take the ride and found being out on the lake very exciting. On the lake, we could see a painted and carved wooden pavilion rising next to the lake. Also, there were lots of weather-beaten lotus and water lily leaves dotted around the lake; and far in the distance was the tall, magnificent Wenbi Pagoda soaring into the blue sky.

After the boat ride was over, we slowly strolled through Plum Flower Park and left via the south park exit entering onto Wuling Road. We walked westward along Wuling Road, next to golden-yellow painted walls, until we stopped to view the grandeur of Tianyun Temple. Three large glittering characters, 天云寺 (Tianyun Temple), were inscribed above the giant door. The temple was fully operational with monks working there daily.

As we walked through the courtyard, it felt serene and holy. We, a bunch of noisy teenage girls, suddenly started to talk very quietly. As we entered the Great Hero Precious Hall, we came face-to-face with giant, golden sculptures of Buddha, dazzling and magnificent. They made me feel small and insignificant. They seemed so powerful, they intimidated me. After glancing at these legendary heroes, I quietly and quickly walked out.

On both sides of the courtyard were two Arhat Halls. There were hundreds of Luohan (罗汉Buddha) stacked in tiers above the ground, lifelike with grand, colorful bodies and varied expressions. One of the girls superstitiously suggested that we count the Luohan. She said you could start the count using any Luohan, but then you had to count consecutively from top to bottom, column by column until you stopped at the number that was your age. The facial expression on the Luohan where you stopped would then predict your future.

I randomly picked a Luohan to start and then counted to 17, my Chinese age (in China, you are one year old on the day of your birth). Luckily, I stopped at a Luohan with a cute smiling face. His right arm reached out with a beautiful bird perched on his hand. Some of my roommates stopped at Luohans with angry, ferocious faces. It goes without saying that I was very satisfied with my good luck and looked forward to a happy life in my future. Of course, the girls that stopped at unhappy Luohan faces said that it was all silly and superstitious.

After returning to school, our vice principal, Mr. Peng, visited us in the dining hall during lunch. Mr. Peng was a very nice, friendly person. Every time I met him at school, he always greeted me by name and asked how everything was. I was always very surprised that, with more than a thousand students on our campus, he could remember my name. Jiangsu Zhongzhou High was a senior high school that taught students from tenth to twelfth grade. There were eight classrooms for each grade, and there were more than 50 students in each classroom. Mr. Peng told us we were the future of China. We were young with growing bodies that needed nutritional food. If we had any suggestions, we should let him know and he would try his best to accommodate.

Schooling in China was free, but only if you were lucky enough to get accepted. We paid eight Yuan per month for the dining plan. The school provided each of us with 28 *jin* of raw rice per month; more than enough for me. At each meal, we individually prepared our own rice. We placed the washed rice with water in an aluminum container (饭盒, *fanhe*) and then stacked our containers in the large steamer in the school kitchen. At meal time, we would collect our rice containers and enter the dining hall, which was next to the kitchen.

The dining hall was made of bamboo and bricks with a thatched roof. There were more than 20 tables with eight of us assigned to each table. There was a stage at one end of the dining hall. The hall was also used as a large assembly hall. For lunch, each table usually received one large basin of soup and one large vegetable dish, together with a small amount of pork. During the summer, the soup was mostly winter melon with seaweed. Mr.

Peng once told us that seaweed was good for our immune system. We were all well behaved and never fought over food, although it was tempting to try to get a little more pork into my bowl. For breakfast and dinner, school only offered pickled vegetables.

The first Sunday was free. YingYing suggested we go to a movie. Several of us joined together and formed a crowd. On the way to the movie theater, I became disoriented and so followed YingYing closely. She seemed to know where the movie theater was and, after all, she was a "city girl." We watched a foreign movie: *Snow White and the Seven Dwarfs*. It was a well-known, classic, American-made cartoon. When I was in school in Yiyang, during school trips, we went to many movies. Most of the movies were about the Eighth Route Army fighting the Japanese, or the People's Liberation Army fighting the Kuomintang. Although *Snow White and the Seven Dwarfs* was subtitled, the story seemed completely disconnected from my life in China. I found it insipid and dull, even though it was my first time seeing a foreign movie, a cartoon.

Although Jiangsu Zhongzhou High was located in a very quiet section of Zhongzhou city, next to Plum Flower Park, the campus didn't have the natural beauty of Jiangsu Yiyang School, where a creek ran right through the middle of campus. As you walked into campus, you faced a huge garden with carefully trimmed hedges and meticulously pruned trees. There were rose bushes uniformly planted in a circular pattern at the center of the garden. The rose foliage was dark green. During late spring and early summer, the red-coral rose blossoms would cover the ground and their heavenly fragrance would spread across the entire campus. This beautiful landscaping gave me an everlasting impression and, even today, still remains fresh in my memory. The rose garden was cultivated by one of our biology teachers, Mr. Gao, who spent most of his spare time laboring in this garden.

On the left side of the garden, there were two large Western-style, two-story buildings. One was for the teachers' offices; the other contained the chemistry and physics laboratory downstairs and the school library upstairs. Towards the east were three, two-story buildings for classrooms. Each building was for one grade, with four classrooms upstairs and four classrooms downstairs. A large campus sports stadium was located on the rear, east side of the campus with a full-size running track. This campus became my home for more than five years.

Boarding school life was rigid. At 6 o'clock each morning, except Sundays, our PE teacher would come to Xindeli to blow a whistle and shout loudly "Everyone, get up!" We would rush out of bed, quickly dress, and then run downstairs to the courtyard to answer roll call.

On the first day of school, I tried to get down quickly from the upper bunk but, in doing so, cut my left hand on the metal foot rail. I covered the bleeding cut with a handkerchief and tried to make sure nobody realized what had happened. I didn't want to be seen as a fragile girl, but the cut hurt and a scar remains on my left hand, even today.

Each morning, we all stood in a line in the courtyard, and then ran around the campus track three times following the PE teacher. After taking a few minutes to wash up, we ate breakfast and, as soon as we finished, we went to our classroom for self-study.

Our classes started at 8 o'clock. There were four classes scheduled for the morning and three for the afternoon with 10-minute recesses between classes. Lunch was from 12 to 1 o'clock, and there were six school days per week. The study load was extremely heavy. Besides the main subjects, Math, Physics, Chemistry, and Chinese Literature and Writing, there was also History, Biology, and a foreign language. Four classrooms were assigned to study English and another four studied Russian. I was assigned to study English.

All students worked very hard. We even studied during class recess except between the 9 and 10 o'clock class. Every morning, physical exercise was held between 9:50 and 10 o'clock, where all the students gathered at the school stadium. We followed instructions from one of our PE teachers who used a loud speaker to shout out "1, 2, 3 ...," while being accompanied by rhythmic gymnastics music.

PE and Labor classes were alternately the last class of the day. The Labor class taught students to develop good work habits, such as weeding the schoolyard and picking up litter. PE was by far my worst subject. I was only 4'11". Every time I came face-to-face with the High-Jump or the Pommel-Horse, I would freeze. The only thing I was okay at was the long-distance run. My PE teacher was nice and never shouted at me, even though she wasn't much taller than me.

After 4 o'clock we had some spare time when local students went home for the day. During this time, soothing, relaxing classical music was played over the campus speaker, such as, "Happiness (喜洋洋)," and "Moonlit Night on the Spring River (春江花月夜)." Most of us did our homework while following the rhythm of the music in the classroom. Dinner time was at 5:00 p.m. After dinner, I started to practice the flute on the balcony in front of my classroom. I wasn't very good, but I tried hard. I guess I had little musical talent.

At 6 o'clock, the music would suddenly shut off and it was time for quiet self-study. By that time, I had finished my homework assignments and would use the evening to review things we had learned in class and prepare for the next day. I also often helped my roommates. A couple of students from the countryside couldn't keep up with the fast-moving lectures, especially those on Chemistry and Geometry, and so they came to me for help.

I always admired my teachers and respected their devotion toward us. During the evening, our young Math, Chemistry and Physics teachers were always there to help us. They walked from one classroom to the other answering questions from students. Each day, our Math teachers would post a challenge Math problem at the front of the building. If I was unable to solve the problem during the day, I would lie awake during the night brainstorming until I got the answer, while everyone else was fast asleep. I loved the challenges and became very frustrated if I couldn't solve the problem. It almost became an addiction to solve those challenges.

Except for sleeping, we spent most of our time in the classroom. The whole school was devoted to achieving academic excellence. At 9 p.m., we had to be back in the dormitory, and by 9:30 p.m. our PE teacher would make sure we were all in bed and the light was turned off.

I soon became homesick. Every time I saw the belt that Grandmother made, tears would well up in my eyes. I missed my grandmother so much, but not just because she was always there for me. I worried about her health. When I was home, I could see she was getting older day by day. October 1st was a holiday — The National Day of the People's Republic of China. We were given four days off from our school, and all my roommates were returning home for the holiday. I decided to also go home and was looking forward to seeing my grandmother again. I spent 2 Yuan to buy a bus ticket. Aunt Zhen sent me 10 Yuan every month: 8 Yuan for school meals and the remaining 2 Yuan for pocket money.

Those days, it took two weeks to send and receive a letter. By the time I decided to go home, it had been too late to send a letter.

As I approached the front door, I was so excited. I shouted out, "I have come home for the holiday!"

My sudden appearance at the front door was a huge surprise for my aunt. It was so sudden; Aunt Zhen couldn't control her feelings. She said, "You only went to school a month ago. It isn't worth spending money to come home for just a couple of days."

Afterward, she realized that she might have hurt my feelings and squeezed out a smile. I had become a sensitive girl. Even though the money my parents sent home supported the entire family, including all my cousins, I always felt like an outsider. Once in a while, my parents' money arrived a few days late and Aunt Zhen would become upset. The anxiety built up in her would make her easily angry. During these times, Grandmother would be quiet and try to keep her emotions under control. Grandmother also told me not to cause any trouble while we waited for my parents' money to arrive. I noted Aunt's comment when arriving at the door and realized I wasn't very welcome at home.

The August moon festival was very close to National Day, but since only National Day was allowed off from school, we celebrated the two holidays together. The August moon festival was the second most important traditional holiday in China, ranked after Chinese New Year. On National Day, Aunt slaughtered one of our home-raised chickens and bought some chestnuts. For the holiday celebration lunch, we made a local delicacy: stewed chicken with chestnuts. In addition, we had stir-fried shredded pork with lotus root, whole fish with sweet and sour sauce, and a soup dish — preserved pork with bok-choy. I not only enjoyed eating the delicious meal, but I was also always excited to be part of the family effort to prepare the food with Grandmother and Xiao Mei, working together as a team.

The local crab was in season, so Grandmother went to the street market and bought three crabs. I heard Aunt say to her, "Crab is so expensive! Why spend that kind of money on this!"

Grandmother said, "It's in season, and I haven't spent much money recently. Adding some crab meat to the dish adds a fresh taste."

During National Day, Grandmother cooked the crab and put some crab meat in the soup. Grandmother also deep-fried some pork fat and put some crab meat and crab roe into the melted pork lard. Then she filled a glass jar with the mixture of pork lard and crab meat.

Four days seemed such a short time. On the fourth day in the early morning I had to take the steamboat back to school. The steamboat ticket was only half the price of the bus ticket and the boat station was very close to my home. It was just across the river, but it would take the whole day on the boat, and then the boat station in Zhongzhou was a long walk to my school.

Before I left home, Grandmother handed me the glass jar filled with pork lard and crab meat. She said, "Add a spoonful into your rice when you have your meal." Today, in America, everybody avoids pork fat, but at that time there was hardly any meat or fat in our daily diet. The pork lard mixed with hot rice tasted delicious, especially with the added crab meat. I hesitated for a moment before taking the jar. I felt guilty to spend Grandmother's money. But then I took it quickly, since I didn't want to make a scene and cause trouble for Grandmother while Aunt was nearby.

Riding on the boat was so different from the bus. The boat was only half-full so there was plenty of space to walk around. The boat headed northward out of Yiyang and passed under the South Gate Bridge along a narrow canal. There were small houses along the riverbank and stone staircases that led down to the river. After leaving Yiyang, the river became much broader, and in some sections, you could only see water all around. Initially I enjoyed the views of the ancient canal and old houses and then the broad waterway, but after a few hours the boat ride became monotonous and boring. Aunt Zhen had been right. It really wasn't worth the money to come home, but seeing Grandmother had relieved my homesickness.

After National Day, I focused entirely on study. I spent New Year's Day (January 1) at school preparing for finals. Most of my roommates also stayed in school. Only a few from adjacent villages went home for the holiday. However, Chinese New Year was a major holiday, when the school would be closed for three weeks. This allowed the out-of-town teachers to return home and spend time with their families.

After admission to Jiangsu Zhongzhou High School, my residence registration (Hukou) was updated to Zhongzhou. Since the school kitchen would be closed during the winter recess, government ration tickets for the holiday period were distributed to each boarding student. Specialties such as dried bean curd, deep-fried bean curd, and soybean sprouts were only sold in government shops once a year, during the time leading up to Chinese New Year. Since Zhongzhou was a large city, Zhongzhou residents received more government rations, and the food sold in government shops was more refined than in Yiyang.

After finals, I visited the government shops and bought everything my rations allowed. I loved my family, and even though Aunt Zhen wasn't my mother, I always had a strong attachment to my home. Grandmother and Aunt Zhen had endured so much suffering while I grew up in Yiyang. I was a child from a poor, underprivileged, Black family. There was an old adage that a child growing up poor would be able to manage the household at an early age — 穷人的孩子早当家. I did not want to waste my rations and wanted my family to share the good food with me. I packed the food I had bought together with a few clothes for the homebound journey. At the last minute, I even put one bar of refined soap I had bought with my rations into my bag, thinking Aunt might like it. Again, to save money, I took the steamboat home.

As was my hometown tradition, preparing for Chinese New Year would take more than 10 days. Aunt Zhen would make new overalls for all of us. The Chinese believed that wearing new clothes on New Year's Day would bring new beginnings and new prosperity. Xiao Mei, Da Di, and I would line up for our rations at government shops. We would start preparing the New Years' eve "banquet" many days ahead. Everyone would take a bath in the local bathhouse a few days before New Year. In winter we usually only took a bath once a month. Since it was so cold at home, we paid for the bath at a public bathhouse. We would do a thorough cleaning of the house to sweep out any bad luck that had accumulated over the past year. It was customary to not do any housecleaning during the first few days of the New Year. Otherwise, you would risk sweeping away all of the New Year's good luck! Therefore, all the cooking and cleaning was completed before New Year arrived.

New Year's Eve was the time to invite our ancestors to come home for a "banquet." That evening, our door would be left wide open, and we would display all the dishes that we had prepared over the previous days on the dinner table. There was whole fish with sweet and sour sauce, braised pork in brown sauce, fresh chicken and preserved salty duck, and many other dishes — a table full of dishes. In the evening, Grandmother, as the head of the household, would lay eight sets of wine cups and bowls of rice and chopsticks around the square dinner table. She would pour wine into each cup and light incense, and then she would say the following as if our ancestors were sitting at the table.

"My ancestors, I feel so sorry that we seldom have you visit our home for dinner. We have so little to offer, but God knows our heart is in the right place. Please enjoy the humble food we have prepared with all our heart."

Then, each of us children would take turns and kneel in front of the table on a prearranged mat. We would bow our head to the floor and listen as Grandmother recited. "My ancestors, please protect our Da Mei (me) and keep her in good health with good progress in her school work."

Grandmother would repeat the prayer for each of us. When we were young, we thought it was funny. Our eyes were fixed at the mouth-watering dishes on the table. Strangely, Uncle Nian always managed to be away from home during the religious ritual, but then would appear once the ritual had ended. After taking our turns, Grandmother would kneel down and bow her head to the floor for several minutes as she mumbled. We could not hear what she said, but we were certain she was begging for help from our ancestors — the mighty and powerful. She probably was asking for help from our ancestors to protect her husband and children who were overseas. People seemed to think the spirits were more capable than the living.

When the time came to say good-bye to our ancestors, Grandmother would burn the ghost paper money on the floor in front of the table. She would move the benches as if the ancestors had stood up and were ready to go. She then threw the wine in the cups on the burning paper and incense, and asked the ancestors to come back next year. To finish the ritual, Grandmother went out of the front door, where she would burn more ghost money for the homeless ghosts (野鬼).

She would say, "My God, please let heaven, earth, and all humans live in harmony, and please let the farmers have a good harvest in the New Year."

Grandmother would whisper many good wishes for the New Year ahead. It always amazed me that Grandmother knew so many fancy words, since she never had one day of schooling.

Once Grandmother had finished the ritual, we all jumped in for the feast. Before we started grasping for the food, Grandmother and Aunt Zhen would remove many dishes from the table. Those dishes would be saved for New Year's visitors. A couple of days after New Year's Day, we would invite Aunt Zhen's brothers and Granduncle, Grandmother's brother, to come to our home for lunch. The New Year's Eve dinner was the only dinner when we could stuff ourselves until we were full to the limit. The sudden intake of fatty food would make me feel bloated for days. We called it New Year Full (年饱).

On New Year's Day we would get up early and run to Grandmother's bedside to wish her good health and longevity. Grandmother would hand out the red envelopes she had prepared for us before New Year's Day. She would offer us many good wishes — good health, strength like a tiger, success in all we do. Each one of us would also receive a glass jar of sweets — caramelized peanuts and rice crackers from Aunt Zhen. I would take the jar back to school with me and nibble from it sparingly for weeks. Of course, I would save the best for last. I had become a frugal teenager. New Year's Day itself was actually a boring, do-nothing day. In the morning we would eat a breakfast of Tangyuan (汤圆) with red dates, symbolizing unity and prosperity. Then, we would run out and greet our neighbors, saying "Happy New Year," hoping to receive some candy in exchange!

A few days before I had to leave home and return to school, Principal Gao from Xinhua Middle School visited us, his face beaming with happiness. He congratulated me for my first semester academic performance in Jiangsu Zhongzhou High. He showed me a letter from my high school thanking Xinhua Middle School for sending them such an outstanding student.

He joked, "In every subject you scored above 95%, except for PE where you raised a red lantern (挂红灯)." In our school system, any score less than 60% was marked with red ink instead of black ink.

Prelude to the Cultural Revolution

In 1964 the school atmosphere suddenly changed. Our dormitory chancellor, Mrs. Wong, seemed no longer interested in our dormitory life. Vice Principal, Mr. Peng, was no longer concerned about our welfare and no longer asked about our dietary needs. Our school no longer promoted "academic excellence." Instead of listening to soothing, classical Chinese music, an army marching song, "Learn from Lei Feng," now blasted loudly from the campus speakers:

Learn from Lei Feng, as a good example;
Loyal to the revolution, loyal to the Communist Party.

At the time, we didn't realize that the prelude to the Cultural Revolution had started. Lei Feng was a member of the People's Liberation Army (PLA) who died a hero. The Learn from Lei Feng campaign was initiated by Lin Bao, the Minister of Defense within the PLA, to emphasize the basic values of service to the party. In 1964 the Learn from Lei Feng campaign expanded and became a mass movement. The campaign gradually shifted from encouraging the performance of good deeds to becoming a cult of Mao Zedong. Lei Feng had studied Mao's work daily and had written what he learned in his diary.

Newspapers were bombarded with articles about the Four Cleans (Siqing) movement where Mao called for mass involvement to rectify problems within the party. Mao kept bringing up the importance of "maintaining vigilance against revisionism within the Central Committee." Anti-revisionism and the promotion of Stalinism was, in fact, the basis of

Mao's secretive plot to regain power and eradicate Liu Shaoqi.[3] Liu Shaoqi had been the pragmatic State Chairman of China since 1959 when Mao relinquished the post after the failure of the Great Leap Forward. For many years, all of us, the students and teachers, had been immersed in a thick cloud with absolutely no idea of the political maneuvering that was taking place within the government. No one ever imagined that Mao's personal vindictiveness would lead to future catastrophe for everyone in China.

During this period, our school introduced a new study subject: Politics. In the Politics class, we studied Lei Feng's diary, which praised Mao with unembarrassed adulation. In addition, of course, we studied Mao's work from a book filled with Mao quotations. The political wind was continuously rising. Again, "walk along the class line" and "class struggle" became pet phrases and political slogans.

Mao targeted the minister for culture and propaganda, Lu Dingyi, an ally of Liu Shaoqi. He accused Lu of allowing schools and universities to accept children with a Black family background. Mao then authorized that the priority for school admission should be given to the sons and daughters with a good background from the proletariat. Mao's political mass movements always divided the people against one another, with the scapegoat always those with a Black family background. Since the Communist Party had taken over China, all the resulting mass movements and political campaigns had led to millions of people with Black family backgrounds being persecuted and sent to reform camps. These mass movements also conveniently eliminated those Mao perceived were disloyal to him.

[3] Liu Shaoqi: The President of the People's Republic of China from 1959 to 1968.

Xiao Mei, an Orphan

During the summer of 1964, Xiao Mei, who was one year younger than me, graduated from Xinhua Middle School but failed to get accepted into any high school. It was a surprise to all of us. It was a devastating blow for Xiao Mei. We grew up like twins. We dressed the same and went to the same primary and middle schools. She also excelled in her schoolwork. She put Jiangsu Zhongzhou High as her first choice and wanted so much to go to the same high school as me.

After the news, she initially felt shame and failure. In hindsight, even if she had performed perfectly, she would never have been accepted by any school. In 1964, the acceptance policy had changed and all the high schools and universities rejected students with a Black family background. At the time, the ordinary population was not aware the admission criteria had been changed.

Xiao Mei used to be a cheerful girl with a lovely chubby, smiley face. Our neighbors used to fondly call her Xiao Mei Mei (小妹妹), meaning the little girl. She gradually grew to be a clever, deft (心灵手巧) teenager. Suddenly, her innocent, budding ambitions had been shattered; a teenager's youthful hopes had perished all at once. She felt ashamed. Her young heart became shrouded in darkness. In the previous year, Da Di and I had both enrolled in high schools and so she was the only one that had failed to get into high school.

That summer was a watershed for Xiao Mei. Grandmother and Aunt Zhen were poorly educated women and probably didn't fully understand the mental impact on Xiao Mei. Our whole family kept quiet about it; thinking that, if they said anything, it would only bring back unpleasant thoughts. Nobody consoled or helped her untie all the bottled-up mental misery. I was so sorry for her, but felt awkward and unable to comfort her.

After all, I had been admitted to Jiangsu Zhongzhou High the previous year. I was afraid anything I said would cause her to resent me. I was a teenager myself. After the summer, I returned to school to face my own challenges, and Xiao Mei's misfortune slowly fell into the background.

The following summer, it soon became apparent to my eye that in both temperament and behavior Xiao Mei was no longer a sweet and lovely girl. She was quiet and was helping Aunt Zhen with her sewing. She also had made some "Society Youth" friends. Society Youth were teenagers who had no job and no school. Instead of trying to help Xiao Mei, Aunt Zhen was complaining behind her back that she played cards with her friends, often came home late, and was not behaving like a good girl. Aunt Zhen was also upset with her for demanding new clothes.

Once Xiao Mei and I became teenagers, Aunt had converted the small added-on room (that used to be our kitchen) into a bedroom for us to share. It was a very small room, no more than 6 ft by 9 ft. While I was in school, Xiao Mei occupied the bedroom herself. She disliked that she had to share the bedroom when I came home. Xiao Mei no longer talked to me. I didn't console her; I didn't know how. Aunt was a snobbish person. Xiao Mei sensed that Aunt looked down on her and had no love for her. In contrast, Xiao Mei felt that I was special in the eyes of our family, since I was attending the best high school. My very existence made her belittle herself, made her feel insignificant, leading to a sense of inferiority. I felt her resentment toward me. As a result, I tried to avoid her.

The lack of communication between us gave her the wrong impression that I was arrogant and self-important. Eventually she couldn't take any more. Her antipathy toward me was so obvious. Her eyes were full of hatred when we were alone in the bedroom. Sadly, I was afraid to talk to her. It was very clear that her feelings toward me had grown from envy to intense jealousness and now to bitter hatred. She didn't shout at me, because I didn't do anything to harm her. Yet her cold looks cast a chill all over my body. During those moments, I wished I was at school. Her resentment toward me became deeply embedded in her heart during that summer and remained with her for years to come.

Once in a while, when I came home during the summer, Grandmother liked to make dumplings for lunch. I knew it cost extra money. The dumpling skins were specially made by a small local shop. One of the ingredients in the dumpling filling was ground pork, which was also expensive. Aunt Zhen did not like to "waste" money. Aunt Zhen liked to squeeze savings from domestic expenses and divert them into her personal savings. The reason she gave for this manipulation was that, eventually, the kids would get married and there would be a whole lot of expenses ahead of us. I was also sensitive that anything done especially for me would arouse jealousy in Xiao Mei, even though everyone in the family would enjoy the dumplings. I told Grandmother not to bother, as it would be too much trouble to make the dumplings. Grandmother did anyway. Before my journey back to school, Grandmother again wanted to have dumplings for lunch. I hurried to prevent Grandmother.

I shouted at her, "Nai Nai, please don't do it. It's too much trouble making dumplings. I don't like dumplings."

Grandmother shouted back, "Since you think it's too much trouble, I will make them for myself. I like dumplings."

Grandmother was the only one in the family that I was not afraid to argue with. She loved me no matter what I did, but I seldom upset her. I remember one evening when Grandmother was complaining about a headache, I handed her an Aspirin pill and a cup of water. Unfortunately, Grandmother had a bad reaction to the Aspirin. That night she was in agony with stomach pain. I was so worried that I hadn't helped Grandmother's headache, but instead had caused pain in her stomach. As she lay there, each painful murmur from Grandmother pierced my mind. I regretted causing her pain and was very worried about her. I didn't sleep all night, and was so relieved when Grandmother felt much better the next day.

In her later years, when she was unable to cook, she would still ask me to go out for a walk with her. I would hold her arm to make sure she didn't fall. When we reached a dumpling vendor, Grandmother would order Xiǎolóngbāo (小笼包, dumpling) for me.

Grandmother started complaining. "I am getting old. My mind is now stronger than my body. The will is there, but not the strength. There are so many things I can no longer do."

Every time I came home from school, I noticed Grandmother seemed a little older than my last visit. It always left me deeply upset. Every time, when I parted from home, Grandmother was the only one I felt I had left behind. By the end of each summer, I was so ready to leave this family. I couldn't understand the constant quarreling over money between Aunt and Grandmother, and the cold treatment I received from Xiao Mei. As a self-centered teenager, I never put myself in Xiao Mei's shoes. She also got no comfort and warmth from Aunt Zhen. Nothing but disdain. Her heart grew colder as she endured the cold that surrounded her.

Xiao Di, my second cousin, was a lucky one just like me. During 1962 and 1963, under Lu Dingyi, government policy changed and the selection process for higher education admission became based solely on an individual's entrance exam results, and not their family background. Therefore, Xiao Di was accepted by Jiangsu Yiyang School for middle school in 1962, and I was admitted to Jiangsu Zhongzhou High in 1963.

Xiao Di was a strong-willed, unruly boy. He made a friend with a boy named Xiao Lan from a Red background family. Because Xiao Lan had a Red family background, he wasn't afraid of anyone or anything. He even mocked the Great Leap Forward that resulted in famine and killed millions. Xiao Di and Xiao Lan would go to see movies without a ticket by climbing over the wall of the movie theater. In the summer of 1965, after he had completed his years in middle school, Xiao Di also was not admitted to high school. One would think, based on his character, that failing to get into high school wouldn't have bothered him. However, as soon as he received the bad news, his face turned white and sweat ran down his face. No one wanted to be a Society Youth like Xiao Mei.

For some reason — maybe the guilt of not studying hard or the sudden realization of the tough road that lay ahead — Xiao Di's behavior suddenly changed course by 180 degrees. He no longer went out with Xiao Lan. He started doing lots of house chores, cleaning the house and going to the river to wash vegetables. During those days, all these chores were considered the work of housewives and girls, but he did them as best he could.

This change pleased my Aunt. Within a few months, Aunt, using all her local connections and bribes, managed to get Xiao Di a clerk job in a local government shop selling various household supplies. Xiao Di was a good worker, and everybody in the store loved him. This job training, at an early age, laid the foundation for future success in his adult years, when he became a shrewd, successful businessman. As Grandmother used to say, "Money makes the mare go." In contrast, Aunt did nothing for Xiao Mei. There was no mother's love for Xiao Mei. Aunt was more worried that my parents' money might be cut in half if Xiao Mei had a job and became independent. Aunt never tried to look for a job for Xiao Mei.

An unloved, lost teenager, Xiao Mei developed a prickly personality and didn't know how to vent her inner anger and grief. Xiao Mei couldn't confront Aunt Zhen, so she vented her anger toward her cousin San Mei. Xiao Di's blustering nature didn't allow Xiao Mei to challenge him. So, San Mei, my younger girl cousin, took the brunt of Xiao Mei's anger. After San Mei finished primary school, she failed to get accepted into middle school, and so started performing many household chores. San Mei was young and did things clumsily without care. Xiao Mei was always finding fault and would continuously shout at San Mei. She often called her stupid, dull-witted, and good-for-nothing.

Sometimes Xiao Mei was so rude that everybody in the family would give her a cold look to show their disapproval. Aunt Zhen would sneer and look on with a cold eye. San Mei was Aunt Zhen's only daughter. It was clear she was heartbroken to see her daughter insulted, but she tried her best to tolerate Xiao Mei. This might have been the result of a guilty conscience that she got a job quickly for her own son, Xiao Di, but did nothing for Xiao Mei.

I only spent time at home during school recess, so I wasn't fully aware of what Xiao Mei had to endure on a daily basis. I never questioned why Xiao Mei still had no job, and yet Aunt Zhen had been able to easily find a job for Xiao Di. My cousins and I were young teenagers and only saw things play out on the surface. We couldn't comprehend the depth of Xiao Mei's pain. We couldn't see the misery that was bottled up inside Xiao Mei's heart, and understand why she was always angry and nasty to San Mei. One day, Xiao Mei was shouting at San Mei again and was being really nasty.

I said to Xiao Mei, "Don't be so rude. San Mei is human too!"

What I said caused a volcanic eruption! Xiao Mei sniffed and looked at me as if I were her worst enemy. "I wondered who was speaking. It turned out to be you, our royal guest! Who could dare argue with you? You are so special. Everyone in the family kisses your ass. You are our shining star and our future university graduate," said Xiao Mei sourly. There was a ring of sarcasm in her words.

"I am only a high school student. Why are you so sure I will go to university? I am not so sure myself," I replied, reflecting on the political turbulence in my school life.

"You are the queen, the untouchable in our family!" Xiao Mei shouted.

I was a forthright sort of person and couldn't understand all the sarcasm. I was poor at articulating my thoughts with words. I couldn't find the right word to shoot back and was left speechless. I loathed confrontation and really didn't like to argue with people. But the years of cold-shoulder treatment from Xiao Mei had driven me to a point where I couldn't tolerate it any longer. The situation had reached boiling point.

At the time, I was holding a bucket of water. With all my pent up emotion, I suddenly smashed the bucket onto the floor and water ran everywhere. Aunt Zhen and San Mei tried to clean things up in a hurry. I walked out of the house with tears running down my face. From Aunt's facial expression, it was very clear she was happy to see Xiao Mei and me fight, especially since I supported her daughter.

After a year or more had passed, Xiao Mei still had no job and no school. The Society Youth life frustrated her so much. The verbal onslaught against San Mei had now progressed to physical abuse. One day San Mei accidentally broke a rice bowl. Xiao Mei immediately smacked San Mei across the head and then started name-calling her again. San Mei was in tears. Aunt's anger had now reached fever pitch.

She shouted at her own daughter. "You are such a stupid girl. You have no brain. If you weren't so worthless, I wouldn't need to listen to my 'little mother' lecture me. Why should I tolerate that evil-tongue, misbegotten bitch?"

Aunt was "cursing the locust tree while pointing at the mulberry" (指桑骂槐). Each time she scolded her daughter she made innuendoes toward Xiao Mei. It was clear to me that Aunt was biased and supported her own daughter. By this time, I felt Aunt had become cold-hearted toward both Xiao Mei and me. Although she was civil to me, it was all just a veneer. Any affection was simulated. There wasn't a hint of motherly love. As Xiao Mei said, I was just a household guest. I never argued with or insulted anybody. I made no demands of Aunt. If it wasn't for my parents' money, we would probably have been kicked out a long time ago. I was sympathetic toward Xiao Mei. We were in the same boat. As the Chinese proverb says, "Grieve for your own kind; when the lips are gone, the teeth will be cold."

I said to Aunt, "If you think Xiao Mei is wrong, please talk to Xiao Mei. You don't need to curse the oak-tree when you mean the ash!"

Xiao Mei suddenly shouted, "I am an orphan. Nobody cares about me!"

The truth finally screamed out from Xiao Mei's heart!

I was Grandmother's first grandchild and her favorite. After entering high school, I lived in school most of the time and so was rarely at home. During those years, Xiao Mei replaced me as Grandmother's soft spot. She was sympathetic toward Xiao Mei. I heard her fondly calling Xiao Mei "my third girl." Xiao Mei was her third grandchild after me and Da Di. Grandmother's eyes were full of compassion toward Xiao Mei, but she had little power to change her daily life.

Dreams of Becoming a
University Student

At the end of each semester, I looked forward to returning home and seeing Grandmother again. Yet even before school recess ended, I was already looking forward to returning to school, though school life offered little enjoyment. Politics had invaded the lives of all the students and teachers.

Our PE class had been transformed into a military training class. Previously, the girls' PE class had a female teacher and was separate from the boys' class. Now the two classes had been combined. Our PE teacher was a tall, muscular man. On the first day of the combined class, we were given wooden hand-grenades. As we lay on the ground, we were ordered to throw them as far as we could toward pretend enemies. My wooden grenade only went a short distance. I had to accept that I was a weak and clumsy person.

After a while, one day, we were given real rifles. The rifle was so heavy, it seemed to weigh more than me. First, we were told to hold the rifle with our right hand in a standing pose. Then we had to lie down and aim the rifle forward as if we were shooting at the enemy. I was totally unbalanced and almost fell over. To avoid embarrassment, I pulled up on the rifle with all my might. The front part of the rifle was much heavier than the handle. When I tried to aim the rifle forward, the front of my rifle stubbornly remained pointed at the floor. At that moment, I was praying nobody saw me. I was so relieved when the class was over. My arms hurt so badly after all the lifting.

Luckily, later on, we were divided into groups. Those students from a good (Red or Gray) background family were assigned real rifles, whereas other students, like me, were given wooden, fake rifles. We weren't sufficiently trustworthy to be given a real one! I felt no shame. The wooden rifle was much lighter than the real one, and, at least, I wasn't the only one holding a wooden rifle.

My English teacher was foreign-born Chinese. He originated from Malaysia and returned to China to make a contribution to his parents' motherland. In our first-year English textbook, there were short essay sections such as: "Campaign for Governor" by Mark Twain and "Oliver Asks for More" by Charles Dickens. Somehow, since my parents were in the US, my English teacher thought I must be interested in learning English. The fact was I hated English class. I had difficulty distinguishing between the "L" and "R" sounds. He often called me up to read a paragraph from the book. He never succeeded in correcting my difficulty with the "L" and "R" sounds.

My poor verbal performance in the classroom actually helped me avoid any criticism that suggested I was working hard in English class with the idea of leaving China for America. By the third year, all foreign references in our English textbook had gone and were replaced with a few pages focused on Mao and the Communist Party, such as: "The East is Red," a song eulogizing and praising Mao, and propaganda slogans such as "Long Live Chairman Mao," and "Long Live the Communist Party."

For my first year of Chinese Literature and Writing, we were taught the classical essays written by the scholars from the Tang to Qing dynasties. The classical essays were written using an ancient form of the language that was very different from modern-day Chinese. It is very difficult for an ordinary person to understand. Our study involved reciting the essays, understanding the essence of the essays, and interpreting them in modern form.

I enjoyed reciting the famous poems from *Tang Shi San Bai Shou* (唐诗三百首), which is a compilation of poems from the Tang Dynasty, and *Song Ci* (宋詞), or Song Dynasty lyric poetry. In these poems, a short verse could embody the quintessence of a particular scene among the lakes, rivers, and mountains. The poems captured my imagination and my heart. It was as if I were there. Some of them sighed and expressed deep feelings about tragic events. They struck a chord with me. They stimulated my artistic sensibilities and triggered deep emotions.

In my second and third years of high school, all the classical Chinese essays and poems disappeared from our Chinese Literature and Writing class. Our studies focused solely on Lu Xun's short stories and Chairman Mao's poems.

Mr. Ding was my Chinese Literature and Writing teacher for both my second and third years. Mr. Ding was a short, skinny man in his thirties. His body always tilted sideways as he walked. One shoulder was higher than the other, and it looked as if someone had removed one of his kidneys. He wore a thick pair of eyeglasses. He was a mystery to me. I could never pinpoint what his goals were. Mr. Ding was actively involved in the Communist Youth League where he was a leading member in our school. He had ambitions to join the Communist Party. Unfortunately, he originated from a Gray class family. He would have to pass many severe tests in order to become a glorious party member. With his political background, he either chose or was chosen to become my Politics class teacher. Teachers of the Politics class controlled students' political life.

None of my Science teachers ever commented on any of the political movements. They remained devoted to the class subject they were teaching. Our homework loads were still very heavy. Our Math teacher still posted the challenge Math problem every day. All of us still quietly worked hard to achieve "academic excellence"; however, nobody mentioned the words "to achieve academic excellence." Everybody knew that without good entrance exam scores there was no chance of entering university, even if you were born of a Red class family. There were very few universities in China and too many high school graduates. Without a university diploma, the future was very dim for high school graduates.

All my roommates were members of the Communist Youth League, except for YingYing and me. YingYing was friendly with one of my roommates, Mei Qin, who was the daughter of the secretary of the Communist Party for her commune. Mei Qin was short, sturdy, and well-built. She, like all of us, had two short braids, but her braids were very thick since she had dense, shiny hair. She was a person of few words, but her authoritative attitude told us she was born of a Red-class peasant family. This gave her the privilege to be a leader no matter what others thought. Her rough edge and unrefined manner led us to be respectful toward her, but also to keep our distance. She had become a leading member of the

Communist Youth League for our school and worked closely with Mr. Ding.

I overheard that YingYing hadn't been able to join the Communist Youth League while in middle school, because her father had been sent to jail for embezzling public funds. No wonder she never mentioned her father during conversations among us girls. In late 1964, Mr. Ding increasingly involved YingYing in many political activities. YingYing gave many speeches in our Politics class:

Although she hadn't emerged from a proletariat family, she was ready for self-reform and to learn from members of the Communist Youth League. She would do her best to eliminate any spiritual pollution her family had transferred to her. She was keen to learn from Lei Feng and serve the people wholeheartedly. She wanted to become a "little screw in the great revolutionary machine"; she strongly desired to contribute to the Communist Party and our supreme Chairman Mao, even at the cost of her own life.

YingYing, talkative by nature, often praised Mr. Ding in front of him and behind his back, but especially in front of Mei Qin. YingYing started to distance herself from me, drawing a clear class line between us. Everybody knew that being a member of the Communist Youth League was a political ticket for future university admission as well as for a future job assignment. After my middle school experience, I knew I had no chance to obtain membership. I had been encouraged to apply for membership by my middle school history teacher, the leader of the Communist Youth League at my middle school, but my application was flatly rejected due to my family background. In addition, I had never been a talkative, ladder-climbing, political person. At the beginning of my third grade, YingYing was accepted into the Communist Youth League.

My teachers and schoolmates knew that I was the daughter of Chinese parents who had gone to America for graduate school education before the Liberation of China. They were also aware that I was supported by my parents financially and, so, enjoyed a better material life. Other than that, they knew nothing. Yet, I always dressed simply, sometimes wearing mended clothes. I lived a simple, humble life as if I came from an impoverished family. Nobody in my school knew that I had actually lived through a tough childhood as my family endured untold suffering.

131

After all the Communist political movements, everyone in China steadily became equally poor except for a few senior-level official families, who became the new high-living aristocrats. So, in response, Mao advocated an austere lifestyle for people in China. I thought that I definitely satisfied Mao's dictate. I was a law-abiding and well-behaved student. I had earned respect from most of my schoolmates. Ling, YingYing, YuYu, and I all got along well. YuYu was my lower bunk-bed roommate. We lived peacefully and in harmony. YingYing was a chatterbox, and I enjoyed her company. Ling, although a daughter of a high official, never seemed unapproachable to me, as she was always friendly toward me.

One Sunday, Ling wanted to buy a pair of socks and asked if anyone wanted to go to the department store with her. YuYu, YingYing, and I went along with her. In the department store, Ling discovered her wallet had been stolen. The department store clerk whispered to Ling and pointed a finger at me, suggesting I might be the thief. Ling flatly rejected her suggestion and said that it could be anybody but me. On the way back, Ling told everyone the story, and they all laughed at me, teasing me because I was dressed like a beggar. They suggested I could dress better. I was always so focused on my studies and never put much importance on clothes. I had never acted as if I was a Thousand-Gold Little Precious Lady (千金小姐) from a bourgeois decadent family.

Initially, I didn't think of university admission or anything else while studying. I just formed a habit of answering the challenges and trying as hard as I could. Besides studying hard, there was nothing I could be criticized for as far as a Communist lifestyle was concerned. As time passed, I suddenly realized that my roommates' attitude toward me had changed. By the third year of high school, it was very clear that a person with my family background would never be accepted by any university. My roommates looked at me with cold eyes and must have wondered, "Why does she study so hard? She has no chance."

A few of my roommates were important members of the Communist Youth League. They hardly talked to me socially, but during the nightly self-study period they shamelessly asked me for help in Math, Physics, and Chemistry. It was as if my existence was only to serve them and help them gain access to university. Although I helped them, inside it hurt. It was as if I was a candle lighting the way for others, while I sat in the shadows slowly destroying myself. Deep inside my heart, I wished there was another Mr. Zong (the admission officer of Xinhua Middle School) who accepted me because of my outstanding exam scores. For that reason, I studied even harder. Hope is always the last thing to die.

Since any word, any writing from or by Mao became an imperial decree, we were asked to recite one of Mao's poems, "Ode to the Plum Blossom":

风雨送春归，
飞雪迎春到。
已是悬崖百丈冰，
犹有花枝俏。
俏也不争春，
只把春来报。
待到山花烂漫时，
她在丛中笑。

Wind and rain escorted Spring's departure,[4]
Flying snow welcomes Spring's return.
On the ice-clad rock rising high and sheer
A flower blossom sweet and fair.
Sweet and fair, she craves not Spring for herself alone,
To be the harbinger of Spring she is content.
When the mountain flowers are in full bloom
She will smile mingling in their midst.

I pondered Mao's poem. I desired to be the winter plum blossom. I had no ambition to claim spring all for myself. I just wanted to "smile mingling in their midst." I just wished to be part of spring.

During winter recess, I went home to celebrate Chinese New Year. I was depressed. A week passed and Uncle Nian arrived home for the New Year. He seemed in a good mood. One evening after dinner, he called me and Da Di for a chat. It was the first time Uncle Nian had talked to me

---

[4] Translation source: https://www.poemhunter.com/poem

directly. He said he had discussed my and Da Di's university admission issues with Uncle Shi Po, my father's older cousin. Uncle Shi Po was aware of the current university admission policy, and that students from a Black-class family had no chance for admission to university.

Uncle Shi Po was now a high official of the Communist Party. He was the Culture and Propaganda Department Director of Zhejiang Province. He secretly joined the Communist Party while he was attending law school at Fudan University in Shanghai before World War II, and afterwards went to Yan'an, which was the citadel of the Communist Party during the war. My father also attended school in Shanghai. They shared an apartment and developed a strong brotherhood bond. During the war, my father retreated to Chengdu, and attended North-West University of Technology. After graduation, he became an instructor in the Chinese Air Force Technical School for the Kuomintang. After the war, in 1945, he became a liaison officer in The Advisory Team of The United States Air Force. In 1948, Father went to America to pursue further graduate school education. The two cousins had traveled totally different roads.

Uncle Nian told us that Uncle Shi Po was still very fond of my father, reflecting on the good times they had together in Shanghai. Since Uncle Shi Po was the Culture and Propaganda Department Director of Zhejiang, he was in charge of all the universities in Zhejiang Province. Uncle Shi Po indicated that there was no problem getting us admitted to Zhejiang University, the best university in Zhejiang Province, provided we did reasonably well in our entrance exams.

He also suggested that, since I was academically outstanding, I should be able to get into a better school. The secretary of the Communist Party of Fudan University in Shanghai was his friend. He could recommend me to him. Therefore, I should apply to the Fudan University's Math Department. Fudan was well known for its Math Department. Da Di should apply to Zhejiang University. We should write down the exam number assigned to us and send that to him immediately after the entrance exams. Studying in Tsinghua University's Physics Department had once been my dream, but beggars can't be choosers. A ray of hope had dawned on me. I had never expected Uncle Nian to be thinking about our university admission. I really appreciated his effort to help us. My negative thoughts of him suddenly evaporated without a trace. Sunny days might come again. I felt a rising hope.

Academic Excellence with Poor Political Behavior

I headed back to school with a brighter spirit. My roommates couldn't understand where my good mood had come from. Some of them looked at me in disdain. Some felt sorry for me. I didn't need anyone's pity. My task was to obtain high scores on the university entrance exams. I quietly pursued that goal.

In the Politics class, Mr. Ding insinuated that, "In our classroom, there are students that display 'academic excellence with poor political behavior' (只专不红, Zhǐ zhuān bù hóng). Everything they do is aimed at obtaining university admission, and not supporting our Communist Party and socialist motherland. We should learn from Lei Feng and study Chairman Mao's work daily."

Mr. Ding's words were full of twists and turns. When he was saying these things, his eyes always seemed directed toward me. I lowered my head. His words were obviously targeting me. He continuously threw out innuendoes toward me. I directed my eyes toward the window and sank into deep sorrow and fear. I didn't understand why I was being targeted. Everybody studied as hard as me. What was I guilty of? I thought my behavior, as a student, was unsullied and clean.

As I reflected on the situation, I thought about one of my local classmates. She was daring. She had two long, thin braids that were tied with brightly colored silk ribbons. She always dressed fashionably, wearing flower-patterned shirts and long, ironed pants. She wore store-purchased leather shoes with a half-inch heel; not like most of us, who wore homemade cotton shoes. She walked gracefully like a swinging, weeping willow. She had full breasts. When she walked, her breasts bounced on her chest with undeniable flirtation. She upset my schoolmates. She was different from all of us. Mei Qin scorned her as a witch, full of bourgeois allure. But because she was born from a Red worker-class family, it seemed she suffered no scrutiny from Mr. Ding.

136

I was a teenager and hadn't fully understood that, no matter how I behaved, I would always be the underdog, a target of criticism. "The tree wants to be still, but the wind keeps blowing" (树欲静而风不止). It seemed there was no peace for me.

One evening, while I was studying in the classroom, Mr. Ding came and asked me to go with him. He had something he needed to discuss with me. Mr. Ding was a local teacher, who seldom came to the classroom during the evening. I suddenly became very tense, thinking that he would lecture me about academic excellence with poor political behavior (*Zhǐ zhuān bù hóng*). I followed Mr. Ding out of the classroom and down the staircase toward the teachers' office building. When we got close to the building, Mr. Ding suddenly made a left turn away from the building toward the campus gate. Mr. Ding told me that his wife was working that night and his apartment would be a quiet place to talk. Mr. Ding's apartment was located close to our campus. We walked very quietly and didn't talk. I thought Mr. Ding wanted to chide me about *Zhǐ zhuān bù hóng* without having other teachers around. I searched my brain trying to figure out how I would defend myself.

We walked toward Plum Flower Park and made a right turn onto Plum Flower Road. From Plum Flower Road, we then walked through an alley and entered a residential complex, where Mr. Ding and his family occupied a small room. He unlocked the door. There was a bed with a mosquito net hanging over it and a table with one side against the window next to the door. Mr. Ding let me sit on a chair next to the table, and he sat himself on the other chair next to me.

He started his inquiry with a wicked smile. "Do you know why I asked you to come here?"

"No, I don't know." I answered as simply as possible.

He continued, "Do you want to become a member of the Communist Youth League?"

"Of course!" I said with a firm voice, thinking Mr. Ding had no idea that my grandfather was an anti-revolutionary element, otherwise he would never have asked me to join.

Mr. Ding moved closer to me and looked at me as if he was admiring a budding flower. His eyes brightened with a hint of sexual excitement. I lowered my head to avoid his searching eyes. Suddenly, his hand touched my shoulder. I was in shock. No man in my life had ever touched me before. I trembled all over.

"Are you hot?" he asked.

Then, he moved his hand toward my neck, intending to untie my overcoat button. It was a cold winter evening. I wore a thick, cotton-padded jacket and an overcoat with a wool sweater underneath. I was fully protected. I firmly pushed his hand away from me, and my facial expression let him know that his advances were not welcome. Within my inner circle of friends, I was straightforward, down-to-earth and easy to get along with. In front of strangers, I was a person of few words, always serious and seldom smiling. My aloofness could be interpreted as "always keep people a thousand miles away" (拒人千里之外). He hesitated...perhaps a guilty conscience? There were neighbors around. His face flushed with shame and anger.

"You can go now," he said in a low, authoritative voice.

I rushed out of the apartment. Initially I felt disorientated and had difficulty finding my way back. As I walked alone on Plum Flower Road, I wanted to scream out loud, but I silenced myself as I walked along the quiet street under the dark sky.

I fell into deep melancholy and fear about the future. I was an 18-year-old girl who had never had thoughts of associating with boys, or dating, or future marriage. I was a lady of antiquity with a feudal young woman's virtue. I always looked down on, and to some extent, hated women who flirted with men to achieve their goals. I always thought that Mr. Ding was an enigmatic, shady person, but never thought him to be such a vile, animal-like creature. I was very disappointed. Teachers were well respected in Chinese society. All my teachers were well behaved and devoted their life to educating the youth. Mr. Ding's behavior was a rare exception. I was saddened and start to wonder how YingYing actually became a member of the Communist Youth League.

The winter was fading, and spring had finally arrived. I had completed my university application with Fudan Math Department as my first choice and Tsinghua Physics as my second choice. I was still in a dreamland, and never gave up hope. I listed Zhejiang University as my third choice. To prepare for university admission, we also had a physical exam to test our eyes, our sense of smell, and hearing.

During my sense of smell test, I mistook soy sauce for cooking oil. When the doctor told me it was soy sauce and not cooking oil, I exclaimed, "Shoot, how stupid I am!" It was a natural response uttered when you discover you're wrong about something. In my mind, I never made the connection between the sense test and university admission. Although the tests were for university admission, I was just trying to provide the right answers, and, at that moment, truly wasn't thinking about university admission.

Recently, I felt a dense, dark cloud had been cast over me. My friend YuYu seemed to want to tell me something, but swallowed back her words.

Mei Qin's suspicious eyes followed me everywhere. YingYing hadn't talked with me for a long time. After she became a member of the Communist Youth League, she seldom associated with me. I sensed something was going on. It was definitely directed toward me, but I didn't know what it was all about.

One day after finishing our Labor class, the local students cleared their desks ready to go home and the boarding students returned to the classroom to self-study. One of the local male students put a slip on my desk and walked out of the classroom quickly. I opened the slip: *See me in the woods behind the campus stadium at once.* I hesitated and wondered why. The student was a tall, well-behaved boy. I had never associated with boys in our classroom. In fact, I hardly associated with any local students, even the female students. We had very little spare time, and the local students came to school when classes started and went home when school ended.

I walked out of the classroom and followed the boy at some distance. We reached the woods. The woods was sparsely planted with trees. It was the beginning of spring. Although tender green leaves had begun to sprout, I could still see clearly through the woods. The student's eyes wandered around, making sure that no one had followed or seen us.

He said in a hurry and straight to the point, "You should be careful what you say in front of people. People heard what you said to the doctor during the sense of smell test. They are criticizing you, suggesting that everything you say and do is focused on obtaining university admission."

I tried to defend myself. "During the sense of smell test, I never thought of university admission. It was just a normal reaction in response to failure."

"You don't need to explain yourself to me. I just wanted to give you a friendly warning," he said quietly and forcefully.

"I don't understand. Is there anyone in our school who doesn't want to go to university? Why do they focus on me?" I protested.

He seemed frustrated with my stupidity and the fact that I couldn't see he was trying to help me. He said in a very serious tone, "Mr. Ding and the Communist Youth League are compiling a detailed file on you. They are planning to use you as a bad example: a student from a Black family whose only focus is university admission and *Zhǐ zhuān bù hóng*. You should be very careful." After telling me these things, he walked away quickly.

A chill penetrated deep into my marrow. I was in shock and despair. I had been blacklisted! A dossier, compiled by the Communist Youth League, would follow me everywhere, including my future workplace. It would affect my job assignment and my future life. It would remain with me my entire life! Any black mark in one's dossier could lead to disaster in one's life and condemnation during any political movement.

I didn't even know the student's name who had tried to help me, but I appreciated his kindness. He had to be a member of the Communist Youth League. There were very few local students that belonged to the Communist Youth League. Most came from Black or Gray families. Their admittance to Jiangsu Zhongzhou High School was a result of their academic excellence. In 1963, the admission policy was to select the most academically outstanding students while giving higher preference to the sons or daughters of Communist Party members. Many local students and I were just the lucky few.

As I walked slowly with a heavy heart toward my classroom, I started to sob. My body felt as though it weighed a hundred tons. My feet were wobbly, as if I were walking on cotton-floss. I felt immersed in a gathering cloud of helplessness and fear. They were slandering me. There was no doubt in my mind that this was Mr. Ding's reprisal against me! I was powerless to respond to the attack. Knowing several roommates were leading members of the Communist Youth League, I spoke to no one as they hovered around me. I was in a state of misery. I was isolated and fell into a deep depression.

One day, I suddenly remembered Lu Xun's words: "unless we burst out, we shall perish in silence" (不在沉默中爆发 就在沉默中灭亡). I was unwilling to perish in silence. I decided to burst out of my depression and put all my energy into my studies. I disregarded what lay in front of me. Living in fear is not living at all. Kill me if you wish!

At the time, I didn't realize that all the political suffering I was enduring was simply a prelude to the chaotic and destructive Cultural Revolution.

A Black Bastard (黑崽子)

The wind blows hard before the storm, 山雨欲来风满楼. The political wind was blowing harder than ever before. From the published articles in the *People's Daily* to the constant promotion of the cult of Mao, the people sensed a storm pressing down on China. In many ways we were getting used to being tossed around. Sadly, we had just experienced a few years of peace combined with a somewhat comfortable life, yet now it looked like another political movement would soon be cast down upon us. Since most articles in the *People's Daily* criticized famous intellectuals and denounced class enemies of the Party, people feared another anti-rightist type movement was on the horizon. However, most people weren't aware of the internal struggles within the Communist Party and did not have the faintest idea that these struggles would lead to devastation in everyone's life.

Mr. Ding devoted himself to the cult of Mao and forced every student to study Mao's work. He worked hard and used this opportunity to try to join the Communist Party. Regardless of all the hearsay around us, our school was immersed in preparing for finals. For the third graders, we had our final exams early so that we would have more time to prepare for the university entrance exams. For us, there were no more classes. We spent all our time self-studying. Mr. Ding was no longer able to use the Politics class to force us to study Mao's work.

Mei Qin and the leading members of the Communist Youth League had disappeared from sight. Students said they saw Mei Qin hiding in Plum Flower Park self-studying for the university entrance exams. Even with her Red bloodline, Mei Qin knew that studying Mao's work wouldn't get her into university without a good entrance exam score.

While the students were preparing for finals and university entrance exams, the teachers and school administrators were strongly encouraged to follow Mao's utterances and the emerging political changes in the country. The report of a Big Character poster published by a teacher (Nie Yuanzi) from Beijing University was announced over the campus speakers. It attacked the University Communist Party administrators and cadres from the Beijing party authorities as "Black anti-party gangsters." The political temperature was rising day by day. We could sense this from the serious faces of the teachers. We, as high school teenagers, hadn't yet fully grasped the seriousness of the situation. Except for a few talking heads, such as Mr. Ding, the school was in deep silence as the heavy political clouds gathered and began enveloping the campus.

Just a couple of days before the final exams for the first and second graders, the campus speakers suddenly announced loudly:

"This is an important announcement, please pay attention. All finals and university entrance exams have been canceled. Students must remain on campus to study the Great Proletarian Cultural Revolution."

The entire campus was shocked. No one could comprehend what had suddenly happened and what lay ahead. Sadly, Mr. Ding was again destined to become the root of my troubles. Politics now became an all-day class. We had to remain in the classroom studying Mao's work; the only time we were allowed to leave was to go to the toilet. In the morning, we would hold Mao's Little Red Book containing Mao's quotations above our head and shout out loudly:

"Long Live Chairman Mao!"
"Long Live the Great Proletarian Cultural Revolution!"

Soon after the following slogan was added and we started shouting, "Sweep Away All Ox Devils and Snake Demons (横扫一切牛鬼蛇神)!"

The "Sweep Away All Ox Devils and Snake Demons" was one of the articles published in the *People's Daily* on June 1, 1966. It was actually directed toward Mao's political enemies. Unfortunately, at the time, very few people knew the true intention of the article.

Afterwards, Red Guard units quickly formed at all the universities in Beijing. Now, the political winds had blown directly into our school. Following the establishment of the Red Guard in Beijing, a Red Guard unit was soon formed at our school. Initially, the Red Guard only accepted high officials' sons and daughters, but, since there were so few in our school, this was extended to include the sons and daughters of commune officials.

Since Ling's father was a high official in Jiangsu Province, she became one of the first members of the Red Guard in our classroom. Mei Qin and a few of the leading members of the Communist Youth League joined the Red Guard soon after. Our classroom was divided into three groups: the Reds (红五类[5]), the Blacks (黑五类[6]), and the Grays — all the undefined. A new proverb spread across campus: "Dragon born dragon, Phoenix born phoenix, Tortoise gives birth to bastard" (龙生龙, 凤生凤, 乌龟生个王八蛋).

I was one of the bastards (王八蛋) born of a Black family — the "tortoise family," a newly classified Black bastard (黑崽子). We, the Black bastards, were ordered to sweep the floors and clean the toilets. Our eyes were dimmed by shame and fear. Our heads were bowed. We avoided looking into anyone's eyes. We were prisoners within our own campus.

Our school's Red Guard followed the Beijing Red Guard. The first Big Character poster was soon posted on our campus wall.

"Exposing and denouncing our school's ox devils and snake demons!"

Apparently, three teachers had been isolated and pressured to self-expose and to expose each other. My third-grade Chemistry teacher Mr. Lu and Biology teacher Mr. Gao were two of the three. No wonder the campus garden had become overgrown with weeds and the rose bushes hadn't been trimmed for weeks. Mr. Gao used his spare time to cultivate the campus garden. The third person selected for exposure was a PE teacher. These three teachers were all out-of-town teachers. They spent

---

[5] 红五类 – "Five red categories" – Revolutionary soldiers, revolutionary cadres, workers, poor peasants, lower middle peasants

[6] 黑五类 – "Five black categories" – landlords, rich farmers, counter-revolutionaries, bad elements, rightists

most of their time on campus and only went home a few weeks a year for the holidays. This *away from home* lifestyle was typical for most teachers at that time. Due to their lonely dormitory life, these three teaches, who were all in their fifties, became friends. They spent a lot of their spare time together.

Mao had ordered the Red Guard to entice and expose all "ox devils and snake demons." The Red Guard had to dig out the "ox devils and snake demons" in our school. With Mr. Ding's help, these three teachers were charged as "ox devils and snake demons." They were seen together a lot and must have said things to each other against the Communist Party and "our dearest Chairman Mao." They were isolated in different cells and forced to confess.

They were told, "Leniency to those who confess; severity to those who resist" (坦白从宽抗拒从严).

They were forced to confess day and night. "Your friend has already confessed. It is now up to you to confess and get lenient treatment."

On a Big Character poster, they were condemned for criticizing the Great Leap Forward and for mocking the Three Years of Famine. Students with serious faces crowded quietly around the posters. No one said anything.

There was a Big Character poster sponsored by the Red Guards in my classroom. It condemned Mr. Lu for only fostering and educating an American daughter, a Thousand-Gold Little Precious Lady (千金小姐), originating from a "bourgeois decadent" family, and ignoring students from families of Communist Party members. After reading this, a chill penetrated deep into my marrow. My body started to uncontrollably shiver. I was the only "American daughter" in my classroom. Since the Red Guards in my classroom wrote this Big Character poster and Mr. Lu was my teacher, it was obviously directed toward me — even though it didn't mention my name.

A throng had gathered in front of this Big Character poster. I felt I had been exposed naked in front of my schoolmates. It seemed all eyes were focused on me. Fearing the worst, I held back tears, avoided direct eye contact, and swiftly walked away. I went to the dormitory and burst into tears from the sheer helplessness of the situation. I was filled with despair.

I was Mr. Lu's favorite student. At the beginning of each Chemistry class, Mr. Lu would randomly pick students and ask questions related to the previous lecture's material. Many students stood up and gave the wrong answers. Then Mr. Lu would ask me to answer the question. I would give the correct answer, and Mr. Lu would give me a little smile of satisfaction. I guessed this made the sons and daughters of the commune officials angry. They had been admitted to Jiangsu Zhongzhou High School with lower scores and had difficulty coping with our school's high academic standard. Behind the scenes, Mr. Ding orchestrated the conspiracy of "Sweeping away all the ox devils and snake demons." Sadly, again, I was a convenient target.

I lived in fear. I was alert to any small movement around me. I felt the Red Guards were always watching me. I was so afraid that I would be "pulled out" for "class-struggle sessions." I secretly asked for divine revelation. I screamed for help from heaven, but heaven was silent. I begged the Earth to show mercy, but the Earth was impervious to my plea. Finally, I became numb. I was lost in this political perplexity. I gave up. Do whatever you like! Go with fate. Whatever will be, will be!

Soon a condemnation meeting was called. We all gathered in the students' dining hall. It was mandatory. Everybody had to attend. The hall was crowded. Many teachers were standing around the room against the walls. They appeared stone-faced. I chose to sit at the back of the hall, far away from the stage. Mr. Ding and several Red Guards were on the stage preparing the meeting.

A few of the Red Guards wore faded army uniforms with brand-new red armbands with a golden inscription "Red Guard." Since these uniforms were their parents' attire from the "old days," they emphasized their superior bloodline. They were the sons and daughters of military generals. These sons and daughters enjoyed preferential treatment and a life of ease and comfort. They were untouchable and arrogant. They were a bunch of spoiled brats. Backed by Mao, they were ready and eager to show their power, and they became ruthless.

Another group of Red Guards wore new, army-style Red Guard outfits. They were the daughters and sons of commune officials. They grew up in the villages and lived a simple, austere lifestyle. Their fathers were the kings of the local kingdoms, and they were the new crop of elitists in their

145

villages. They envied city life. They were jealous of those city children from the bourgeois families for their superior material lifestyles. The Cultural Revolution was their opportunity for revenge. They were the Red Guards that occupied my classroom.

Suddenly, a Red Guard appeared wearing a faded army uniform with a 3-inch-wide leather belt cinched around his waist. He led us in the shouting of slogans.

"Long Live Chairman Mao!"
"Long Live the Great Proletarian Cultural Revolution!"
"Expose and Denounce Ox Devils and Snake Demons!"
"Sweep Away and Crush All Ox Devils and Snake Demons!"

Fearful, I followed the crowd, and waved Mao's Little Red Book above my head. As my mouth moved with the slogans, my heart was heavy. I steered my eyes around. Most of the students were like me; shouting without enthusiasm, but afraid of getting into trouble. If we didn't follow the crowd, we would be black-marked. We had to wave and shout.

After the slogan "Sweep away and crush all ox devils and snake demons," three Red Guards dragged out the three teachers. Each of them wore a wooden placard on the front of their chests. The signs were hung around their necks with a thin wire. They were identified as Ox Devils and Snake Demons. The Red Guards pushed the teachers' heads down, pulling their hair with one hand and twisting their arms backward behind their back with the other. After many days without shaving, I could hardly recognize these teachers. They had all lost so much weight and looked horrible. Dark circles around their eyes made them appear as if they had just been pulled from hell. The cruelty of the Red Guards was unbearable to watch.

People were shouting loudly, "Sweep away and crush all ox devils and snake demons!" The loudest shouting came from the front rows where the Red Guards stood. I shouted with my eyes looking forward. I was afraid I was under surveillance. My heart was pounding. I couldn't believe that these ruthless animals were actually human beings.

Then a new slogan, "Smash the Rightists," was shouted out, and two other teachers were pushed onto the stage by the Red Guards. They received similar treatment to the three Ox Devils and Snake Demons, except their placards identified them as rightists.

One of the rightists was my third-grade math teacher, Mr. Chen. He was the best Math teacher in all of Zhongzhou city. In order to ensure high percentage entry into university, the school administration always selected him as the third-grade math teacher. He was a local teacher. Besides teaching math, he never said anything extra in our classroom. When math class ended, he always walked out quickly. I had never seen him talk to any other teachers. No wonder, it turned out he was a rightist. He had learned his lesson during the anti-rightist movement: "People should seal their mouths and say nothing."

Mrs. Chang was the other rightist. She taught Russian to second graders. She lived downstairs in our dormitory with her husband, a history teacher, and their two children. Mrs. Chang was always well dressed, not gaudy but refined. Her manner was gentle. You could tell that she was from a bourgeois, intellectual family. Before the condemnation meeting, we didn't know they were rightists.

Mr. Ding, representing all the schoolteachers, gave the condemnation speech. He glorified his own achievement. He had been able to dig out what these three teachers had discussed privately between themselves. I was sickened to listen. My brain refused to participate anymore. I blanked out. I bowed my head, keeping my eyes fixed on the floor. I had no idea who the next speaker was and what was said in the following speeches. The meeting finally ended. People swiftly dispersed in silence. The three "Ox Devils and Snake Demons" were placed in isolation again.

After that day, these five teachers were ordered to stand outside the school gate with their bodies bent downward, their heads bowed toward the floor, and the heavy placards hanging from their necks. They stood there for many months from 7:30 to 10:00 o'clock every morning. It was dreadful. I had to pass the school gate every morning as I went to the classroom. It was during the middle of a hot summer. The thin wire that held the placards sunk into their skin. I could only imagine the suffering they were experiencing. I wished someone could have shown them some compassion, and allowed them to place a cotton pad around their neck to ease the pain. It lasted for many months until those sons and daughters of the high officials discovered that their own parents had also become targets of Mao's Cultural Revolution! At that time, the five teachers no longer stood outside the school gate, but they were still held in isolation.

During the Cultural Revolution, students no longer ate in the dining hall. We would go to the kitchen to pick up our rice container. The cook would then put some vegetables on top of the rice, and we returned to the dormitory to eat. On one sunny October Sunday, I picked up my lunch from the kitchen and hurried back to my dormitory. As I walked, I came face to face with Mr. Lu who was on his way to the kitchen for some hot water. He was being closely escorted by a Red Guard and was holding a thermos bottle. He was thin. His hair had turned all gray, but his face seemed oddly calm. After many months of isolation and mental torture, it appeared as if he had become resigned to whatever fate would bring him.

His eyes looked toward me, as if wanting to say "Hi." I gave a quick glance at the Red Guard. He was watching. I turned my head and walked away as fast as I could. Afterward, I was so ashamed of myself. I was a wimp, a weak person afraid to be out of step with the political tide, even in a small way. I could have given Mr. Lu some indication to show that I still respected him as my favorite teacher. It would have been a tremendous comfort to him, but I hadn't been able to look at him eye-to-eye. I felt unworthy to be his student.

Three years later, I heard that Mr. Lu had killed himself. He was kept in confinement until his death. He was beaten by the Red Guards and was insulted continuously, but he kept his desire to live through all of these atrocities. It wasn't until he learned that his only son had committed suicide that he finally also lost his will to live. His son had also been persecuted as an anti-revolutionary element. He hanged himself in his cell at the school. I also learned that Mr. Gao committed suicide during his confinement.

Mr. Ding remained busy punishing the devils and the demons, and the Red Guard were busy writing the Big Character posters. We now were ordered to self-study Mao's work. No one could leave school without permission. After early morning assembly, all the Reds left the classroom, while we, the Blacks and the Grays, remained studying Mao's work. It was so boring. All day our eyes stared at Mao's book, yet our minds were thousands of miles away. I had started to copy Mao's quotations and poems onto paper, so that time could pass faster. Then I became worried that the Red Guard and Mr. Ding might manipulate my writing and then accuse me of insulting Mao and having ulterior motives. This had happened to many condemned rightists during the anti-rightist movement. Hours seemed extremely long. Days passed so slowly. After months of grinding, our patience started to wear off. At the same time, the Red Guards were slowly losing their grip on us. They were busy making connections with their "big brothers" (Red Guard) in Beijing.

My classmate, Jin, told me there were many students from other classrooms in the school library. They were studying books by Marx and Lenin. Chairman Mao encouraged us to study the thoughts of Marx and Lenin. She asked me if I would like to go to the library with her.

Jin was a local student who sat next to me. She was a nice girl. Her father was a factory clerk before the Liberation of China, and that made her a Gray student. She was thin, petite, and held an ancient young girl's beauty. We went to the library. There was a roomful of students already there, but no Red Guards. Besides Mao's books, there were books by Marx, Lenin, and Engels. All other books had been removed from the bookshelves. I became fascinated with Marx and Lenin's personal biographies. They were far more interesting than reciting the dry, tasteless written work of Mao.

In the library, I was introduced to another local student. Her name was YeYe. Her father was a clerk, which also made her a Gray student. YeYe was a tall, very reserved girl. On the surface, she seemed arrogant and unwilling to swim with the tide, but when you got to know her closely, she was a very kind person.

Jin and YeYe were city-grown girls. They were polite and gentle, speaking with a quiet voice. In the library, I learned from them that the local students in our classroom held a huge resentment against the sons and daughters of commune officials. They were aware that these rough-edged, no-brain students worked closely with Mr. Ding, while they also bullied other students. Since the start of the Cultural Revolution, almost all the local students were classified as Grays or Blacks, even though some of them were members of the Communist Youth League. They were sympathetic toward me because I had to live with those idiots. Academic excellence was continually criticized politically. My high performance in the classroom had created jealousies among many of my Red roommates and had resulted in condemnation from Mr. Ding. However, it had also earned me the respect of many local classmates.

YeYe and Jin became my close friends, and the library became our sanctuary.

"Destroy the Four Olds"

In August, Mao called upon the Red Guards to attend the Revolutionary Tours (大串联). The Central Cultural Revolution Committee expressed support for students across the country to visit Beijing and exchange their revolutionary experiences. The "Sweep Away All Ox Devils and Snake Demons" was Mao's way of firing up the students against Liu Shaoqi[7] and Liu's supporters. Unfortunately, the young students all over the country were so naïve. They were "Sweeping and Smashing" their own teachers. A few collateral victims of the "great revolution" never bothered Mao. He was a self-centered tyrant. As he said himself, "better that I betray the world than let the world betray me" (宁可我负天下人；天下人不能负我). However, Mao wanted to inflict his evil goals without actually pointing his finger at Liu Shaoqi. He wanted to kill Liu and his supporters, but didn't want the people to see blood on his hands. He plotted to have these young, full of energy, fearful of nothing, yet ignorant, naive students be the slaughterers on his behalf.

All Red Guards in our school rode the train and went to Beijing for the Revolutionary Tours (大串联). On August 18, 1966, millions of students from all over the country gathered in Tiananmen Square. Mao, wearing a Red Guard armband, stood atop the Gate of Heavenly Peace with Lin Biao next to him to review the students' rally. Mao expressed his "strong support for their actions" and steered the Red Guards to attack the supporters of Liu Shaoqi. He ordered the students to "Bombard the Headquarters," pointing toward the local government officials, the Liu supporters. Lin Biao also gave the Red Guards their directive: "Destroy

---

[7] Liu Shaoqi: The President of the People's Republic of China from 1959 to 1968.

151

the Four Olds." These were: "Old ideas, old cultures, old customs, and old habits."

While the Red Guards were exchanging their revolutionary experiences in Beijing, we, the Grays and Blacks, were able to take a breather from the daily harassment inflicted by the Red Guards. After the Red Guards returned, at one morning assembly, the leader ordered all of us to get involved in the Destroy the Four Olds movement. They had identified a family who owned Four Olds, and they planned to raid this family. The Red Guards wanted Blacks and Grays to join the raid to "reform" ourselves. From the start of the Cultural Revolution, we, the Blacks and Grays, had never been asked to join the activities of the Red Guard. Since the Red Guards in our classroom came from villages and had seldom visited the homes of people from the city, they now wanted to boost their courage and bully city families. The more students that became involved, the more olds would be destroyed.

Around 9 o'clock in the morning, all my classmates gathered in the schoolyard. In front of the gathering, a Red Guard held a microphone to give out instructions. There were Red Guards holding red flags followed by more Red Guards playing drums, cymbals, and gongs. We marched out of the school gate and walked down the street toward the unfortunate, hapless family. The family wasn't aware that within an hour devastation would befall their home. We loudly shouted the slogans:

"Long Live Chairman Mao!"
"Long Live the Great Proletarian Cultural Revolution!"
"Smash the Four Olds!"

The slogans were accompanied by loud drums and the deafening sounds of cymbals and gongs. The residents all came out, watching us with fear and curiosity in their eyes. I felt so ashamed, I turned my head downward.

We stopped at the front of a traditional Chinese courtyard complex. The head of the household was a famous Chinese brush painter. Due to his artistic talent, this family enjoyed a better life than the average Chinese family and still lived in a multi-room courtyard house. At the front door of this house, the Red Guards shouted slogans, beat drums, and crashed gongs. Once the slogans ended, the Red Guards led us into the courtyard and then we were dispersed into all corners of the household.

I followed my roommates to a room upstairs. There was an old lady crying in fear. She was in her late sixties, sitting on a rattan armchair next to her bed. My roommates opened all the drawers and trunks. They enthusiastically dumped all the brush paintings and clothes onto the floor in the center of the room. Their wolfish eyes seemed filled with curiosity. After they emptied all drawers and trunks, they moved on to search a different room. They ordered me to stay in the room to watch over the old lady.

On the floor, there was a large pile of beautiful paintings. There were paintings of water lilies, flying horses, and peony flowers — many beautiful paintings. So sad, very soon all of these would be set on fire and turned to ashes. I wanted to put some paintings back into the drawers, but I was petrified. On this hot summer morning, it seemed my hands and feet were frozen. I was afraid to move.

The old lady was sobbing. She could have been my grandmother. I wanted to say something to comfort her, but didn't know what to tell her. After this, I started to worry about my own family. Growing up in a Black family where you were continuously harassed by the residential neighborhood committee and the local Public Security Bureau, you became sensitized to political movements. I had to let my family in Yiyang know what had happened in Zhongzhou so that they could prepare.

The Red Guards returned to pick up the paintings. Pearl, one of my classmates, a Red Guard who was lame and had crossed eyes, saw me standing there in a daze.

She scolded me and came down on me like a ton of bricks. "Are you a blockhead? This is your chance to reform yourself and draw a clear line between you and your Black family. It seems that you, the Black Bastard, can never be reformed."

She ordered me to pick up some of the paintings and carry them to the courtyard. I secretly cursed her. "What a vile character, a good-for-nothing! You will die like a dog."

In the courtyard, the Red Guards had already dug up the tiled floor. All my classmates encircled a huge pile of paintings, books, and already broken porcelain antiques. A scholarly looking old man in his seventies, with a

153

long white beard, had been forced to kneel in front of the pile. His head was held down by a Red Guard. His body was uncontrollably shivering as if he had a bad flu. Tears welled up in his eyes. The Red Guards set the pile on fire with smoke and flames soaring toward the sky. We were shouting slogans: "Long Live Chairman Mao, Long Live the Great Proletarian Cultural Revolution, Destroy the Four Olds," again accompanied by the deafening drums and gongs. We left the family in disarray with a wall of worry: What might happen tomorrow? Are they coming back again? Are we going to jail?

We returned to the classroom. I was very worried about my family. How could I let them know the current situation as soon as possible? At any time, there could be a raid on my family. Political movements normally started in the big cities, and then trickled down to the county towns. Back in those days, information transfer was very slow. It would take a couple of weeks for a county town to pick up any new political message. However, it would also take a week or more for me to get my letter home! There were no phones available for the public or individual families.

It would be devastating if my letter reached Yiyang when the Red Guards were in the midst of raiding our home. I would be identified as the Black Bastard that could never be reformed, couldn't even draw a clear line between her and her Black family. I would likely be pulled out for class struggle session.

After dinner, I took a notebook and walked quickly toward Plum Flower Park. My brain was preoccupied. Tree-lined Plum Flower Road was empty. The dense green foliage of the old trees cast cool evening shadows upon me. I crossed a stone bridge and walked alone into Plum Flower Park. The weather-beaten, light-brown water lily leaves were floating on the lake. The tall, magnificent Wenbi Pagoda was silhouetted against a setting orange-red sun and summer evening clouds. The park was deadly quiet. Practically no one was in the park. Walking in the park could be considered "old culture" and a "bourgeois" lifestyle. A fragile evening moon was rising in the east as the sun slowly withdrew its rays and finally hid behind the mountains under the darkening sky. The pavilions, plum trees, and lake surrounded me in the stillness of a summer evening.

The scene around me evoked memories of the past. I remembered the first week of my high school when Mrs. Wong took us for an outing to

Plum Flower Park and Tianyun Temple. She told us: "During winter time, the Plum Flower blossoms will form pink-red clouds set against white snow. It will be fantastic scenery." Sadly, I never had a chance to visit Plum Flower Park when the plum flowers were blooming. Three years had passed, and Plum Flower Park seemed depressingly desolate. I reflected on that time three years ago. It was also a late summer day, and we were a bunch of innocent, gay, 16-year-old girls. Three years later, it was a whole world of difference. Those grown-up-in-the-countryside girls had shown their tiger claws. We were no longer friends. Political clouds had darkened the sky and obscured everything.

As I strolled through the park, I found a man-made rock hill. I hid behind the hill, sat on a Tai Lake rock, and started composing my letter to Aunt Zhen. I began the letter with an enthusiastic statement: I had answered Chairman Mao's appeal and participated in the "Destroy the Four Olds" movement. I had joined my classmates and raided a bad element's family. I gave a detailed description of the raid. I emphasized that we opened all the drawers and trunks. I also let Aunt know we dug up the courtyard floor. I gave a subtle hint that the two trunks of fur coats and picture albums left by my mother could belong to the Four Olds. I didn't dare mention mother's trunks directly. At the end of the letter, I exclaimed that I felt so proud I had followed Chairman Mao's instructions, and then I ended the letter with many slogans. I thought, even if the Red Guards confiscated my letter, it wouldn't prove me guilty of anything. Next morning, I handed the letter to the school gatekeeper and asked him to place the letter in the outgoing mail slot.

A week later, the Red Guards destroyed Plum Flower Park. They also completely destroyed Tianyun Temple. All the Buddha and Luohan (罗汉) were smashed to pieces. The Tianyun Temple gate was defaced. All the monks were confined, and some were tortured. What an unbelievable tragedy. No one dared say anything or challenge anybody. After all, these were the orders of Chairman Mao, "our greatest leader."

I was eagerly looking forward to Aunt's response to my letter. A letter from Aunt eventually came, but it never mentioned a raid. I assumed our family was okay. When I returned for Chinese New Year, I found that the Red Guards did raid our house. Prior to the raid, Aunt had burned all the picture albums and my diary. It was from those picture albums that I remembered how my parents looked. Aunt also gave the fur coats to our God Pond Valley relatives.

Xiao Mei and Xiao Di claimed that my cousin, Da Di, led the Red Guards raid on our house! Da Di was a senior high school student in Jiangsu Yiyang School. He was an easygoing, nerdy-looking young man who was easily bullied. One morning the Red Guards in Jiangsu Yiyang School encircled Da Di and shouted slogans at him: "Down with the capitalist anti-revolutionary element!" They called Da Di "Black Bastard." The Red Guards pushed and barked at him. They ordered him to lead the way to our home.

The Red Guards were ready to go. They were holding red flags and had their drums and gongs prepared. They were aligned in a procession. They pushed Da Di to the front of the line and forced Da Di to shout the slogans and march toward our home. The sound of the drums and gongs stopped when they reached our front door. Slogans burst out:

"Down with the capitalists!"
"Smash anti-revolutionary elements!"

Two Red Guards pasted the Big Character poster on our front door and exposed us as the family of a capitalist, anti-revolutionary element. The neighbors started gathering around our house. We were the first family raided in Yiyang town.

Although Aunt was prepared, she felt ashamed in front of the neighbors and shivered with fear. The Red Guards flocked into the house. The house was so small. They squeezed into the small spaces between the beds. Grandmother suddenly had chest pains and was in agony. Grandmother was 70 years old. Her face was pale, and she looked frail. Aunt asked the Red Guards to let Grandmother lie on the bed. One of the Red Guards was kind and said okay. There was really not much to discover in our little house. We had so little. Aunt had hidden her cash.

They started digging the floor. Aunt was nervous. She had buried gold underneath the floor near Grandmother's bed. Some gold jewelry had been left by Mother, and the rest belonged to Aunt Zhen herself. Grandmother's heart was pounding. She started wailing in pain. The gold had been buried for more than 15 years, the day when we moved in. The floor had caked up hard like cement and the gold had sunk deeper. With Grandmother groaning in pain, the Red Guards soon lost interest and stopped digging. Luckily, the Red Guards found nothing. Many families were persecuted for hiding gold underground.

Two naive teenagers, Xiao Mei and Xiao Di, blamed Da Di for bringing the Red Guards to raid our home. Sadly, it was nothing to do with Da Di. If they had been in Da Di's shoes, they would have done the same thing. Who dared resist the Red Guards? Poor Da Di had not only been pushed and humiliated by the Red Guards at his school, but he had also been shouted at by his own family members.

Our family stayed indoors for many days. They were ashamed to meet our neighbors. Grandmother felt she was suffocating at home and wanted to visit one of her friends. Xiao Mei was a sensible girl and worried that Grandmother might cause trouble. She was getting older and becoming forgetful and might say something foolish in front of her friends. With the current environment, the less you are seen the better.

Xiao Mei told Grandmother, "In the midst of the Cultural Revolution with our family just being raided, I think it would be better to stay home."

Grandmother became upset and replied, "I am sick and tired of sitting at home. If I go out, is someone going to eat me up?"

It seemed Grandmother was determined to go out! Xiao Mei became more nervous and wanted to stop Grandmother. Xiao Mei wasn't thinking clearly and started to say some things she would regret. "You shouldn't rely on your old age and think you can simply do anything you wish. After all, you are an anti-revolutionary element's wife. You are lucky you haven't been pulled out for class struggle session. You are asking for trouble!"

Grandmother was now in a towering rage. Her own granddaughter had called her an anti-revolutionary element's wife. "Who do you think you are, calling me an anti-revolutionary element's wife? You little bitch. Yes, I am an old woman. I have lived long enough. Dying doesn't scare me. I will go out even though they might cut my head off. It would only leave a hole in my neck! I haven't done anything to offend anyone in my entire life. Why should I be afraid of anyone? Almighty earth and heaven, what's there to do?"

Grandmother was old and had become stubborn. Tears ran down her face. She stumbled out, hobbling along on her cane. Soon after,

Grandmother returned. She was constantly heaving sighs. Probably, after the raid, her friend hadn't been keen to chat with her. After all the stress, Grandmother had developed chest pains.

Since I had been forced to stay at school in the summer for the "Great Proletarian Cultural Revolution," I hadn't seen Grandmother and my family for over a year. I was eager to return for the Chinese New Year celebration. However, this year there wasn't going to be a New Year celebration. Heavy, dark thoughts pressed down on Grandmother and Aunt Zhen's hearts, especially when they found out that Uncle Nian couldn't come home.

The Red Guards had confined and isolated Uncle Nian at his work unit in Shanghai. Aunt had discovered his situation from his neighbor. Other than his confinement, we knew nothing else. I could imagine his suffering after seeing the treatment received by my three "Ox Devils and Snake Demons" teachers at my school. We didn't have the usual New Year's Eve ancestor worship ritual because it was considered old culture — one of the four olds. On New Year's Eve, our door was kept shut tight!

Back in 1964, my grandfather passed away in Hong Kong. That summer, Grandfather's concubine, Uncle He-Shen's mother, visited us for the first time. Although she was in her sixties, she still held an elegant figure. No wonder Grandfather liked her. She called my grandmother "my respected sister." They shed mournful tears together for Grandfather's passing. These two rivals finally reconciled after Grandfather's death. Since then, during the New Year's Eve ancestor worship ritual, Grandmother always added two new dishes, Grandfather's favorites. One was meatballs with sweet, sour sauce, and the other was whole eggs with brown sauce.

We didn't have many dishes for this New Year's Eve, but meatballs with sweet, sour sauce and whole eggs with brown sauce were still displayed on our dinner table. Without a New Year celebration and with Uncle Nian's absence, it was very quiet at the dinner table. Before the food, Grandmother begged our ancestors to protect us and asked our ancestors to help Uncle Nian keep out of danger and return safely home. Aunt Zhen held back her tears.

Uncle Nian didn't return home for more than three years. Later, Uncle Nian told Aunt Zhen, that once his work unit found out his father was an anti-revolutionary element and had escaped to Hong Kong, the Red

Guards pulled him out for class struggle session. After further investigation of his family background, they discovered not only that my parents, his brother and sister-in-law, were residing in the US, but that his older sister and half-brother were living in Hong Kong. This made Uncle's family background extremely complicated and strongly connected to foreign countries. The Red Guards accused him of being a foreign spy. They isolated him and forced him to confess. Before the Cultural Revolution, Uncle Nian had been so brainwashed by the Communist Party that he wrote to my father to encourage him to return to China and contribute to our great motherland. Now, the Red Guards accused him of being a foreign spy!

Raid on Our Dormitory

After the siege and ruin of Tianyun Temple, YeYe told me to be careful. After seeing the raid of the famous brush painter's home, I had a hunch that something might happen to me. I just didn't know when it would occur and what would happen.

Both YeYe and Jin invited me to their home, and I visited many times. YeYe's father, Mr. Yin, was a very reserved person and seldom made comments on any political issue. However, in front of me, I sensed a hint of cynicism in him. He seemed to possess a lot of worldly wisdom. He loved antiques and admired all the famous scholars in Chinese history. On the surface, he seemed he could grin and endure any attack that might come his way, but I could see that he had a set of unspoken standards. I always suspected he was actually from an aristocratic or intellectual family prior to the Liberation of China. He seemed to have a cultural upbringing. In spite of all the chaos of the Cultural Revolution, he allowed no glimmer of resentment to appear on his face. He joked and smiled as usual. However, he encouraged YeYe to be friendly with me, a Black student, and to participate less actively in the Cultural Revolution.

I had saved up about 200 Yuan, which I kept hidden in my trunk. This cash had been saved from Grandmother's red envelopes during Chinese New Year and the monthly pocket money sent by Aunt. I seldom spent money except for necessities such as soap and toothpaste. 200 Yuan was a large sum of money, especially in the eyes of some of my Red Guard roommates. In the library, I quietly handed the cash to YeYe, and asked her parents to keep it for me. YeYe took it without hesitation.

One Sunday morning we were fast asleep. Because there were no academic classes and exams, we tended to get up late. Suddenly we were woken by a loud whistle, which hadn't been heard for a while. This was followed by the sound of many random footsteps. One of our female PE teachers and a party of female Red Guards suddenly burst into our room as we were waking up from our youthful deep sleep. At first, we were at a loss as we tried to open our lazy eyes, but slowly we realized abnormality and urgency.

Mei Qin was one of the Red Guards. She declared, "Destroy the Four Olds is part of the Cultural Revolution. To make sure there aren't any Four Olds in our room, we want everyone to open their trunks and let us search for Four Olds."

Then she walked to her bunk bed and pulled out the trunk from underneath. She would do her part to Destroy the Four Olds first, to set an example. She opened the trunk and let other Red Guards rummage through her personal belongings. Not surprisingly, no four olds were found.

"She knew about the raid ahead of time. How could it be different?" I questioned silently.

The Red Guards proceeded with the search. Each of us stood by our trunks and opened them up as the Red Guards came to check. The Red Guards came to me. Resignedly I opened my trunk. The Red Guards paid extra attention to my trunk and searched it slowly and carefully. They wanted to find something to incriminate me. Luckily, nothing of interest was found in my trunk.

The Red Guards approached Ling's bed. Ling didn't move. Mei Qin said, "Everyone has opened their trunk. Why not you?"

Ling replied unhappily, "Why should I do what you say?"

"It is our great Chairman Mao's order to destroy the four olds, and you are no exception!" Mei Qin replied, blushing scarlet with anger.

Mei Qin was already fed up with Ling for her recent passive attitude. She felt that Ling had been unwilling to participate in many of the Red Guards' activities and often presented herself as a "little bourgeois lady," yet she was a high official's daughter. Now, she was challenging Mei Qin's authority.

Mei Qin continued to criticize and disparage Ling. "It is Chairman Mao's order. Just because you are a high official's daughter, you think you can disobey Chairman Mao?"

Ling immediately barked back at Mei Qin, "You are a self-important, meddlesome busy-body. Did Chairman Mao tell you to search a Red Guard's trunk?"

Mei Qin looked angry and flustered. I was secretly delighted to see Mei Qin getting the rough side of Ling's tongue.

Other Red Guards smiled ingratiatingly and tried to calm Ling down. "We are simply following orders. Please don't get offended by this. Once you open your trunk, we will be out of here in no time, and will leave you in peace."

Ling stood up, pulled her trunk out, flung open the lid with a bang, and pushed the trunk in front of Mei Qin. Mei Qin was exhausted by Ling's attitude. She quickly glanced through the trunk and left without making a careful search.

During the raid, surprisingly, nothing was discovered related to the Four Olds, not even a trace of classical poems. After the Red Guards left, we were all upset and felt our dignity had been demeaned. However, in Communist China, what is dignity? YingYing ridiculed the dormitory raid. "It's similar to Raid on Prospect Garden."[8]

Although YingYing was a Communist Youth League member, due to her family background she was still classified as Gray. Obedience and endurance were reserved for the Black Bastards. I had no guts to say what I thought. I didn't dare mumble a word.

Later I learned they were looking for my diary — a Black Bastard's diary. Thank God, due to the heavy workload preparing for the university entrance exams and, more recently, the repercussions from the Cultural Revolution, I had stopped writing in my diary a long time ago. My old diary had been left at home, and Aunt Zhen had burned it before the family raid. The search was intimidating. I was glad I had handed my cash to YeYe.

---

[8] "Raid on Prospect Garden" was described in *"Dream of the Red Chamber"* written by Cao Xueqin during the Qing Dynasty. It is one of the most renowned Classical Novels in China.

Member of the "Leisure Club" (逍遥派)

After a big rally in Tiananmen Square on August 18, 1966, many more rallies followed. The Central Cultural Revolution Committee expressed support for students across the country. They encouraged them to come to Beijing and learn about the revolution first-hand from the Beijing students. They wanted all students to follow the Red Guard in Beijing — "Bombard the Headquarters." They also wanted the Beijing students to extend the revolution across the country. In response, all the cities established Revolutionary Tours (大串连) reception stations to offer free food and accommodation for the Red Guards. The Red Guards only needed to provide proof of student status, such as a school badge, and the Red Guard armband. The Red Guards took advantage of the opportunity to visit relatives and see the sights. Beijing was no longer the only focus. People went south to Guangzhou, north to Harbin, west to Xinjiang, and even as far as Tibet.

The Red Guards were in the Revolutionary Tours mood. They left the "Ox Devils and Snake Demons" in their cells and took turns guarding the devils and demons. They also set the Blacks and Grays free. Morning assembly was no more. The local students came to school or stayed at home; it was their choice. I was no longer a social outcast. YeYe, Jin, and I started to visit the People's Park near Jin's home. An old man, in his seventies with a long, white beard, practiced Tai Chi every morning in the park. His eyes shone brightly. He was so calm and peaceful. He seemed untouched by the chaos around him. I wondered, "How come no one had removed his long beard? Surely, that must be one of the Four Olds. He must belong to the Reds." He was so relaxed. His movements were so gentle and flowed so gracefully. People told us he was practicing Yang-style Tai Chi. We decided to follow him and practice Tai Chi.

The People's Park was a small inner-city park. There was a man-made rock hill and a few trees. Mostly it was a grassless open space. It had been spared a Red Guards' assault. The park was becoming more and more crowded. Many young high school students took refuge in the park. Besides studying Mao's work, we were not allowed to read anything else. The old man seemed not to mind that we followed his movements. The Tai Chi activity started with only a few of us, but later expanded to a larger group. We also started sword-dancing (舞剑). Sword-dancing is a traditional Chinese martial art that uses faster movements than Tai Chi. Jin borrowed three bamboo-made fake swords from her family friends. Between Tai Chi and sword-dancing, we spent most of our mornings in the park.

Released from the suppression by the Red Guards, we were happy for the moment. We didn't plan for our future, didn't think of our future. No one knew what future lay ahead of us. After a couple months practicing martial arts, my spirit became brighter and I was physically stronger. While climbing the stairs to my dormitory room, I could spring upward without much effort.

My roommates wondered what I had been doing. The Red Guards in my dormitory were out of sight. Ling had disappeared from school. She had gone to Beijing to visit her Aunt. YingYing and a few Grays remained in the school dormitory, and no one told us to go home.

At the beginning of 1967, the Red Guards movement took a drastic turn and was elevated to the level of a nationwide mass campaign. The Central Cultural Revolution Committee had called on not only students, but also "the masses consisting of workers, peasants, soldiers, revolutionary intellectuals, and revolutionary cadres" to support the Cultural Revolution. Red Guard units formed in all workplaces in China. The original Red Guards seemed unable to fulfill the task to "Bombard the Headquarters." Most of them were children of high officials in local governments and military generals. They were not up to the task of overthrowing their own parents. Mao was convinced the parents were supporters of Liu Shaoqi. Mao wanted "Shaking the Heavens and Splitting the Earth" to uproot Liu Shaoqi. Mao and the Central Cultural Revolution

Committee had encouraged students and workers to form "Rebellion" groups and to purge local government leaders.

A Rebellion (造反派) unit was formed in our school. They called themselves simply the Rebel Group (造反团). All the Grays joined the Rebel Group. During the earlier part of the Cultural Revolution, the Grays were viewed as second-class students. They were excluded from Cultural Revolution activities and felt they had been superseded and abandoned. During the beginning of the Cultural Revolution, the Red Guards also exposed any black marks on their family members. They were humiliated and sometimes harassed by the Red Guards. The Grays joined the Rebel Group enthusiastically. They had at last found a place where they belonged. Some students sought revenge. The local male student, Chen Ming, who revealed that Mr. Ding compiled a personal dossier about me, also became a member of the Rebel Group. They started calling the original Red Guards the Loyalists (保皇派) — loyal to their parents, loyal to local government officials.

The Rebel and the Loyalist groups posted Big Character posters attacking each other. Those Red Guards from high official families became subdued. They worried about their own parents and were angry about the current situation. Most of them went home or sightseeing. Children of commune officials now ran the original Red Guards group. Grays wanted to participate in the Cultural Revolution so that they could engrave some positive marks on their personal resume that would give them a better chance of acceptance at universities. At that time, both students and their parents thought school would eventually resume. They still dreamed of going to university. Dreams always come when the world is dark.

No one could have imagined that the Central Cultural Revolution Committee would have used the Grays as a tool. Due to their parents' political connections, only the children of high officials sensed the real motive of the central government. A few individuals in the worker Rebellion units were under direct control of the Central Cultural Revolution Committee.

After Mao's death, it became clear that the Gang of Four controlled that committee. One of the Four was Mao's wife, Jiang Qing. Most of the members of the Rebellion units were innocent victims of the Cultural

Revolution. Sadly, at the end of the Cultural Revolution, many of the Rebellion members were persecuted as anti-revolutionary elements.

YingYing, Lin Da, YeYe, and Jin became members of the Rebel Group. Lin Da was my roommate. Although she was the daughter of a commune official, after further investigation the Reds discovered that she had been adopted. Her biological father was a landlord before the Liberation of China, and so Lin Da became classed as Gray. Since that time, resentment toward the Loyalists became deeply rooted in her.

YeYe and Jin inquired whether I could also join the Rebel Group. I was rejected since my family background was too complicated. At that time, they couldn't accept anyone from a Black family. The Reds, the Loyalists, would accuse them of being anti-revolutionary. They couldn't allow one rotten apple to spoil the whole barrel. The Rebel Group was new and was afraid to take a second step until completing the first!

YeYe and Jin were busy with Rebel group activities. All my roommates were either preoccupied with their revolutionary activities or were sightseeing across the country. I was all alone with nothing to do. I became a member of the so-called Leisure Club (逍遥派). No Leisure Club actually existed. This was what we, the undesirable Black students, called ourselves and the word used by the Grays to tease us. It was the loneliest time for me. Amazingly, I didn't think about the future or the possibility of attending university. Young people have never been sophisticated enough to worry about the future. I needed to do something to occupy myself. Studying Mao's books was out of the question. After being forced to study the "Holy Bible" — Mao's work — for many months, I became bored stiff with Mao's work. I loathed even glancing at it.

There were rumors that Chairman Mao loved to read all four of the Great Classical Novels: *Water Margin* (水浒传); *Romance of the Three Kingdoms* (三国演义); *Journey to the West* (西游记); and *Dream of the Red Chamber* (红楼梦). It was said that he read *Dream of the Red Chamber* five times. Since Chairman Mao had read the novels, it gave me the green light to also read these four great classical books!

Most classical books were burned and destroyed during the Destroy the Four Olds movement. Now there were many of these books circulating in the underworld. As described in the poem, "Farewell on the Ancient Grassland" by Bai Juyi, "wild fire can't burn all, the spring wind will rejuvenate anew" (野火烧不尽，春风吹又生). I borrowed books from YeYe and Jin's local friends and started devouring the books one by one. *Water Margin* didn't suit my taste. Too much fighting and killing. *Journey to the West* is a popular folktale in China; even children know the story of Monkey (孙悟空) and Pigsy (猪八戒). I glanced through these two books once.

Romance of the Three Kingdoms (三国演义) was quite interesting: a Chinese historical novel based on events during the turbulent years of the Three Kingdoms period. The novel focuses on the conflict between the three kingdoms, Wei, Shu, and Wu, with the plot evolving around the struggles between the three powers. The main character is Zhuge Liang (諸葛亮), a master warfare strategist and political leader for the Shu kingdom. Zhuge Liang possessed a wide range of innate abilities. His war strategies and battlefield tactics were often topics of hot discussion among the people.

It was clear that Mao had explored and then utilized Zhuge Liang's superior talent in his own version of *Sun Tzu's Art of War* (孙子兵法)[9] during the Chinese civil war. No wonder Mao liked *Romance of the Three Kingdoms*. It enabled him to win the war!

Dream of the Red Chamber is considered a masterpiece of vernacular Chinese literature. It is the pinnacle of Chinese classical novels. It was written in the Qing Dynasty by Cao Xueqin, and extended by Gao E. *Dream of the Red Chamber* is believed to be semi-autobiography of author Cao Xueqin. It reflects the rise and fall of his own family during the Qing Dynasty.

I loved this book and read it many times. Each time it gave me new understanding. I admired the author's remarkable talent. He created amazing, true-to-life, vivid descriptions of the characters. After reading the book, I formed a life-like image of each character described by the author. Due to the turbulent events within Cao Xueqin's family, the book presents a philosophical perspective on life and the sighing vicissitudes of the world. Facing the "ups and downs" in my own young life, Cao Xueqin's "cynical,

---

[9] "Sun Tzu's Art of War" is an ancient Chinese military treatise attributed to Sun Tzu who was a high-ranking military general and strategist during the "Late spring and autumn" historical period.

misanthropic perspective" (愤世嫉俗) and his "totally enlightened outlook on life" (大彻大悟) struck a resonance with me.

Cao Xueqin wrote,

Truth becomes fiction when the fiction's true;
Real becomes not-real where the unreal's real.

I asked and sighed. "In today's world, what is true? What is real?"

Cao Xueqin wrote,

好了歌
世人都晓神仙好，只有功名忘不了！
古今将相在何方？荒冢一堆草没了！
世人都晓神仙好，只有金银忘不了！
终朝只恨聚无多，及到多时眼闭了！

Won-Done Song[10]

Men all know that salvation should be won.
But with ambition won't have done, have done.

Where are the famous ones of days gone by?
In grassy graves they lie now, every one.

Men all know that salvation should be won.
But with their riches won't have done, have done.

Each day they grumble they've not made enough.
When they've enough, it's goodnight every one!

A Chinese Old Saying: "Adults shouldn't read *Romance of the Three Kingdoms*; the young shouldn't read *Dream of the Red Chamber*."

Romance of the Three Kingdoms promoted insidious intrigue and encouraged deceit. *Dream of the Red Chamber* described the love story of a young couple and had descriptions of sexual interactions. It was unsuitable for young people in a traditional, feudalistic society. The philosophy of

---

[10] Translated by David Hawkes

168

"being disillusioned with this human world" was viewed decadent, and unprogressive. Oh, well, at least there was something in common between Mao and me. We both loved to eat these two forbidden fruits.

During this time, I felt completely incapable of controlling my own destiny. I became more philosophical, nihilistic.

Mr. Ding

One morning while I was reading my book, YeYe and Jin ran into my room. They had never come to my dormitory before. They hated to talk to some of my roommates who they viewed as hypocritical. They pulled me down from my upper bunk bed, and told me there was something they thought I would want to see. We ran into school and came to the front of the teachers' office building. There was a throng of students and teachers gathered in front of a Big Character poster. People seemed excited, and many were beaming with joy.

The title of the Big Character poster was "Expose our school's *Jumping beam clown* (跳梁小丑)[11] — Ding Li-quan." Ding Li-quan was Mr. Ding's full Chinese name. He was my second and third grade teacher for Chinese Literature and Writing as well as Politics class. He had caused so much misery in my life both before and during the Cultural Revolution.

The Big Character poster started with Mr. Ding's first name, Li-quan (立权), which translates as "establishing power." The poster was questioning Mr. Ding's evil intentions. It asked what kind of power he was trying to grab — the power of our Communist Party or the power of our supreme leader, Chairman Mao? The poster exposed that his wife, Mrs. Ding, was the daughter of a landlord, so Mr. Ding was the son-in-law of a landlord. The poster also pointed out Mr. Ding's father was a capitalist, owning a business before the Liberation of China. In fact, Mr. Ding's father was only a small street vendor. The poster exaggerated the true facts, but during the Cultural Revolution, all Big Character posters were done this way with exaggeration and false accusations. Mr. Ding did the same thing when he exposed the "Ox Devils and Snake Demons." Now this

---

[11] jumping beam clown (跳梁小丑): a Chinese phrase describing a petty scoundrel fond of playing tricks and creating trouble

poster was using Mr. Ding's own spear to penetrate his shield and force his own poison down his throat. On the bottom of the poster, it stated someone had seen Mr. Ding and Mei Qin walking in Plum Flower Park on a dark night, insinuating that Mr. Ding misbehaved as a teacher. The Rebel Group had composed the poster. People surrounded the poster with a "couldn't help but smile" look on their faces. Wow, I didn't realize Mr. Ding was so unpopular and hated.

Zhongzhou city is located in the rich southeast of Jiangsu Province in Eastern China. During its history, it attracted many notable people and famous scholars. Most Zhongzhou people are gentle and respect traditional Chinese moral integrity. During those days there were very few universities in China. Most universities were located in Beijing and Shanghai. There were one or two universities in the capital city of each province. Jiangsu Zhongzhou High School was the highest educational institute in Zhongzhou. There were no universities in Zhongzhou at that time.

Jiangsu Zhongzhou High School students were highly regarded by the local people. The Grays, most local students, disliked the way they had been treated during the start of the Cultural Revolution. They were sympathetic toward the teachers who were condemned by the original Red Guards and Mr. Ding. They felt bullying our teachers was distasteful and inhumane, and yet they felt they couldn't speak openly in their defense. Such protests would have led to attacks on themselves. Speaking in defense of revolutionary enemies was a big taboo. They were disgusted with Mr. Ding, who stepped on the shoulders of others to climb the political ladder. They viewed Mr. Ding as a clown, jumping around for his own political gain. The brutal treatment that Mr. Ding exerted on the three teachers caused great anger among many students. In order to silence him and teach him a lesson, the Rebel group came down hard on Mr. Ding. Since Mr. Ding was exposed as the son of a capitalist, and the son-in-law of a landlord, there was now a clear class line between the Reds and Mr. Ding. The Reds couldn't defend Mr. Ding.

A quote from Mark Twain states, "I have never killed a man, but I have read many an obituary with great satisfaction." This described my feelings as I stood in front of the poster among the crowd of smiling faces.

The next day, Mr. Ding declared he had changed his first name from Li-quan (立权) to Li-xin (立新), which means "to become a new person." Since then, Mr. Ding silenced himself. Sadly, a year later, a truck killed his only son. Many people said, "What goes around comes around" (恶有恶报). I was sad for his wife. I never wished anyone to be punished this way.

Later, one of my roommates, Tin, became my friend. Tin was a member of the Communist Youth League and a Red. She knew what Mr. Ding had compiled in my personal dossier. She told YeYe and Jin that it was very damaging to me. They didn't tell me what was inside my dossier, as they didn't want to hurt my feelings. Before school was dismissed, they encouraged me to obtain the dossier from Mr. Ding. I was nervous, and hesitated since I had no desire to see Mr. Ding again. Going back to Mr. Ding's home would bring back bad memories. My friends pushed me to go ahead. They would go with me.

It was the second time I visited Mr. Ding's apartment. This time I was with my three friends. Mr. Ding was lying in bed alone and sick. His face was pale. He had just lost his only son, which was a huge blow to him. The place was dreary and sad.

I summoned my courage and said to Mr. Ding in a weak voice, "Mr. Ding, they told me you had gathered information about me and compiled a personal dossier on me. It is very important to me. I want it back."

Mr. Ding looked at my friends, paying special attention to Tin. He couldn't deny the existence of the dossier, but Mr. Ding replied quietly, but firmly, "I don't have anyone's dossier. I destroyed all the student files."

He wasn't apologetic. To him I was still a Black Bastard. I suddenly felt sick. I told my friends: "Let's go." We walked out fruitlessly. What else could we have done since he had already destroyed the file? In the future, if the dossier reappeared and push came to shove, my friends could confirm the dossier was full of lies and completely false. At the age of 20, I was still full of innocence and naivety. In reality, during the middle of a political storm, no one would dare to speak up for you if you were condemned as a political enemy.

"We Counted the Mighty No More than Muck" (粪土当年万户侯)

In February 1967, the power-grabbing Jiang Qing, with support from Mao, insisted that the class struggles be extended to involve the military. Many old cadets of the People's Liberation Army, who were instrumental in the founding of the PRC, voiced their concern and opposition to the Cultural Revolution — calling it a mistake. A political explosion had erupted between the military and the Central Cultural Revolution Committee. At the same time, many large and prominent Red Guard groups rose in protest against other Red Guard groups who ran dissimilar revolutionary messages.

Very soon, the Rebellion Red Guards and the Loyalist Red Guards both received weapons from different factions of the Peoples' Liberation Army. This exacerbated the chaos between the Rebellion and Loyalist groups, and fights sprung up like bamboo shoots. The fighters were the diehard few. They were dyed-in-the wool followers. The Rebellions believed they were following Mao, and the Loyalists were obviously protecting their parents and local government against chaos. They were both backed by strong groups. The public realized the danger and started to recognize that political manipulation was going on behind the scenes.

YeYe and Jin were told by their parents to stay home and not get involved in any school activities. School life became so boring. Very few students were involved in the fighting. Most stayed in school with nothing to do. Some students were still sightseeing. I started visiting YeYe's home every evening.

There was a girl called Huayi who lived across the alley from YeYe's home. Huayi was the same age as YeYe and me. She was the only daughter of her family. She had a humble, small bedroom all to herself. It was similar to YeYe's bedroom. It only had enough room for one small bed and a small desk. In contrast, YeYe had to share her bedroom with her sister. The three of us would stay chatting in Huayi's bedroom most evenings. Huayi had many local stories to tell. We sometimes talked until midnight.

From YeYe and Huayi I learned there were people committing suicide every day. They were the political victims of the Cultural Revolution. These people couldn't suffer the mental isolation and physical abuse anymore. Death became a better option than life. They found ways to kill themselves. Zhongzhou was a major textile city. Many people in the textile factories killed themselves by jumping into big dye vats.

Rumors started to spread that some Red Guards in both groups had died during the fighting. We never dared openly criticize the Cultural Revolution, and especially Mao. Deep resentment toward the Cultural Revolution began to sprout from our young hearts. We started whispering and calling Jiang Qing, Mao's wife, "the Empress Dowager Cixi" who unofficially but effectively controlled the Qing Dynasty. We were still too afraid to mention Mao, but inside my heart I hated him so much — the evil tyrant. I wished a brave soul would assassinate him, and get rid of the tyrant for China and the Chinese people. Hadn't we suffered enough?

We enjoyed the evening chats as we disgorged the anger bottled up for so long inside our young hearts. As Mao wrote in his own poem:

长沙
问苍茫大地，
谁主沉浮？
………
恰同学少年，
风华正茂；
书生意气，
挥斥方遒。
指点江山，
激扬文字，
粪土当年万户侯。

CHANGSHA

Brooding over this immensity,
I ask, on this boundless land
Who rules over man's destiny?

....

Young we were, schoolmates,
At life's full flowering;
Filled with student enthusiasm
Boldly we cast all restraints aside.
Pointing to our mountains and rivers,
Setting people afire with our words,
We counted the mighty no more than muck.[12]

We now started to view today's mighty leaders as no more than muck.
After giving vent to our deeply buried political opinions, I walked to my
dormitory alone. In the dark, deep night, on the quiet, deserted street, I
felt released and without fear.

---

[12] English translation is from https://www.yeyebook.com

The Mini "Long March"

The fighting between different Red Guard groups continued, while nobody was in charge of our school. My roommates from the outskirts of Zhongzhou city started to take time off from school and only showed up occasionally for their food rations. I wanted to go home to see my grandmother, but it was spring and I had just returned from Chinese New Year recess. It was costly to go home for no reason.

Tin, one of my roommates, who was a Red and a Loyalist, had become friends with YeYe, Jin, and me. Tin lived only 6 miles from school, and so she often walked back and forth to her home. One day she suggested we walk to our homes together. When you are young, you often do things in a moment of passion without ever thinking it through carefully. During those days, transportation was very poor and there was no detailed road map between Zhongzhou and Yiyang. I didn't realize Yiyang was more than 60 miles from our school. Tin lived in a village close to the Zhongzhou to Jintan highway. Jintan was a small county town, like Yiyang, located halfway between Zhongzhou and Yiyang. One of my roommates, Wong Li, was from Jintan, and so she also decided to join us.

I packed a small bag, and the next day we got up early and started our Mini Long March. We followed Tin and cut through Zhongzhou city heading westward through many stone-paved alleys. We passed many residential courtyard complexes and crossed many canals and stone bridges. Finally, we reached the highway. It took us more than an hour. I now realized Zhongzhou was vastly bigger than my hometown. We then headed off along the highway, which was made of sand and mud. Once outside the city, we were surrounded by vast farm fields. Farmers had started their work early. Many groups of farmers dotted the boundless fields. They were preparing the soil for the spring seeding season.

When we reached the crossroad to Tin's home, Tin invited us inside to rest. We gladly accepted the invitation. Tin's home was a bright farmer's house with a compacted dirt floor. There were proper wall separations and doors between the bedrooms and kitchen. I envied Tin's house: simple, but much bigger and brighter than my home. Her father was a commune official. The home was either confiscated from landlords or specially built for her family. Tin's parents weren't home because they were out working in the fields. Tin took out some flour and made pancakes for us. We filled up our stomachs with pancakes and warm water from their thermos. We thanked Tin for her hospitality and headed off on the next stretch of our journey.

It was near noon, and the bright sun was casting its warmth while a spring breeze gently brushed our cheeks and hair. We were in high spirits. After several miles of walking, we started feeling tired. The sun was setting in the west, and orange-tinted clouds embellished the western sky. Wisps of smoke rose from the chimneys of village houses as farmers' families started preparing for dinner. Farmers were still working in the fields. We continued our march, but our stomachs started to grumble. Dusk was descending. The farmers, shouldering their tools, were returning toward the village.

Wong Li and I realized we were nowhere near our homes and needed to find a place to eat and sleep. We searched for a small town with food vendors and a school. The night had already cast down, and the dotted villages had disappeared into the darkness. The sky was studded with stars with an occasional flickering light far in the distance indicating life. Wong Li and I were hungry, cold, and tired. We were scared of the creepy darkness and emptiness.

Finally, we saw several lights flickering not too far ahead of us. We walked toward the lights. Luckily for us, it was a small town. We found a small food vendor selling rice crumpets. We ordered some crumpets and gobbled them down in no time. We told the vendor that we were students from Jiangsu Zhongzhou High School and were headed towards Jintan High School for Revolutionary Tours activities. We asked whether there was a local high school, where we could take shelter for the night. The vendor told us there was a high school in the town and pointed the way.

We walked into the girls' dormitory, and told the students the same story. The students welcomed us. There were two empty beds. The owners of the beds had gone on their own Revolutionary Tours. We fell sound asleep as soon as we lay down in the strangers' bunk beds. We were exhausted. Early next morning we thanked our kind "roommates" and ate crumpets from the same vendor.

We started the second day of our journey home. We were refreshed and full of energy again. We saw the bright sun rising in the eastern sky. Farmers had already started their work before dawn. They were using water buffalos to plow the fields. We were enjoying the scenery of "the Yangtze River Delta, land of plenty" (江南鱼米之乡).

We reached Jintan at noon. Wong Li was happy that she would soon be getting home. After Jintan, I would be all alone for my return to Yiyang. Before Wong Li said good-bye to me, we asked a local resident how far it was to Yiyang. He told us it was more than 25 miles away and that I definitely shouldn't walk home alone. I wouldn't reach Yiyang today. The local told us there was a steamboat to Yiyang this afternoon and, if we hurried, I could catch the steamboat home. Wong Li accompanied me to the boat station. I was lucky and managed to catch the boat on time.

When I arrived home, it was late evening. I had a slight fever and so went to bed without saying too much. Grandmother would be upset if she found out that I had walked more than 30 miles to come home. This journey must have struck me deeply. Since then, I often dream about standing on a highway in the middle of fields while dusk descends as I search for the way home; or sometimes I dream about trying to catch a bus or boat home, but miss the bus or boat. I wake up lost and desperate.

Da Di had just returned from a Revolutionary Tour. He had been to Beijing and visited his Aunt, Aunt Zhen's younger sister. He toured the Summer Palace and climbed the Great Wall. After he came home for a short break, he meandered southward to Guangzhou, and then wandered all the way to Yunnan. In between, he visited Uncle Shi Po and went sightseeing at the famous West Lake in Hangzhou. I admired Da Di. He had guts. A Black bastard who dared to attend a Revolutionary Tour. I envied Da Di. He had toured so many wonderful places. I wished I could do the same thing.

In Yiyang, fights between Red Guards hadn't escalated to as large a scale as in Zhongzhou, but the factories were semi-paralyzed. Da Di and Xiao Di had started mingling with two young factory workers. They started smoking cigarettes and came home late at night. Grandmother had been worried to death when Da Di went on his adventure to the Revolutionary Tours. Now Grandmother was anxious and agonized when her grandsons came home late for dinner. She stood by the door hoping to see a sign of her grandsons' return.

She kept nagging Aunt Zhen. "They are your sons, and you have no control of them. I am only their grandmother. By the time they have grown up and are able to show their filial piety, I will be resting-in-peace in my grave and you will enjoy their revered respect."

Grandmother wanted Aunt Zhen to look out for her grandsons, and Aunt Zhen was becoming more and more upset with Grandmother's continuous nagging.

She snapped back. "I don't have the good fortune to receive their filial piety. Where do you expect me to find them? It's a big place. It's like shooting a gun without a target."

Of course, Aunt Zhen was worried about her sons. In fact, she was planning for Da Di to do carpentry work. It would be like killing two birds with one stone. Da Di would learn carpentry skills and at the same time it would prevent him from getting into trouble during these chaotic times. Also, if push came to shove, carpentry could become a means of livelihood. Aunt knew a master carpenter working in an adjacent factory. She showered him with gifts and money to take Da Di as his apprentice.

Xiao Mei was still a Society Youth without a job and with no livelihood skills. The thought that Xiao Mei's future was being damaged by my parents' monthly subsidy to the family never entered my mind. Grandmother, who was older and wiser, knew better. Obviously, Aunt Zhen never had any concern or worry over Xiao Mei's future. After all, she was not her daughter. In addition, if Xiao Mei became independent, it would reduce my parents' subsidy to the family. Grandmother didn't dare challenge Aunt Zhen.

My Belated Revolutionary Tour to Beijing

After a few weeks at home, I returned to school. I worried that if I stayed home too long, I would find myself in trouble. I should discover what had happened in school while I had been away. The fighting between the Rebellions and Loyalists was getting more and more intense. Many young people had died in the fighting. The Culture Palace was the headquarters of the Rebellions Group in Zhongzhou city. We heard that the Rebellions had piled dead bodies at the Culture Palace.

The Culture Palace was very close to Xindeli, my dormitory. At night we could hear noises from the Culture Palace. I was on the top bunk bed next to the window. When I sat up in bed, I could see the Culture Palace through the window. At night, the wind rustled past my window and gave me an oppressive feeling of dread. I felt chills and had ghostly thoughts. I could feel my skin crawl as fear turned to terror.

Lin Da was in an adjacent bunk bed and also slept on top. She often woke up at night screaming. She was quiet during the day. Her friends must have been killed in the fighting. Lin Da was originally a member of the Rebel group at our school, but then had followed a more radical group called 501. Ling again went to Beijing to visit her aunt. YingYing also went home for a break. Although the central government had announced a stop to the nationwide Revolutionary Tours, people were still out sightseeing.

It was early summer 1967. The dormitory was quiet. My roommates were in and out of school. One day, Tin told me that a few boys in our school were getting together and planning a visit to Beijing. The last time they went to Beijing was to attend the big rally in Tiananmen Square, and, so, they never had a chance to tour Beijing.

I asked, "The central government has ended the Revolutionary Tours. The train ride is no longer free. How will they get there?"

Tin said, "They are going to take cargo trains."

She asked me if I wanted to go along with them. She told me that she was tempted to go.

I said, "Let's ask YeYe and Jin if they want to come along with us?"

In fact, Tin had already asked them and their parents had said no. I agreed with their parents. It was a dangerous proposal. Many young students had been killed journeying to the Revolutionary Tours. I didn't blame their parents. I'm sure my grandmother would also say "no." Still, I was tremendously tempted to go with Tin, since I had never gone anywhere during the Revolutionary Tours. Even Da Di had visited Beijing and Guangzhou. I decided to go with the group. Three local boys from my classroom were organizing the trip. One of them was Chen Ming. Ever since he told me about Mr. Ding's damaging personal dossier on me, I had trusted him. He seemed a kind, steady, and unruffled boy.

Next evening, we walked along the boundary wall of the train station. When we reached the end, we snuck inside. There were many cargo trains parked on the rails. Chen Ming told us to search for cargo going to Nanjing. As soon as we found what we were looking for, the boys told us to spread ourselves across several freight cars to avoid the attention of the station workers. During those days, most of the freight cars were big open box cars. Tin and I climbed over the top rim of one containing cabbage and jumped down inside. We crawled to a corner where we hid ourselves well below the top rim of the car. After 10 minutes of quietly waiting, the train started to move. It chinked, chunked past the station boundary wall. Yay! We were out of the station and free.

We stuck our heads up and looked as the villages passed us in a blink of an eye. The green rice fields were flying past us, dashing in the opposite direction. The wind tossed our short braids around, smashing them on our faces. It was a hot summer evening, and so we didn't mind the hasty wind.

The train stopped, and the boys called us to get out. The train stopped at Nanjing station. It was pitch-dark. The cargo trains were parked some distance away from the passenger trains. Using flashlights, we searched for a train to Beijing. We couldn't find one, but we found one heading to

Xuzhou. Xuzhou was a city situated on the main Shanghai-Beijing rail line. Tin and I clambered into a freight car loaded with steel rods. Luckily, the rods were only piled halfway up the freight car.

The night was getting a little chilly, so we hid ourselves in the corner to avoid the wind. We waited for the train to start. After a good half hour, the train eventually began to move. We closed our eyes, dozed off, and had some sleep. We woke by the rose-pink light of dawn, and soon the sun had risen high into the blue sky. Early that morning, bathing in the sun's rays was wonderfully refreshing. However, very soon, the sun became more and more unfriendly, as it cast its unpleasant burning heat down upon us. We stuck our head out to cool ourselves from the incoming wind. The train stopped, hooked and unhooked freight cars, and then left and reached Xuzhou in the afternoon.

We jumped out and walked along the rails to the station. We were so thirsty. A tap with flowing water near the station was our savior. We held our heads under the tap and drank the heavenly cool water. We washed the dust and sweat off our faces, and then marched out of the station exit hidden among the legitimate train passengers. We entered a small restaurant and replenished ourselves with bowls of noodle soup. We didn't have train tickets, so we again walked along the station wall and snuck into the station. We searched for cargo heading to Beijing but couldn't find any. Instead, we found cargo heading for Jinan and took the free ride.

The landscape quickly became bare, and we were surrounded by yellow, gray, dusty land. In the far distance, toward the northeast, there were mountain ranges in the midst of clouds. We were in Shandong Province. I had heard Mount Tai was the most famous of the Five Sacred Mountains in China. Mount Tai is located in the center of Shandong Province. It is surrounded by green pines and giant rocks, as well as ever-changing clouds and mists. These all combine to make it the most majestic, beautiful, and mysterious mountain in China. I asked Tin to remind me when we were passing Mount Tai. I wanted to see the famous mountain. Unfortunately, we saw nothing. We passed the Tai mountain range in the middle of the night when it was pitch black.

Next morning, we reached Jinan. We went out searching for food. Since Jinan was a northern city, none of the food used rice. We stopped at a small vendor selling golden steamed buns. They looked so delicious. The golden color enticed our appetites. I ordered two buns. After just one bite, I realized it wasn't as good as I had imagined. It was rough and had a slightly sweet taste. It wasn't the bun I knew from southern China, the Yangtze River Delta, the region where I came from. It turned out these golden buns were called Wō wo tóu (窝窝头), and were made from corn meal. After eating, we snuck back into the station and caught a cargo train to Tianjin.

At noon, the sun's rays were torturing us again with no place to hide. The inland summer scorching heat made me feel a little sickly. Braving the sweltering heat, I looked forward to seeing the ancient city of Beijing. As we approached Tianjin, the landscape became much greener. There were green orchard farms scattered across the distant hills. It finally cooled down as evening approached and the train entered Tianjin City. Tianjin was one of the historical big cities in China. Originally, we planned to have a short stop in Tianjin to see the city, but once we jumped out of our trailers, we saw a cargo train marked for Beijing. It was late in the day, and we didn't want to miss the opportunity. We decided to jump into the Beijing cargo train.

We reached Beijing before midnight. The Beijing train station was huge. We had to walk along the railroad for a long time to reach the passenger area. We exited again with all the legitimate passengers and entered a huge hall. The hall was crowded, but was brilliantly illuminated. Most of the passengers were young students. It seemed students with special permits could still travel free. I was the only one in our group visiting Beijing for the first time. As we walked among the huge, noisy crowds, I had no time to admire the grand Beijing station. I was afraid I would be lost in the crowd, and so followed our group closely.

We reached a bus station and caught a bus. The bus took us to Tiananmen Square where Mao had, on several occasions, rallied millions of Red Guards. We got off the bus and walked past the famous Forbidden Palace. The palace doors were tightly shut and guarded by armed soldiers. A huge portrait of Mao was placed above the gigantic gate at the entrance to the magnificent palace. Large slogans, "Long Live the Peoples' Republic of China," "Long Live the United People in the World," were inscribed on the front wall of the palace entrance on each side of Mao's portrait. If it hadn't been for Premier Zhou Enlai's quick actions, the Red Guards would have destroyed the Forbidden Palace during the Destroy the Four Olds movement.

During those days, I knew so little of Chinese politics, but Premier Zhou had always held a large place in my heart. During all the political movements, when the class struggle went out of control, he calmed the situation and mitigated the damage. For us, the Blacks, we had put so much hope in Premier Zhou Enlai. When we were suffocating during political movements, we prayed for Zhou to come out and say something.

The central government protected the Forbidden Palace as an historical cultural heritage. Entrance was forbidden to all visitors. Within the Forbidden Palace walls, many power struggles and tragedies had played out during Chinese history. Now, today, history was going to be made again. It would not only involve people within the palace, the powerful people, but, tragically, it now would involve everyone in China – people with absolutely no desire for power.

We entered the People's Culture Hall located next to the Forbidden Palace. Originally part of the Palace, it was now the Beijing reception station for the Revolutionary Tours. We waited in a long line to register, but, when we reached the desk, we were told we didn't qualify for accommodation in Beijing. We were on our own. Chen Ming had a phone number from Ling. Ling had told him that while we were in Beijing, he could call her aunt and let her know we were here. Since it was the middle of the night we decided to wait until morning to call for help. In the People's Culture Hall, there were many students randomly lying on the floor sleeping. We found an empty spot and slept on the cold, hard, tiled Culture Hall floor.

Next morning, we, using the station phone, called Ling's aunt who said she would let Ling know we were in Beijing. An hour later, Ling met us in front of the Culture Hall. We took a bus to the home of Ling's aunt, who very much resembled Ling. She had a slender figure and a clean-cut face. Her haircut lined up with her ears. She wore a perfect-fit, faded army uniform. She had the look of a typical high official. She seemed relaxed and cheerful. I guessed she hadn't been condemned during the Cultural Revolution.

When we arrived at Ling's place, Ling's aunt had already prepared lunch for us. There was a huge bowl of stir-fried Napa cabbage on the kitchen table, together with cooked white rice. We devoured the cabbage and rice quickly. I had sorely missed cooked rice on the journey to Beijing. Oh boy, this was one of the most delicious meals of my life. I must have been really hungry.

Ling's aunt and her family lived in a reasonably new residential compound that must have been built after the Liberation of China. They were two-story buildings and reminded me of high-class army barracks. Ling took us to a room with many bunk beds and told us to rest. We lay on the beds and soon fell sound asleep.

We didn't wake up until the following morning. Ling brought us some steamed buns made of flour, not corn meal, and asked us where we would like to visit. We all shouted in chorus that we would like to climb the Great Wall. Sadly, for us, the Great Wall had already been closed to visitors. It was under protection of the central government as an ancient heritage site, just like the Forbidden Palace.

We decided to revisit Tiananmen Square and some adjacent parks. We walked across the huge square and stood next to the massive granite monument of the People's Heroes. From a distance, we admired the Gate of Heavenly Peace with its golden roof and red wall. The magnificent grandeur of the Gate of Heavenly Peace was enhanced by the morning light. It was supposed to represent the past, failed feudal imperial history of China, but Chairman Mao inherited its glory. It now signified the power of the Communist Party and Chairman Mao.

We walked past the gate of Zhong-nan-hai where two armed guards stood to prevent entry. Ling told me that Chairman Mao and his wife Jiang Qing lived in this new "forbidden palace" with gardens and lakes. Mao had called for an austere lifestyle for everyone in China, except, of course, himself and his family.

We leisurely strolled through Beihai Park, one of the most carefully preserved imperial gardens in China. In the park, most buildings were no longer open for visitors. From the lakeside, we stared into the distance admiring the famous White Dagoba. Our hands also touched the dragons on the Nine Dragon Screen, hoping they would transfer some of their power to us so that we could overcome ominous devils.

Beihai Park led us straight to Jingshan Park. Standing at the commanding height of the Everlasting Spring Pavilion, we gazed across the golden roofs of the Imperial Palace as they stretched into the distance. From our high vantage point, we overlooked Beihai Lake, the Drum and Bell Towers, and the ancient Beijing city. We paid a visit to an old tree where Chongzhen, the last Ming emperor, was supposed to have hanged himself. We lamented the vicissitudes of Chinese history and its famous, powerful people.

Afterwards, we caught a bus to visit the Temple of Heaven, where the Emperors communicated with God in Heaven and prayed for good harvests. We had a long, fun day and eventually returned to Ling's home. We again ate cooked white rice and stir-fried Napa cabbage for dinner.

The next morning, we ate the steamed buns that Ling's aunt left on the kitchen table and then headed out to enjoy the grandeur of the imperial gardens at the Summer Palace. The Palace was the summer residence for the Qing imperial family. It was a beautiful Beijing summer morning. We climbed Longevity Hill to overlook the entire garden, and then descended to the side of Kunming Lake. We walked along the Long Corridor, admiring the ancient paintings on its upper wooden structures. We boarded the Marble Boat; Empress Dowager Cixi had rebuilt the boat with funds originally earmarked for a new imperial navy.

Then we strolled leisurely toward the Seventeen Arch Bridge. On the way, I walked with Ling, staying some distance behind our group. I wholeheartedly thanked Ling and her aunt for their hospitality. I told Ling that her aunt was a very nice person. She was so thoughtful and unassuming, in spite of her rank. I was envious of Ling with such a loving aunt. To my surprise, Ling told me a family secret. Her aunt was actually her biological mother. She was the illegitimate child of her father. After Ling was born, her "aunt" was banned from her father's family.

Adultery was a big taboo for Communist Party members. Mrs. Zhao, Ling's "stepmother," claimed Ling as her own child in order to protect her husband and her younger sister. Ling grew up with four stepsiblings under the care of her maternal grandmother. Since her father felt guilty toward his wife, he acted as though Ling didn't even exist. The very existence of Ling reminded her "stepmother" of her husband's unfaithfulness. Ling was always a thorn in her flesh, and so Ling grew up unloved by her parents. Her siblings treated her as an inferior stepsister. The only person who loved her was her grandmother who had passed away a few months earlier. Ling was deeply sad. During the burial of her grandmother, Ling's aunt invited her to Beijing for a short visit.

Feeling "the fox's sympathy for the hunted hare" (兔死狐悲), sensing a similarity between us, I was both sad and sympathetic. It turned out that, even though Ling was from a privileged family, she was the "ugly" stepchild. Suddenly Ling's mood changed, and she was cheerful again. She told me that her aunt had always been accommodating and supportive toward her. After Ling revealed her secret to me, we became much closer.

After lunch in a canteen, we went boating on Kunming Lake. The boys handled the paddles, and we girls enjoyed the beautiful lake scenery: the blooming water lilies, the long causeways, the stone bridges, the magnificent halls and pavilions. After fully enjoying the beautiful and elegant Summer Palace, we headed back to Ling's place. On the way, we visited the famous Tsinghua University and glanced at the ancient-looking student dormitories. At one time, I had dreamed of being a student here. Now, I had met reality. I was awakened, and realized I had no chance of ever fulfilling that dream. Knowing it would be bothersome to Ling's aunt for us to stay longer, we decided to head back to Zhongzhou.

We had seen most of the historic attractions in Beijing. I was very satisfied with our trip. If I had come earlier, the only additional thing I could have seen was the pathetic, old, evil Mao. Many people were dying to see Mao, but not me. The next morning, we caught cargo trains back home. Again, I missed seeing Mount Tai. It was midnight as we passed. After jumping from one cargo train to another and, as before, experiencing chilly nights and torching hot afternoons, we eventually returned to Zhongzhou.

Feeling dirty and tired, I immediately gave myself a good wash and fell asleep on one of the empty lower bunk beds. I didn't even bother to climb into my own bunk bed. I was totally worn out. Next day, Tin and I met with YeYe and Jin. We gloated about our adventure. YeYe and Jin were worried about us, as many young students had been killed on self-made journeys to the Revolutionary Tours. Some students had been decapitated as they passed into tunnels on the mountain range during dark nights on the open box cars. Without adults to constrain us, we dared to challenge. As Mao wrote:

Filled with student enthusiasm
Boldly we cast all restraints aside.

Thoughts of Going to America

After Xiao Mei and I were born, my maternal grandparents never paid any attention to us. Grandmother and Aunt Zhen had told us that, before the Liberation of China, Mother's father had been an executive officer of the Central Bank of China. He had been educated at Yale University in the US. My biological maternal grandmother had died when my mother was only an infant. My mother's first stepmother was also a daughter of a distinguished family and a highly educated lady. Sadly, she committed suicide after her husband abandoned her and married a girl 24 years his junior. Mother's second stepmother was beautiful, charming, and alert. I called her Grandma Chow. My grandmother had met her once in Shanghai before I was born. She told us that Grandma Chow's "eyes could speak" — Chinese slang for resourcefulness.

A few years ago, Grandma Chow suddenly started to inquire about us. My mother had a cousin, Mr. Lou, who was the only remaining relative of Mother's biological mother (daughter of the Lou clan). He lived in Hangzhou, Zhejiang Province, and Mother was very close to him. Mr. Lou gave Grandma Chow the home address of their lost-for-the-ages granddaughters. One day, before the Cultural Revolution, we were invited to visit Grandpa Chow and Grandma Chow in Shanghai. I was in school, loaded with schoolwork and preparing for the university entrance exams, and, so, was unable to visit them.

Xiao Mei visited many times, and every time stayed for a long period. Grandma Chow treated Xiao Mei very well. Xiao Mei was the only child living with them. Grandma Chow taught Xiao Mei how to cook Shanghainese food. Xiao Mei was happy with her grandparents in Shanghai. An ugly "stepchild" in Yiyang suddenly received the full attention of her newly introduced grandparents. Xiao Mei always stayed in

Shanghai for an extended period, and so Mother's money started flowing from the US to Shanghai. Longing for her father, Mother sent more money to Shanghai than was sent to Yiyang. A week after I returned from Beijing, I received a letter from Grandma Chow that was sent directly to my school. She invited me to Shanghai to meet with my elderly grandfather, Grandpa Chow.

I took the night train to Shanghai to save money and arrived before dawn. The food shops were open near the train station, so I ordered two rice crumpets and stayed there waiting for the morning hours to arrive. I took a bus to a Hutong (a small neighborhood) on Huaihai Middle Road. There were many three-story buildings on both sides of the Hutong. Each building consisted of two townhouses next to each other with little lanes in between that provided access to the entrances of the residences.

I followed the instructions from Grandma Chow and walked to the end of the Hutong, turned right into the last lane and walked all the way to the last townhouse on the right side. I was told to enter through the back door. Grandpa Chow bought this townhouse before China was liberated. It was originally one of his rental properties. After the Liberation of China, he disowned all other properties, including mansions next to West Lake in Hangzhou. He and his family then moved into this townhouse to lower his stature after the Communist Army took over Shanghai. As the children grew up and moved out, the residence committee "persuaded" them to share their townhouse with two other families.

The first-floor living room and front courtyard were occupied by one couple, who "owned" the front door entrance. Therefore, other residents had to enter through the back door into the kitchen, which was shared by all the residents of the townhouse. The second-floor bedroom now belonged to a couple with two young kids. There was also a Western-style bathroom on the second floor. The bathroom was shared by all three families.

The bathroom had a bathtub, a sink, and a toilet. To me it was absolute luxury. It was the first time I had ever seen a flushing toilet. Every time I went to the toilet at my school or in Yiyang, I had to sit over other people's shit and endure the stench. Wow! This is how rich people lived!

Grandpa Chow and Grandma Chow now only occupied the third floor and two small rooms located between the floors next to the staircase.

These small rooms were known as *tíngzijiān* (亭子间). They used the tíngzijiān between the first and second floors as a dining room, and the tíngzijiān between the second and third floors as a guest room. This was where I would sleep.

Grandpa Chow was in his late eighties. He never said a word to me while I stayed with him. Grandma Chow took good care of him. At breakfast, he read the newspaper. Once he finished his meal, he quietly left the dining room. To him, I was a stranger. Sometimes, I did wonder why he had bothered to invite me to his home. He ate quite well with a good appetite.

A few years later, he died at the age of 90, and I was called by Grandma Chow to his hospital bedside. I was there when he passed his last breath. He lay on a sickbed unconscious in a big ward. The ward was occupied by approximately 15 other patients. Grandma Chow wanted me to report Grandpa Chow's death to my parents. I had no particular feelings toward Grandpa Chow or his passing and didn't understand why I had been called by Grandma Chow to his death bed.

Grandma Chow was in her sixties. She took care of Grandpa Chow attentively. She spent a good deal of time every day to cook three meals. In the early morning, she took me to an open market to shop for vegetables, meat, and fish. She prepared delicious Shanghainese food for Grandpa Chow and me. It was the first time I had tasted seafood, such as ocean crabs and lobsters. She was pleasant toward all her neighbors, but remained distant. Grandmother was right that Grandma Chow was a smooth, intelligent, quick-witted lady. In contrast to my mother's birth mother and first stepmother, Grandma Chow had very little schooling and grew up in a poor family. This tough upbringing had equipped her with the common sense to easily handle the swirling trickery and chaos that surrounded her. Willing to serve and eager to conquer, she had won Grandpa Chow's heart. Her goose-egg face together with her big brown eyes radiated smartness and confidence. I could imagine how beautiful she was as a young girl. However, I did have reservations about her, since her "existence" led to the first step-grandmother committing suicide.

Grandma Chow had enjoyed the good life with Grandpa Chow, but also suffered family tragedy. Her older son was prosecuted as a rightist and sent to a gulag camp in Xinjiang in 1957. Since then she never saw him again until his rehabilitation after Mao's death. Her second son committed suicide while he was a student at Tsinghua University in 1958. The university claimed his suicide was due to a failed romance. Grandma Chow always doubted this claim. My grandmother believed that my first step-grandmother's ghost might have haunted Grandma Chow. Her misfortune was retribution for the first step-grandmother's suicide. Oh, well, what can you say, my grandmother was an uneducated, superstitious old woman. All Grandma Chow's children attended an elite American Christian School before the Liberation of China. After the Liberation, they all went to highly ranked universities. The only thing comforting Grandma Chow was that her three daughters had all married into well-matched, distinguished intellectual families.

Grandma Chow's second daughter, I called her Aunt Wei, graduated from The First University of Medicine in Shanghai. She worked in Hangzhou as a doctor, and together with her husband had a young son. Xiao Mei was in Hangzhou babysitting her son. Now, Aunt Wei also invited me to Hangzhou for a short visit.

Aunt Wei had inherited the best of her parents' looks. Grandpa Chow was a tall, handsome man, and Grandma Chow was beautiful with big, attractive eyes. Aunt Wei had a slender figure and a goose-egg shaped face embellished with big, shining eyes. She gave me the overall impression that she was a beautiful and graceful person. Aunt Wei and her family lived in a traditional courtyard complex. They only occupied a small unit — a living room at the front of the unit with a bedroom in the rear. The only furniture in the living room was a square table and a bed, which Xiao Mei and I would share while I was there. The cooking area was located outside on the corridor facing the courtyard. Aunt Wei and her husband seemed to enjoy their young, simple, yet happy life.

Coincidentally, Aunt Wei and her husband, together with their college friends from Shanghai, were holding a reunion in Hangzhou. They took Xiao Mei and me to meet with their friends at West Lake. West Lake is a man-made lake divided by two causeways, *Su Di* and *Bai Di*. West Lake is located on the west side of Hangzhou City and surrounded by green mountains on three sides. West Lake is the most famous scenic park in China. It is adorned with ancient pavilions, arched bridges, tree-lined walkways, verdant islands and hills.

Following Aunt Wei and her husband, we walked along the Bai Di causeway under the hot summer sun. The heat didn't inspire me to admire the surrounding scenery. Even though Kunming Lake in the Summer Palace was an imitation of West Lake, I found it was more exciting and more fun being with my own friends to enjoy the scenery.

We met their friends at the front of the tea house on Gushan Island. They were all in their early 30's and spoke with a Shanghai dialect. From their manner and use of words, you could tell they were highly educated and had elite upbringings. Aunt Wei introduced Xiao Mei and me to their friends and told them that my parents were in America. One of her friends, who had foreign connections, was surprised that we were still in China and hadn't applied for a passport to unite with our parents. He told us that many of his relatives had gone to Hong Kong and the United States after the Liberation of China. He added that now there were a few of his relatives starting again to look into applying for an exit visa.

His words moved me. I started having thoughts of going to America — yes, the evil, imperialist country. Its people were suffering there. It was a dark hell there!

It was a hot and humid day. We went inside a tea house. Aunt Wei and their friends bought bottles of cold soda and offered two bottles to Xiao Mei and me. I opened the bottle. The bubbling gas shot out, and liquid started overflowing from the bottle. I swallowed a mouthful of the cool liquid, and the bubbling brew gushed out of my nose. I couldn't stop myself from coughing. Since I didn't want to embarrass myself in front of these highly educated elites, I quickly handed the bottle to Xiao Mei and rushed out of the tea house. This was the first time I had tasted a carbonated beverage.

After cooling down in the tea house, we climbed up the hill. From the high ground, I looked north and saw Baochu Pagoda on top of the Precious Stone Hill (宝石山). Uncle Shi Po lived in Precious Stone Hill. Da Di visited him during Revolutionary Tours. Aunt Wei told me, Uncle Shi Po had now been condemned as a "capitalist-roader" and was under class struggle. She told us, with the current situation, it was best that we not pay him a visit. Our visit would only make things worse for him. Uncle Shi Po was the Director of the Culture and Propaganda Department in Zhejiang Province.

Uncle Shi Po was eventually rehabilitated in the late seventies after Mao's death. After years of isolation and mental and physical torment during the Cultural Revolution, his health had deteriorated to near death. In the early 1980s, my father went back to China for a visit. Uncle Shi Po was gravely ill with cancer. These two cousins had been torn apart in their twenties by their different political beliefs and life circumstances. At that time, they were bright, vigorous, full-of-hope university students. Finally, they had met again under such sad circumstances. Now they were gray-haired old men. They held each other's hands, unable to speak, with their faces puckered up and wet with tears. On his death bed, Uncle Shi Po asked my father a favor. "While we were in Shanghai, we had a brotherly friendship. For the sake of our friendship, I beg you to help my son leave China." My father promised him that he would do his best. Soon after, Father managed to arrange for his son to leave China and arrive in America. At that time Uncle Shi Po had already passed away.

As we stood looking down at West Lake from the hill, the clouds started to gather and the wind began to blow. It was typical Hangzhou weather. During summer there were often thunderstorms. We entered a pavilion to take shelter. Facing West Lake in the powerful wind, I reflected on a verse from a poem: *"wind blows, filling the pavilion before the rainstorm"* (山雨欲来风满楼). The dark, heavy clouds were hanging oppressively in the sky. Looking eastward toward the city, it could be said that *"dark clouds bearing down on the city threaten to crumble it"* (黑云压城城欲摧). I was suddenly in a poetic mood. I wished my friends were here. Within a few minutes, big drops of rain came down hard and stirred up the dust on the ground. I could smell the soil. The rain was pouring down, accompanied by flashes of lightning and rumbling thunder all around. The lake was steaming, and, in the distance, the green mountains were veiled by the rain and mist. It was a beautiful, picturesque panorama. It was no surprise many famous poets and poems originated from this beautiful area.

The rain came suddenly, and ended quickly. It was blue sky again. West Lake returned to its calm. The blooming lotus plants were refreshed with shining water drops embellishing their large green leaves. The green mountain peaks flitted in and out of the clouds and swirling mist. The lake, the pavilions, the causeways, and the mountains, everything around me took on an entirely new look.

The next day, Aunt Wei hosted a tour of Lingyin Temple. I don't remember much about the temple itself. I do remember walking along a tree-lined canyon road where it was cool and pleasant. Lingyin Temple was a tranquil place. I only stayed with Aunt Wei for a couple of days, yet she gave me a deeply positive impression. She was beautiful, happy with her life, and was also a smart, successful doctor.

I never anticipated, and never had the slightest hint, that three years later she would kill herself in this Lingyin canyon. Aunt Wei's death gave me the inspiration to get out of the madding crowd. This land couldn't distinguish between right and wrong. I became determined to leave China, for better or for worse.

The Lost, Hopeless High Schoolers (老三届)[13]

In our dormitory the class line became murky. The Reds, the Grays, and the Blacks all lived in harmony again. We awoke from all the chaos and fighting. We were the participants and the witnesses of all the chaos. We were also the victims of the Cultural Revolution. We were desperately hoping for a future, but there was none. We were filled with anguish. Disappointed and depressed, we played cards all day and began to display a youthful rebellious nature. We sat on chairs with our feet up on the table! For girls, this was unknown in China at that time. We were originally a group of well-behaved youths. "Putting our feet on the table" was the start of our rebellion against everything going on around us. We were fed up of being tossed around.

Ling returned from Beijing. During the early stage of the Cultural Revolution, her father had been condemned as a capitalist-roader and had been brought out for class struggle session many times. He was now sick with lung disease. Ling knew more than us about the early period of the Cultural Revolution. No wonder she hadn't been keen to participate in the Cultural Revolution from the beginning. Ling brought a bottle of wine. We started drinking. I had never drunk before. Alcohol was not my friend, but I let Ling pour some into my cup.

Ling held her cup up high and loudly exclaimed, "the drinker's mind is other than wine" (醉瓮之意不在酒).

She continued, "drinking to forget the worries" (借酒消愁).

---

[13] 老三届: the high school students who were supposed to graduate in the three years of 1966, 1967, and 1968.

I recited a verse from Li Bai's poem, "toast and dispel worry, more of worry" (举杯消愁愁更愁).

YingYing joined in. "Drink for today, tomorrow's worry for tomorrow to worry" (今朝有酒今朝醉, 明日愁来明日愁) (Luo Yin's poem).

Lin Da sighed. "Seize the moment for tomorrow may never come."

We were all 20-year-old youths. We never thought we could strike a resonant chord with those old, disillusioned poets from ancient dynasties.

I went home for Chinese New Year. Xiao Mei was home. Mother wrote to Aunt Zhen asking Xiao Mei to "move her butt back to Yiyang." Mother had become annoyed. Grandma Chow kept hinting for more and more money. All of the letters Mother sent to Aunt Zhen never showed a hint of affection toward Xiao Mei and me.

At home I learned that Aunt Wei had suddenly been confined and isolated by her hospital Red Guards while pregnant with her second child. Her good looks and success as a highly regarded doctor had caused some of her coworkers to become jealous and harbor grudges against her. One of the hospital officials had been condemned as a capitalist-roader, and she had become a collateral victim. She had a close working relationship with the capitalist-roader, and, in order to establish guilt, the Red Guards also exposed any of his close associates.

Aunt Wei was educated in an American-run Christian school. She was baptized a Christian follower when she was a teenager — well before the Liberation of China. This led them to search her home where they found a Bible in one of her drawers. Hiding a Bible at home was an anti-Communist offense. Soon a condemnation and class-struggle meeting against her was called. Immediately after the condemnation, she was confined and isolated in a hospital cell without a chance to talk to her husband. She was accused of being a "running dog for America" — an American lapdog or spy. She was coerced to expose other Christians and friends.

Uncle Nian again didn't come home for the New Year celebration. He was still under confinement. On New Year's Eve, our door was tightly shut. This time, we secretly conducted our family's yearly ancestor worship ritual. It was my turn to kneel on the floor to bless our ancestors. As Grandmother stood by my side praying to the ancestors for my good health, I continued kneeling for a good couple of minutes. I silently begged my ancestors to help me escape from this chaotic, upside-down world. I had become superstitious. Once all tangible hope had gone, I gave free rein to fantasy.

Fear, insecurity, and hesitation occupied our entire being. We, the Black Bastards, were the opposite of the unruly Reds. They dared do many things that we Blacks were afraid to do. Fear of being accused of truancy and of lacking enthusiasm for the Great Proletarian Cultural Revolution, I returned to school after only a few weeks at home, even though school was still paralyzed. No one was in charge.

Jiang Qing and Lin Biao continued a massive campaign aimed at promoting the already adored Mao to a godlike status. Everywhere you went there were large posters of Jiang Qing and Lin Biao together holding Mao's Little Red Book. This excessive flattery of Mao made me want to vomit. I started wondering what Lin Biao was up to: promoting Mao or actually destroying Mao? Are people really that stupid? It was like "The Emperor's New Clothes." Did Lin Biao really believe what he was saying?

Very few students remained in school. Most of my roommates were at home. Fighting between different factions of the Red Guards was getting fiercer. YeYe and Jin's parents worried about their children as they floated uncontrollably in a city full of chaos and danger. They finally made some connection with distant relatives in the countryside and decided to send their children there for shelter.

Therefore, in the spring of 1968, YeYe, Jin, and I took a steamboat and traveled to a village about 30 miles from Zhongzhou. We took shelter at the home of the village official who was a distant relative of Jin's family. They felt obliged to help their relatives. In return, we offered all our city rations and provided money to cover our living expenses while we stayed with them. We would also obtain a letter from the village official stating we participated in the spring seeding and reformed ourselves in the village. We hoped the letter would help us obtain future university admission or a job assignment. The villagers cleaned up their small attic and laid some rice straw on the floor. We all brought our own cotton wadding quilts. The attic had just enough room for the three of us, as we squeezed and snuggled together.

Farmers worked very hard. Before dawn, a loud whistle brought all the village laborers to the fields. They were plowing and weeding the fields. A quick break for breakfast came after the sun had risen, a bowl of rice porridge and some pickled vegetables. After about 30 minutes, the loud whistle blew again, and everybody quickly returned to the fields. Lunch lasted an hour. We usually had cooked rice with stir-fried cabbage or stir-fried onion. The farmers stopped working at dusk.

Since we were all volunteers and were the village official's "relatives," little pressure was placed on us to perform. We followed the farmers' schedule and were assigned to a team of older women spreading seeds. Seeding wasn't hard labor work, but walking and throwing seeds all day did tire us out. We ate well and slept like a rock. We hardly had a chance to talk among ourselves.

A farmer's life relies on the yearly crop harvest, yet after working hard all year, they were still the poorest people in China. After the harvest, they were only allowed to keep a small amount of rice for their family. This had to last until the next harvest season. Most crops had to be sent to the government to feed the people in the cities. Many farmers had very little rice left to feed their family as the next harvest season approached. I remembered back to my youth when every year, before harvest time, my relatives from God Pond Valley used to visit Grandmother to ask for help.

After many weeks of working in the farm fields, we were tanned like farmers and had even built up some muscles. Away from all the political chaos, we found some inner peace. After we returned to Zhongzhou and were stepping off the steamboat, we saw the terraced houses along the riverbank were all painted bright, bloody red. It was dazzling and hurt our eyes. Lin Biao had a new phrase. "Red represents the supreme leader Chairman Mao — the red sun from the east." Lin Biao, unscrupulously, let his flattery reach a pinnacle. There were jumping clowns, like Mr. Ding, who took all Lin Biao's words at face value. They painted walls and store facades red. We looked at each other with knowing smiles. Here we were, back to this chaotic, crazy world.

After the Wuhan Incident[14], leaders within Mao's clique began to realize that things had gone too far. In October of the same year, Mao began a campaign to purge officials disloyal to him. They were sent to the

---

[14] The Wuhan Incident: in July 1968, big bloody battles occurred between military soldiers and rebels in Wuhan.

countryside to work in labor camps. At about the same time, Liu Shaoqi was "forever expelled from the Party." Mao had settled the score with Liu Shaoqi. The mass movements became irrelevant to him. He wanted to calm the already stirred and now boiling, bloody mass movements.

Mao had his "great strategic plan" handy. Mao sent the "Workers' Mao Tse-tung's Thought Propaganda Teams" to colleges and schools. These teams were primarily composed of industrial workers with participation from the People's Liberation Army. The slogan was "Using Mao Tse-tung's Thoughts to Educate the Masses of Teachers and Students."

In the fall of 1968, we were all called back from home, sightseeing, and fighting to study Mao Tse-tung's Thoughts. Mao had called for "Firmly Grasping Class Education." The older, previously poor workers in the propaganda team held meetings with students and teachers. These workers recounted their own life experience of suffering prior to the Liberation of China, and spoke of their happiness and sweet life after the Liberation (忆苦思甜). Mao was using his old trick and promoting class war again. This time, we were like "little monk reads scriptures, moves his mouth without troubling his mind" (小和尚念经，有口无心). We were forced to study Mao Tse-tung's Thoughts even though we didn't believe.

The central government also started cracking down on the Bad Elements of the Cultural Revolution. Most of the Bad Elements came from the Rebel side. They were no longer useful to Mao, but might cause trouble for the Communist Party. The scapegoats were, again, those from Black background families. I was so glad that no group accepted me as their member during the Cultural Revolution. Instead I enjoyed membership of the Leisure Club (逍遥派). One of my schoolmates, whose father also resided in America, was sent to jail for 3 years during this period of political crackdown. He was involved in one of the rebel groups during the chaotic times of "Right to rebel! Right to revolution!" (造反有理革命无罪).

One day in the winter of 1968, I walked out of my dormitory heading for school. Just before I started to cross Xinghe Road, I noticed trucks full of people gushing toward me from the south. I stopped walking and watched the trucks as they passed. They were full of young students and teenagers. All their hands were tied behind their backs and their heads were shaved. One of the boys, who looked roughly 15 years old, had tears streaming down his bloodless, pale face. He looked so scared. People said they were Bad Elements and were being taken to be sentenced. A deep sorrowful pain speared the center of my heart. These boys' parents must be devastated. Human life seemed worth nothing to tyrant Mao. He slaughtered people as if they were chickens. I have never forgotten that boy's tearful, sniveling face. It is engraved into my brain and remains fresh in my memory.

Every day we went to class to study Mao Tse-tung's Thoughts. Behind this calming surface, we contemplated our school might return to normal soon. We started worrying about university entrance exams again. Since Uncle Shi Po in Hangzhou had been condemned as a capitalist-roader, he could no longer help me get into university. I felt an urgency to leave this country as soon as possible. An intelligent, successful person such as Aunt Wei was locked up without any warning. It could easily happen to me, a Black bastard. I felt I was on the edge of a cliff. Any time I could be pushed into the abyss.

I started writing to my parents in America. I couldn't describe my real motive for leaving the country. All letters to foreign countries were censored. I told my parents that I was sad growing up without ever being able to see them. I wanted to meet them and asked them, almost begged them, for help. Father never wrote back. Later, I learned that he worked for a defense company in the US and was not allowed to contact people in Communist China. If discovered, his secret clearance would be forfeited. My mother's letters were always cold and businesslike. She said that from what she had read in the newspapers, the current policy of Communist China was rigid. It seemed no one was allowed to leave China. She said she would like to reunite with Xiao Mei and me and would look into the matter.

Near the end of 1968, we suddenly realized the "up to the mountain and down to the countryside" (上山下乡) movement had been initiated at our school. The Workers' Mao Tse-tung's Thought Propaganda Team had started planning our future. Mao said, "The intellectual youth must go to the countryside, and be educated by living and working in rural poverty."

Mao's words were the "holy" golden rule. We, the high school students, suddenly crowned as "the intellectual youth" (知识青年), must be reformed by doing hard labor in the rural countryside or at a desolate frontier. After nearly three years of the violent Cultural Revolution, no one could anticipate the next step of the central government and Chairman Mao. This time the propaganda team was more civilized. They didn't viciously attack the students, who had nothing more to lose. Nothing could be worse than working as a hard-labored peasant in a rural village unable to feed yourself for life.

For local students, their resident registrations (Hukou) were not at school. The propaganda team informed their parents' work units and residential neighborhood committees in order to persuade students to leave the city and transfer their Hukou to villages in the countryside. All the parents were in agony. They were in a difficult situation — between a rock and a hard place. If they didn't send their children to the countryside, they could lose their jobs, which were the livelihoods for their families. If they delayed their decision until the local surrounding villages had filled their quota for accepting the "down to the countryside" students, then they might be forced to send their children to a desolate frontier, such as Xinjiang or Inner Mongolia, places so far away from home that they would hardly ever see their children.

YingYing's mother was a middle-school teacher in Wenjiang, and she was wavering. Her school's propaganda team had exerted tremendous pressure on her. If she didn't let YingYing "down to the countryside," she would lose her job. YingYing said her mother hoped to find a village near Wenjiang for her. She could then easily come home for visits. YingYing was very depressed and not her usual chatterbox. Ling was gone, disappeared. Ling was a daring person. She didn't worry about the consequences of her own actions. Most of my other roommates came from farmers' families in the countryside. The propaganda team didn't need to do anything for them. They would be sent back to the villages from where they came. I was a problem for the propaganda team who had to transfer all boarding students' Hukou to villages in the countryside or in a remote frontier. The transfer needed consent from a parent or student. My Hukou was registered at my school, and I had no parent in China. Therefore, they put me on their back burner for later attack.

Only a few weeks later, at the beginning of 1969, all schools in China were dismissed. I remember the last day at my high school. It was a miserable day. All my roommates left quietly with sad, gloomy looks on their faces. It seemed we were all sentenced to jail. No one said "good-bye" or "will write to you." For those daughters of the commune officials, the dream of being a city resident was crushed. They had hoped Jiangsu Zhongzhou High was a stepping-stone to a university and thereafter a well-paid city job. For students like me, there were many uncertainties and fears. We sensed a dim future. People say, "There isn't an endless party." Now the party was over. For all those good and bad times, I suddenly felt a great loss coupled with sadness. I would miss the dormitory life and my roommates.

Before I left Jiangsu Zhongzhou High, the place I had lived for almost 6 years, I went to say good-bye to YeYe and Jin. YeYe's Mom and Dad, and Jin's Mom and Dad were still holding ground. They wouldn't budge. They were desperately searching for some other means to keep their daughters in the city. Before I left YeYe's home, I asked her to go back to school every month and pick up my monthly ration food tickets. YeYe gave me her promise.

An "Intellectual Youth"

As soon as I stepped through the door, I immediately sensed turmoil. Da Di had been forced "down to the countryside." In the tornado of the "up to the mountains and down to the countryside" (上山下乡) movement, many of Da Di's schoolmates had signed onto a "glorious" list known as the "Up to the Mountains and Down to the Countryside" Intellectual Youth list. No one was inspired by Mao's call. Rather they were fearful of their parents losing their jobs, or they had been harassed by the residential committee. Who in the world would think a better future was waiting for them in rural villages or a desolate frontier?

Uncle Nian was still confined at his work unit in Shanghai. Aunt Zhen was a housewife, and so there was no job to lose within our local family. For many years Aunt Zhen volunteered in the community and tried hard to fit in. She kissed up to the residential committee members, gave them gifts, and made them new clothes without charge.

But during this critical time, no one came to help. Instead, committee members visited our home daily to threaten Aunt. "Zhen, we have treated you very nicely in recent times. Years ago, Mrs. Chen and Mrs. Shi and their families were forced 'whole family down to the countryside' (全家下放). We could have done the same thing to your family. There are many students who have a better family background than Da Di. Why should Da Di stay in the city and these others go to the countryside? Does it make sense to you?"

Every day the residential committee members incessantly pressured Aunt Zhen, until eventually she gave in and Da Di was assigned to a village about 20 miles from Yiyang town. Da Di was Aunt Zhen's oldest son and Grandmother's oldest grandson. In Chinese tradition, the oldest son and oldest grandson hold a very special position in the family. As they contemplated Da Di doing hard labor for the rest of his life with no future, Grandmother and Aunt Zhen became increasingly devastated and heartbroken.

Da Di was a top student in Jiangsu Yiyang School excelling in all subjects. Aunt Zhen had placed much hope in him. Xiao Mei recalled that before the university entrance exams, just before the start of the Cultural Revolution, Aunt Zhen would get up early every day and cook two poached eggs for Da Di. It was a mother's true love. She wanted Da Di to study hard so that he would be able to enter university, but, at the same time, she worried about her son's health. If he worked too hard, he would become exhausted. She hoped that the poached eggs would keep Da Di strong.

As I walked through the door, Grandmother was busy preparing some food for Da Di to take with him to the village; pork cooked with pickled vegetables. This type of dish would last longer in the warm spring. In those days no one had a refrigerator. Aunt Zhen was getting Da Di's bedding ready. The entire family was filled with despair and was in a gloomy mood. Now I, another jobless youth, namely an "Intellectual Youth," would rejoin this household and add to the challenges facing the family.

After Da Di went to the village, pressure transferred to Xiao Mei. Since we moved to Dayin Lane, Mr. Yu, the government eye in our neighborhood, had always set his sights on the condemned families. Now all the condemned families had moved out except us. We became his focal point. Under pressure from his own work unit, Mr. Yu's daughter, Xiao Fang, had signed up for "up to the mountains and down to the countryside." Mr. Yu was also a member of the residential committee, and so had to set a good example for everyone else. He certainly glorified his action to everyone in the neighborhood. Xiao Fang was the same age as Xiao Mei and also a Society Youth in the neighborhood.

Xiao Fang cried out, "Why can Xiao Mei stay in the city, but I have to go?"

Mr. and Mrs. Yu couldn't let that happen, and so Xiao Mei had to also be sent "up to the mountains and down to the countryside." It seemed our household had no peace. Committee members started visiting again. Aunt Zhen said to them, "Da Di is my son. I have already answered Chairman Mao's call and sent my own son down to the countryside."

Aunt Zhen sobbed bitterly and continued, "Xiao Mei isn't my daughter. She was left here by her parents for me to look after. I can't make this decision. If I say 'yes' to you today, my brother-in-law and sister-in-law will blame me. I would love to give you her parents' address so that you can write them directly."

Xiao Fang was extremely jealous and started verbally abusing Xiao Mei. "We, the working-class families, must go 'up to the mountains and down to the countryside.' Why should an American daughter remain in the city?"

Every time Xiao Fang met Xiao Mei in the alley, she would laugh sneeringly. "Someone has American parents backing her. Is America not an imperialist country?"

Xiao Mei swallowed her anger and bowed her head to avoid looking directly at Xiao Fang. Xiao Mei became more worried. Her anxiety built up over time. There were several Society Youth in the neighborhood. Some, under pressure, had already signed up for "up to the mountains and down to the countryside." Xiao Mei didn't know how long she could hold out. For many nights she couldn't sleep and complained about her ears ringing all the time.

One day while she was walking in the alley near the neighborhood hospital (Mr. Wu's family home had been converted to a hospital), she fainted and fell to the floor. People hurried and immediately carried Xiao Mei to the hospital. Xiao Mei regained consciousness and was sent home to recuperate.

Dr. Hu was a friendly young doctor. He was in his thirties and always came to chat with Grandmother when free from patients. Aunt Zhen asked him to write a diagnosis statement for Xiao Mei.

Dr. Hu wrote the following. "Xiao Mei had a seizure yesterday. The diagnosis is that Xiao Mei has an incurable disease called epilepsy. Periodic seizures will accompany Xiao Mei for the rest of her life."

Afterwards, Xiao Mei was no longer harassed to go "up to the mountains and down to the countryside."

I became an Intellectual Youth or Society Youth, but regardless of what you called me, I was an obvious target for "up to the mountains and down to the countryside." Since my Hukou was still in Jiangsu Zhongzhou High, the residential committee could do nothing. In order to avoid trouble, most of the time I just hid indoors.

Xiao Mei and I were now both part of the hopeless Society Youth. When Xiao Mei visited Shanghai, she learned cooking techniques from Grandma Chow. She loved to cook, and we all enjoyed Xiao Mei's food. In the mornings, besides practicing calligraphy, I would cut and wash the vegetables in preparation for Xiao Mei. In the afternoons I would help Aunt Zhen with her sewing. After a while, I started needlework, embroidering pillow covers. Our relatives from God Pond Valley praised me. What a virtuous, well-behaved girl! Oh, well, the virtuous girl was sad and depressed.

Very soon a rumor started spreading in the neighborhood. A young worker at the rice-processing factory located behind our house had told his coworker that I was a pretty girl and had an air of great natural refinement. He would love to have me as his future wife. The coworker spread his words among others. He was criticized for fancying an American daughter. Grandmother and Aunt Zhen knew the boy, but I did not. For the last 6 years, I had been in school most of the time and hadn't paid attention to the people in our neighborhood. In fact, I wasn't interested in any boy. I just wanted to get out of China.

In a feudal, gossiping, tight-knit neighborhood, being a topic of boys' chatter wasn't at all flattering. This was especially true since my name always seemed to be accompanied by "American daughter." I became tremendously upset. "The tree wants to be calm, but the wind keeps blowing" (树欲静而风不止). How could I be free of this nonsense?

I wrote to Mother again and asked her to write to Premier Zhou Enlai for help. Mother seemed to treat my request lightly. She again indicated to me that, with the current situation, coming to America was a hopeless dream. We should let heaven control our fate. She added that one shouldn't fantasize that America could bring "wealth and high rank" (荣华富贵). She complained about her own life in America. Her husband was only a "lowly engineer" and couldn't afford to hire a maid. Mother had to do the house chores herself while she also took care of my two American-born younger sisters. She was a housewife. Mother absolutely didn't understand the poverty and political harassment we experienced in China. In all of my dreams there was never "wealth and high rank" (荣华富贵). It might have been Mother's own dream when she landed on American soil. She had become disillusioned with reality.

Melancholy was bottled up inside me, but no one knew. The anxiety had even affected my menstrual period. I was dripping blood all the time. Every month, there were only a few days without blood. Grandmother became worried. She cooked two poached eggs with cooking wine and forced me to swallow. She told me that eggs poached with red wine would improve my blood circulation; it might get rid of my blood sludge and promote new blood, but it didn't work.

I went to see an herbal doctor in Xushe, a neighboring town where the doctors were famous for curing female diseases. The doctor prescribed an herbal medicine for me. I moved our little coal stove to the alley to simmer the herbal mixture. I sat on a little wooden stool watching the medicine slowly simmer down. I made sure it didn't overflow. The herbal smell filled the little alley.

Suddenly, two of my teachers from Jiangsu Zhongzhou High appeared before me. One was my first grade Chemistry teacher Mr. Jin, and the other my first-grade Math teacher Mr. Young. Mr. Jin said to me in his soft Suzhou dialect, "Lee Yu, how are you? It has been so difficult to find you. You live here?"

He glanced at the surroundings: a small alley without a proper sewer system, garbage and chicken droppings scattered everywhere, muddy water puddles next to the dirty, dank walls. They were a little shocked that I lived in such a poor neighborhood. Since both my parents were college educated before the Liberation of China, they had assumed my family was originally an aristocratic, highly cultured family. Surely, they thought, the next generation of aristocratic families still lived above ordinary people.

I saw pity in their eyes. I stood up and greeted them with reservation, feeling uneasy and unsettled. Mr. Jin and Mr. Young were two young, unmarried, boarding teachers. They worked very hard. I remembered they came to the classroom every night during self-studying time and helped students with their homework. I had a lot of respect for them.

Mr. Young started the conversation softly. He was also Suzhounese, "We were sent by the propaganda team in our school to persuade you 'up to the mountains and down to the countryside.' We didn't have a choice."

I could sense a hint of resentment in his voice. I stood quietly. I hung my head and said nothing.

"Are you cooking herbal medicine? Who's it for?" Mr. Jin asked.

I replied, "For myself. I recently developed some sort of chronic illness, and the doctor prescribed this medicine for me."

They looked at me. My face was pale. I was thin and frail. Both of them looked knowingly at each other. They said, "Okay, we'll let you simmer your medicine. You take care of yourself. We have other students to visit."

They walked away quickly. I appreciated that they didn't make a big fuss over me. They seemed to excuse me for the time being, but it stirred up my worries.

The days passed cheerlessly. Very soon many of my schoolmates, whom I didn't know very well, visited me. They were Zhongzhou city residents, local students, but were not in my classroom. After the villages surrounding Zhongzhou city had filled their quota, many of my high school students had now been assigned to villages near Yiyang. However, transportation was poor with only one bus and one steamboat from Zhongzhou to Yiyang each day. Also, to complicate things further, there was only one steamboat each day from Yiyang to their future home villages. This meant that my schoolmates couldn't reach their villages in one day and so sought shelter overnight in Yiyang town. Sometimes a group of two students would turn up seeking shelter, sometimes even three.

Grandmother and Aunt Zhen had soft hearts for these young students and welcomed them without hesitation. Each time, we placed a thick layer of dry rice straw on our mud kitchen floor for them to sleep on. Even with such a humble sleeping arrangement, they thanked us profusely. Grandmother was brokenhearted. She heaved a heavy, sad sigh. "Poor kids! What have they done wrong? Why should they be punished this way?"

I felt very sorry for my schoolmates. I was still in the city counting my lucky days, yet fearing they would end soon. With my petite stature, I couldn't imagine working in the fields and shouldering heavy loads of human waste to fertilize the land.

After the majority of high school students had gone "up to the mountains and down to the countryside," the central government still seemed determined to break apart every family. This time it targeted the "bad background" relatives of urban dwellers. It was determined that they should also be sent "down to the countryside."

209

Aunt Phoenix, in Shanghai, wrote to Aunt Zhen. Her mother, we called her Wu Nai Nai (the fifth grandma), was coming down to a village close to Yiyang town, and Aunt Phoenix asked us to pick her up at the bus station. Wu Nai Nai's husband was Grandfather's younger brother. We called him Wu Ye Ye (the fifth granddad). After the Communist Party took over China, Wu Ye Ye had been classified as a landlord during the Land Reform Movement. All his land and properties were confiscated by the government.

Under these harsh circumstances, Aunt Phoenix, with reluctance, immediately married a middle school principal 12 years her senior in Shanghai. She then invited both her parents to live with her. Although Wu Ye Ye had passed away a few years ago, Wu Nai Nai had continued living with her daughter and taking care of her four grandchildren for the last 15 years. Now over 60 years old, she should be enjoying her golden years with her family, but, since she had been a landlord's wife, she had been forced "down to the countryside." Aunt Phoenix had arranged for her to stay with a distant niece in a nearby village.

Aunt Phoenix had a very close relationship with Uncle Nian. The lonely life in Shanghai led Uncle Nian to often visit Aunt Phoenix. My family was glad to have an opportunity to receive Wu Nai Nai who was a Lee family elder. Aunt Zhen went to the market to buy pork and seasonal vegetables to prepare a "little banquet" for Wu Nai Nai. Aunt Zhen also slaughtered a chicken. We raised chickens for eggs and only slaughtered chickens twice a year; once during the autumn moon festival and once for Chinese New Year celebration. Chicken was very precious in China during those days.

Although Wu Nai Nai was our special guest, she insisted on doing the cooking herself with my help. Wu Nai Nai seemed to have a tender heart toward me. When the chicken bok choy stew was ready, she picked up a piece of chicken and offered it to me to taste. I told her, "Wu Nai Nai, you taste it." But she insisted I taste the chicken. At lunch, Aunt Zhen picked up a piece of chicken and put it in Wu Nai Nai's bowl. Less than a minute later, when no one was paying attention, Wu Nai Nai placed the chicken in my bowl. She only stayed in our house for two days, but I had felt her soft heart toward me. Thinking back, she probably felt sorry for me: a poor unfortunate girl, living under a relative's roof without her own mother or father.

Wu Nai Nai's niece lived more than 5 miles from our home. Wu Nai Nai had some luggage, and so I voluntarily accompanied her to the village. In the early morning, after breakfast, we cut through Yiyang town and walked northwest. We reached Matou Street, and then passed the Xin Yuan factory complex that my grandfather used to own. Wu Nai Nai sighed. "Time flies. It seems not so long ago that I visited your grandfather and grandmother at Xin Yuan."

She was thinking back to the good times. We walked along Matou Street lined on both sides with terraced store facades; one side lay along the riverbank. We stopped at the Twin Bridges where the river splits. We crossed one of the bridges and continued on our journey, turning toward the north. After crossing the bridge, we left the residential areas and were surrounded by farmlands. It was the middle of summer. Summer in Yiyang was hot and humid. We reached Wu Nai Nai's village in the late morning. Without much delay, I started off for home.

The sun was excruciatingly hot, and, without much food in my stomach, I hurried home. When I reached home, I suddenly felt nauseous and started vomiting. I was probably dehydrated. I felt dizzy, and my body was burning hot. Finally, I fainted away. Grandmother put me to bed, laying me on a cool bamboo mat. She also placed a cold, wet washcloth on my forehead.

Suddenly in the midst of this chaos, my teachers, Mr. Jin and Mr. Young, again knocked on our door. Grandmother led them through our dilapidated home into my humble little bedroom. There I was lying unconscious on the bamboo mat burning with fever; a sad, depressing scene. They squeezed together and stood next to my bed. They must have thought I was dying. The last time they saw me, I had also been sick. They didn't realize I had just walked more than 10 miles in the sweltering heat. In all the confusion, they must have forgotten the purpose of their journey: to persuade me "up to the mountains and down to the countryside." Their eyes turned red. They must have been thinking, "Such a bright student has come to this kind of end!" They walked out without a word and never showed up at our door again!

After I regained consciousness, Grandmother recounted the whole event to me. She added, "Still, some good came of it. It was a lucky coincidence." She was referring to the fact that my "illness" had occurred just at the time when my two teachers visited me.

Whole Family Down to the Countryside (全家下放)

In the autumn of 1969, well after the start of "up to the mountains and down to the countryside" movement for Intellectual Youth, a new movement began called "whole family down to the countryside" (全家下放). It was directed toward Black families, such as ours. The residential committee had already warned Aunt Zhen about it when they persuaded Da Di "up to the mountains and down to the countryside." We knew we would be a top target for the "whole family down to the countryside" movement. Aunt Zhen couldn't bear the daily visits by the residential committee members and decided to "escape" to Shanghai where she stayed in Uncle Nian's empty room. While there, she could also learn more about Uncle Nian's situation. The God Pond Valley relatives had invited Grandmother to visit them many times. It was also a good time for Grandmother to leave town.

Aunt Zhen left some money with San Mei, her 17-year-old daughter, to manage the daily expenses. Regarding money, San Mei was the only one Aunt would trust, even though I was 5 years older. As far as money was concerned, I was an outsider. Xiao Mei and I could only be trusted to do all the household chores. It didn't bother me at all during those days. I guess I wasn't old enough, or sophisticated enough, to be bothered by such domestic details. Besides, Aunt Zhen wouldn't even trust Grandmother to manage the household expenses. Years ago, when Aunt Zhen visited Uncle Nian in Shanghai, she preferred to let San Mei be our household's financial executive instead of Grandmother. At that time, San Mei was only 14 years old.

As a result of the harsh living conditions in the countryside, the heavy physical labor, the time away from their intellectual culture, and a refusal to accept the rural life that Mao had planned for them, most Intellectual Youth eventually snuck back into the cities. Families willingly exhausted their own food rations to share with their "down to the countryside" children. "Pitiful parents' heart!" (可怜天下父母心). The poor parents felt guilty and commiserated with their children. They continuously worried about their children's future, and couldn't accept that they would have to stay in the rural villages all of their lives. Parents refused to order their children back to the villages, and so there were many depressed, resentful Intellectual Youth floating in cities all across China.

Da Di was back from the countryside. He was the only one in our family sent down to a village. Da Di was 21 years old and had never left home before except for a few weeks for the Revolutionary Tours. Although he didn't say much, he was certainly depressed — a lost soul. We were all very sorry for Da Di. San Mei was in charge of the family's daily expenses. San Mei occasionally bought some small fish or pork for Xiao Mei and me to cook. We liked to treat Da Di well while he was home. I felt that Da Di had been the sacrificial lamb for our family.

Da Di started doing carpentry work with one of his high school friends, Xiao Song, in our kitchen. They were making a dresser for Xiao Song's relative. In our neighborhood, house doors were kept open during the daytime, even during the cold winters. Open doors were one of the few ways for daylight to enter houses. Da Di and Xiao Song were working in the kitchen near the door so that they could have the benefit of the light. Da Di was a sloppy person. Hammers, wood saw, and chisels lay everywhere. The floor was covered with wood chips and shavings. The kitchen was in terrible disorder. It made it appear that there was a huge project in progress.

One of the residential committee members, we called him the blind man because he had one blind eye, had been walking past our house many times over the last few days. Each time he would tilt his head and look into our home. The blind man was a loafer who, before the Liberation of China, exhausted his parents' family wealth by gambling and drinking. When the Communist Party took over the country, he was jobless, penniless, an absolute proletariat, owning nothing. Relying on his Red background during every class struggle session and Communist movement, he was arrogant and one of the cruelest men in our neighborhood. Xiao Mei, the one in our family with street-smarts, became worried. She said, "The blind man has a dubious character. He is up to no good."

She told Da Di to be sensible and prepare to return to the village. Da Di was reluctant and said he would like to finish the dresser first and then go back to the village.

The next morning, Da Di and Xiao Song started working on their dresser. Xiao Mei and I were preparing to cook the fish that San Mei had bought from the street market. The fish were small, only two inches long. Removing the scales and gutting these small fish was a tedious job. We were all busy and hadn't noticed the blind man entering our house.

The blind man sneered. "Big fish and big pork (大鱼大肉)[15], having a banquet? What an extravagant, bourgeois decadent lifestyle!"

"What big fish? Most people feed these fish to the cat," Xiao Mei responded, holding up the fish in her hand. She couldn't help but correct the blind man.

"You shut up!" the blind man said furiously. He shouted at Xiao Mei scornfully, "Is it your place to speak?"

Xiao Mei didn't dare utter another word.

The blind man turned to Da Di. "Shouldn't you go back to your village to reform yourself? Who allowed you to come back to Yiyang, 'big fish and big pork,' and enjoy this bourgeois decadent lifestyle?"

Da Di stuttered, "I will go back to the village soon."

The blind man shot us a cold look, and then abruptly walked out. We all agreed that the blind man's uninvited visit was a bad omen. Da Di had to return to the village as soon as possible.

The next morning San Mei bought some pork. Xiao Mei and I were going to cook pork with pickled vegetable for Da Di to take to the village with him. It was a small amount of pork, so most of the dish was pickled salty vegetable. The small amount pork just added some flavor to the dish. The fat in the pork would soothe Da Di's stomach for a few days. Hopefully, Da Di could stay strong during the heavy physical labor. Da Di and Xiao Song had decided Xiao Song would finish the dresser by himself.

---

[15] Big fish and big pork (大鱼大肉): a Chinese idiom, describe the richness of the dishes.

Xiao Song was at home preparing his own workplace, and Da Di was hurrying to do as much as he could to help Xiao Song.

Suddenly, several security guards from the local Public Security Bureau flocked into our kitchen. One guard exclaimed, "No wonder people reported you to us. You hold a banquet at home and eat 'big fish and big pork' every day!" He had seen a piece of pork lying on our kitchen table. The blind man had reported us to the Public Security Bureau.

One guard, who appeared to have a higher rank, asked Da Di, "Shouldn't you be at the village?"

Da Di said, "I will return to the village tomorrow."

Pointing to the pork on the table, I added persuasively, "We were preparing for Da Di to return. We are cooking some pork with salty vegetable so he can take it with him to the village."

The security guard totally ignored me, and continued pressing Da Di. "What are you doing at home?"

Without waiting for an answer, he questioned Da Di threateningly, "Are you opening a private business at home?"

Then he put on bureaucratic airs and using official jargon said, "Conducting a private business in our socialist country is against the law! You must come with us to the Public Security Bureau."

Da Di was suddenly really scared. Pea-size sweat trickled down his face, and he turned white as a sheet. But he still tried to argue. "I wasn't conducting a private business. I was making a dresser for my friend."

Da Di was immediately pushed out by the security guards. We became panic-stricken. We were all stunned and in shock. Little Tiger, my youngest cousin, burst out calling for "big brother" (大哥哥). He cried out loudly and chased his 大哥哥. Xiao Mei held Little Tiger tight.

Little Tiger was only 7 years old. When Aunt Zhen was pregnant with him, she wanted an abortion. She mulled it over in her mind. "My youngest child is already 10 years old. I already have two sons and a daughter. This pregnancy is unwanted."

She was tempted many times to go to the hospital for an abortion, but Grandmother convinced her otherwise. She told Aunt Zhen, "Now our situation is much better. We shouldn't be worried about having an extra mouth to feed. I don't care what other people say. I believe abortion is bad and might harm your health."

Since the day Little Tiger was born, he became Grandmother's favorite. Xiao Mei was suffering with her own life, but she also always had a soft spot for Little Tiger. Any place she went she would bring Little Tiger along. Any food she had; she would share with Little Tiger. Xiao Mei was trying to calm down Little Tiger. San Mei's eyes welled up with tears as she swept up the wood chips and shavings on the floor. All of us were at a loss and didn't know what to do.

A thought suddenly flashed into my brain. I should ask Xiao Song to clarify the situation. Da Di was making a dresser for Xiao Song. He wasn't conducting a private business. I told Xiao Mei and San Mei that I was going to see Xiao Song.

Xiao Song lived in the Song Clan Village just past the North Gate Bridge on the outskirts of Yiyang town. I hurried out, crossed the South Gate Bridge, and quickly walked along "up Riverside Road" to the north. Near the steamboat station, I met Aunt Zhen's older sister, Da Yi. I told Da Yi what had happened to Da Di. Da Yi was very concerned — a houseful of kids without an adult. She said she would write to Aunt Zhen and ask her to hurry back home. She told me she would go to our home right away to make sure everything was okay. She encouraged me to hurry to see Xiao Song.

I went to Song Clan Village and asked Xiao Song to speak in defense of Da Di. At least, when the security guards came to ask, he should have the same story that Da Di had previously given. Xiao Song was a Red peasant's son. Xiao Song told me not to worry. He would do whatever he could.

That evening Da Di was released from the Public Security Bureau. We didn't know whether Xiao Song had talked to the security guards or they had just wanted to teach us a lesson and force Da Di to go back to the village. It might also draw Aunt Zhen out from hiding in Shanghai. Da Di came home like a defeated rooster. He was very quiet with tears welling up in his eyes. He refused to elaborate on what happened during the time he was confined in the Public Security Bureau. The next day he took a steamboat and returned to the village.

Soon Grandmother and Aunt Zhen returned home. There was a daily meeting in our neighborhood organized by the residential committee. The meeting encouraged residents to voluntarily "whole family down to the countryside." We were on tenterhooks again. Soon National Day arrived on October 1st; the day Chairman Mao stood atop the Gate of Heavenly Peace and declared, "The Chinese people have stood up!" and announced the creation of a "People's Democratic Dictatorship" — the People's Republic of China.

Every year since we had moved to Dayin Lane, Public Security Bureau officers would visit our home on National Day eve and New Year's Day eve. It was called "Cha Hukou — checking residency registration" (查户口). We had been classified as an anti-revolutionary element's family with foreign connections. They made sure no foreign spies were hiding in our home. Year after year it had become a routine humiliation. It would occur during the middle of the night, when everybody in the neighborhood was in deep sleep. The security guards would knock on our door and shout loudly: "Cha Hukou!" which, of course, woke everybody in the neighborhood!

Aunt Zhen would open the door and let the security guards enter. She would hand our residency registration book to the security guards who would then perform a thorough search. They would open the mosquito net of each bed, and shine a flashlight on our faces. One by one, they checked our names against the names in our residency registration book. There should be no one less and no one more; otherwise, we had to explain.

The next day, Grandmother and Aunt Zhen would pretend nothing had happened. They would present themselves with smiling faces to greet our neighbors. It was so awkward. Mr. Chang's family, across the alley from us, was always kind and would greet us as usual. Mrs. Qian, our next-door neighbor, wasn't so nice. She would let us know that she had been awakened by the security guards. "Last night they knocked so hard, I woke up and couldn't go back to sleep." She made sure we understood that we were beneath her and had better bow to her!

I hated the whole thing, but it was a fact of life for our family. For the next few days, I tried to avoid dealing with our neighbors. Luckily, I had been in boarding school for the last 6 years and so had mostly avoided these yearly harassments. This year my school was dismissed, and I had come back home; but my Hukou, my residency registration, was still in school, not at home. So my name wasn't listed in our household residency registration book. Under normal circumstances, when kids came home from school, it wasn't a big deal. Everyone in our neighborhood knew I had grown up there. But now in the midst of the "whole family down to the countryside" movement, they could nitpick at me and cause trouble for our family.

That evening, Aunt Zhen told me, "Tonight, the security guards will come to us. Cha Hukou. I have arranged for you to stay with my sister, your Da Yi."

On National Day eve, I slept with Da Yi. After the Communist Party came to power, very few families had the luxury of an extra bed for guests. An extra bed in a household was reserved only for high officials' families or some selective rich intellectual families. That night, I couldn't sleep as I curled up in a small portion of the bed, trying not to disturb Da Yi. I didn't want Da Yi to have trouble sleeping because of me. I hadn't slept under the same bed quilt with anybody for a long time. Xiao Mei and I used to share a small bed under the same quilt when we were children.

The residential committee members started visiting again. They were trying to persuade Aunt Zhen to agree to "whole family down to the countryside." They told her, "At the moment you have three girls at home doing nothing. If your family moves to a village, you could open a sewing business. The three girls and you together could make clothes for the village people. You could really make a good living there."

How kind you are? I thought secretly. I didn't dare ask them, "If moving down to the countryside is so good, why haven't you moved your families down?"

The fact was that once we agreed to "whole family down to the countryside," we would have to surrender our city residency registration book and, then, there goes our government food rations! Without government rations, you were unable to buy food even if you had money. Peasants worked so hard all year long and still couldn't feed their families. Since we were from the city and not used to heavy labor, there was no chance we would be able to feed ourselves. Also, Xiao Di, my second cousin, had a job in the city. If we agreed to "whole family down to the countryside," Xiao Di would have to give up his job and come down with us. He would then also become a poor peasant. Aunt Zhen wasn't stupid

219

and couldn't be fooled. She held her ground, but she was worried. The whole family was worried.

There was a woman, Mrs. Lin, who lived a few houses away from us. Mrs. Lin wanted Aunt Zhen to make a new jacket for her husband in a hurry. Aunt Zhen was glad to make a new jacket for her husband, because her husband was a local town official.

During their chats together, Mrs. Lin told Aunt Zhen that, during an official town meeting a few days ago, a new policy from the central government was discussed. It said no family should be forced "whole family down to the countryside" unless the family had done something against the law or the major breadwinner of the family, normally the husband, had been condemned and sacked by his work unit in Yiyang town. "Whole family down to the countryside" should be voluntary.

In those days, if someone in power accused you of breaking the law, then, by dictate, you had broken the law. False accusations wouldn't surprise anyone because they occurred everywhere during the Cultural Revolution. From the information provided by Mrs. Lin, Aunt Zhen knew in her heart that, no matter what the committee members said, she should not budge from her position. They couldn't point a gun to her head and force us to go. Nevertheless, we had to be extremely careful.

New Year's Day, January 1st, was fast approaching. There would be Cha Hukou, checking residency registration again. To make sure no unexpected issues arose, Aunt Zhen told Da Di to stay in the village and not come home for the holiday. Although my Hukou was at my school and the "up to the mountains and down to the countryside" movement for the Intellectual Youth was basically over, three girls at home "doing nothing" looked worse than only two girls at home "doing nothing." Aunt decided to send me away to a distant relative, Aunt Gou, to hide for a while.

A few days before New Year's Day, Aunt Zhen and I took a bus to a small town, Zhuze, in a mountainous region. As we left Yiyang town, there were farmlands all around us. It was an overcast, chilly winter's day during the slack farming season. Crops were already harvested, while seeding season hadn't begun. The land was bare. I gazed out of the bus window. In the distance, a flock of birds flew across the sky. I pondered a poem verse, "*the sea is so broad that fish may swim freely, and the sky so vast that birds may fly as they want"* (海阔凭鱼跃, 天空任鸟飞). People say the sky's the limit. Sadly, on this boundless earth, no place could shelter me.

Soon, we entered the wilderness. The road became primitive and bumpy, causing the bus to jolt around. On both sides of the road were uncultivated hills covered with loose granite stones. Not a soul was in sight. A scene of total desolation. The hills became higher as we entered the mountainous region, which was covered with large granite boulders. In the distance, I saw a small, booth-like structure halfway up the mountain, made of granite stones. For miles there'd been no hint of a human soul, and so this small structure caught my attention.

Although there weren't any "green hills or clear water," no picturesque scenery, my mind entered a fantasy zone. I wished I could live in that little stone booth where no one would bother me again and I could live in peace and tranquility. At that moment, I didn't even think about how I would survive in such a desolate wilderness. Then my mind wandered off into the Land of Peach Blossoms (桃花源).[16]

We were dropped off at a small bus station. Aunt Zhen and I started climbing uphill. The village was 3 miles away from our drop-off point. Aunt Zhen carried my pillow and some daily washing stuff, and I carried my cotton-padded bed quilt and a couple pieces of underwear. This time I insisted to myself that I wouldn't sleep under the same quilt with anyone else. My justification was that I would wake Aunt Gou during the night. Carrying the luggage and climbing the stone-covered hills were exhausting.

Finally, we reached Aunt Gou's home. Aunt Gou's house was located on the edge of the village well away from the rest of the houses. The house was small with a thatched roof, and the walls were made of brown clay. The whole village was very primitive. There were only a few trees. The surroundings were bare with brownish yellow soil and granite stones scattered around. It was very different from God Pond Valley with its vast rice fields crisscrossed by ponds and rivers. In my depressed mood, everything in front of my eyes seemed to cast such a cold and desolate winter scene. I suddenly became overwhelmed with sadness.

---

[16] "Land of Peach Blossoms (桃花源)" is a self-reliant, self-sufficient, self-contained, peaceful village. It was depicted in an essay by Jin Dynasty scholar Tao Yuanming.

As we walked into the house, on the right, near the front, was a cooking stove with a chimney. On the right, at the back, was a muddy animal pen. A huge pig oinked loudly from within the pen. Facing the door was a square table set against the back wall with three benches surrounding the open sides. On the left was a bedroom. In the bedroom there was a window with a wooden plank cover. It was the only window in the house. Under the window sat a sewing machine that Aunt Gou used to make clothes for the village people. There was only one bed, and I started to wonder how we would sleep that night.

Aunt Gou was in her early forties, about the same age as Aunt Zhen. She was a simple and kind countryside woman. Aunt Gou sent her husband to share a bed with his friend in the village. That night, Aunt Zhen, Aunt Gou, and I, all three of us, squeezed into a full-sized bed. Aunt Zhen had made a financial arrangement with Aunt Gou. She gave Aunt Gou my monthly ration tickets for rice and cooking oil. Aunt Zhen also paid Aunt Gou some money to cover my expenses while I stayed in the village. Next day, Aunt Zhen returned home.

I stayed with Aunt Gou for over a month. I helped Aunt Gou with her sewing work and cooking lunch and dinner. I seldom left the house. Although Aunt Gou was a very nice person, there was a huge generational and cultural gap. There was no common "language" between us. During my time there, I didn't read any books or practice my calligraphy. It just wasn't the environment for it. Most people were illiterate, and I wanted Aunt Gou to like me. I thought the best thing I could do to make Aunt Gou happy was to help with her sewing. By my nature, I was slightly aloof and never found it easy to socialize with people I didn't really know. But village life was very lonely. I felt as if I was in solitary confinement.

It was a pleasant surprise when Aunt Zhen appeared just a few days before Chinese Lunar New Year. She had come to take me home. The situation had improved for our family. An article in the *People's Daily* claimed that China intended to join the United Nations. The government started promoting better relationships with overseas Chinese. The government reestablished the Committee for Overseas Chinese General Affairs. The government also encouraged overseas Chinese to send money to their relatives in China. With overseas money, the government rewarded relatives of overseas Chinese with additional ration tickets. Most importantly, the relatives of overseas Chinese were no longer accused of being foreign spies.

During my absence, the "whole family down to the countryside" movement had become increasingly intense. Under daily coercion and humiliation from the residential committee, Aunt began to waver. She was worried the worst might yet come to our family. Aunt knew the husband of Xiao Mei's nanny who was a village official. So, in case the worst came, she arranged for us to move down to the nanny's village. This way, we would at least be protected by an official.

Aunt Zhen also told me that Mrs. Qian, our next-door neighbor, kept inquiring about my whereabouts. Aunt Zhen told her I had returned to school. Her son had a business trip to Zhongzhou, so she sent her son to check if I was at school. She was so nosy and despicable and just had to try to expose Aunt Zhen as a liar. She warned Aunt Zhen that her son had told her that all Jiangsu Zhongzhou High School students had been dismissed. No one was at school when her son visited my high school. Aunt Zhen didn't know what to say. She just mumbled.

Luckily, over recent days, there were no more visits from the residential committee. Aunt Zhen was no longer under the gun. The residential committee had started to loosen its grip.

Uncle Nian had finally been released from confinement and would come home for Chinese Lunar New Year. Grandmother also wanted Da Di and me home for the holiday, so that there could be a family reunion. Living in China was just like being in stormy weather. Chaos was always present, yet unpredictable. The political wind could change direction in a flash. Daily life was more or less dependent on the whims of "our supreme leader, Chairman Mao."

On Chinese New Year's Eve, during the ancestor worship ritual, I again asked my ancestors to help me get out of China. I wrote to Mother again and asked her to write to the Committee for Overseas Chinese General Affairs. Later when I came to America, Mother gave me the reply letter from the Committee. The letter started with a bureaucratic slogan.

最高指示
我们的责任；是向人民负责。

The Supreme Instruction:
Our responsibility; we are responsible for our people.

Then the letter indicated they had received Mother's letter requesting that the Chinese government allow her two daughters to travel to Hong Kong.

Following the "Supreme Instruction," the brief response avoided all culpability by simply stating, "It wasn't the committee's *responsibility*!"

The letter chided my mother. "By the way, the capital of the People's Republic of China is Beijing (北京), not Peiping (北平)! This is common knowledge that you should know. Using Peiping instead of Beijing in your letter was a serious error. You should correct yourself in the future."

Mother couldn't believe the committee had nitpicked on such a small matter, but I knew the committee members were just leaning to the left to cover their own asses. This was still during the chaotic Cultural Revolution. No one in China knew the direction of the next political wind.

Aunt Wei's Suicide

In the summer of 1970, Uncle Nian wrote to Aunt Zhen to tell her that Aunt Wei had committed suicide in Lingyin canyon near Lingyin Temple. She used a shaving knife to cut an artery and bleed to death.

Toward the end of 1967, the Red Guards found a Bible in her home. She was accused of being a "running dog" for the American imperialists, and was condemned as a foreign spy. Aunt Wei was pulled out for class struggle session, and was thereafter confined and isolated in a cell at the hospital where she had worked. During the confinement, she found out that she was pregnant with her second child. She was released for the birth, but kept under surveillance by her coworkers. The class struggle sessions, the confinement, the pregnancy, the birth of her second child, all drove her into a profound depression. Finally, she had a nervous breakdown.

She often screamed out during the middle of the night. She told her husband that she often saw her stepbrother walk toward her holding a ragged bed quilt. She said her stepbrother's ghost-spirit was coming to settle a score on an old grudge. The stepbrother was the son of my mother's first stepmother. During the anti-rightist movement, he was a college student and ended up having a nervous breakdown. Grandpa Chow wanted his son to stay with him so that he could care for him, but his son was insane. The stepbrother would stick his head out the window and scream out loudly, disturbing the neighbors. Sometimes he shouted out political statements that endangered the entire family.

Aunt Wei was a medical school student at the time. She arranged for her stepbrother to enter a mental hospital. A month later she went to see her stepbrother. He was in bad shape, a mess. His hair was long. He hadn't shaved for a month. He was dirty, held a ragged old quilt, and mumbled words that no one understood. A few months later he died, and the guilt became buried deeply in Aunt Wei's heart.

Now, she was insane herself. One night she went to Lingyin to end her life and leave all her troubles and sadness behind. She also hoped to free herself of the guilt she felt for her stepbrother's demise. She was desperately searching for peace and tranquility in heaven, but sadly she left behind her husband and their two young sons; one was only a baby.

Aunt Wei's suicide shocked me to the core. It was a warning for me. If I stayed in China, I would also end up like Aunt Wei. I was determined to leave China, no matter what. I was ready to bet my life on it. I decided to go to the Public Security Bureau, and ask for permission to see my parents. I knew it was a risky move. I could be locked up right on the spot. Living in fear was worth nothing. I would rather die for freedom. I didn't tell anybody what I was thinking. I walked toward the Public Security Bureau.

Standing in front of the entrance I hesitated. "Am I ready for whatever could happen to me?" I asked myself.

I plucked up courage and walked into the office. There were three security guards. There I was, standing in front of these guards, a petite young woman looking like a teenager.

"Are you lost?" one of the guards asked me.

I spoke to the point. "My parents in America asked me to come to your office to seek permission to meet them in Hong Kong."

The guards suddenly realized who I was. They knew our family very well. They came to visit us every year to Cha Hukou — check our residency registration. Xiao Mei and I were the only two girls in town whose parents were in America.

They started laughing and jeering at me. "Are you kidding? We didn't go after you, yet you come to provoke trouble for yourself and invite death!"

One of the guards bullied me. He was extremely haughty and treated me with contempt. He shouted at me, "Can't you distinguish day and night? Do you not know what era we are in now? We are in the middle of the Cultural Revolution, and you dare to ask permission to go overseas. Do you know the meaning of American imperialism? Have you eaten a leopard's gall-bladder (豹子胆)? What a nerve!"

226

The third guard seemed to have some humanity. He told me, "Go home and never show your face here again. Go, go!"

He pushed me out. I was never a bold and vigorous girl, always timid and shy. I walked back home, hopelessly disappointed and disillusioned.

Labor in Training

In the spring of 1971, I unexpectedly received a letter from Jiangsu Zhongzhou Senior High School. The letter informed me that I had been assigned a job at the Red Flag Construction Company in Zhongzhou and that my school had already arranged transfer of my Hukou (residency registration) to the Red Flag Construction Company. I was excited. There were no more threats of "up to the mountains and down to the countryside," and my Hukou would stay in Zhongzhou. I would receive government rations, and the Zhongzhou Hukou surpassed the Yiyang Hukou. I didn't second-guess the job. It would mean one chapter of my life — being an Intellectual Youth or Society Youth — had finally come to an end.

I immediately took the bus to Zhongzhou. The Red Flag Construction Company was also located on Xinghe Road between the train station and Jiangsu Zhongzhou High School. It was in the same district as my high school. It turned out that the Red Flag Construction Company was a collectively owned (民办) unit. Unlike workers in state-owned companies, workers in collectively owned units didn't have a job guarantee. Collectively owned units could be dissolved at any time.

The entrance to the Red Flag Construction Company was on a side alley connected to Xinghe Road. After entering, I found myself in a courtyard. The company seemed in the midst of construction. To my surprise, Ling and another girl, whom I also knew from my high school, were there talking to a middle-aged man. The middle-aged man wore a faded military uniform and looked like a demobilized soldier. I was so happy to see them, and right away sensed we would work together.

The middle-aged man was the Communist Party committee secretary of our company, Mr. Hua. He greeted me and told me that the three of us would temporarily live in the attic above the accounting office. He apologized for such an inferior living arrangement. He pointed to the left where a building was in the middle of construction and said, "We are building a four-story building for our new semi-conductor factory. Hopefully, we will have a better living arrangement for you in the near future."

He added that in response to Chairman Mao's call to modernize our country, our company was going to be transformed from a construction company into a semi-conductor company. The three of us would be pioneers in this new adventure. Mr. Hua was a friendly and pleasant man. After being away from school for 2 years, I knew little about what my roommates had been doing. I was eager and anxious to talk to Ling. After Mr. Hua left, we didn't ask each other how we managed to dodge the "up to the mountains and down to the countryside." We greeted each other enthusiastically. Right away, the quiet courtyard was filled with noise and excitement.

The other girl I would work with was Orchid. She was an ordinary-looking, medium-built girl who had an open and candid nature. She was a second grader in our school (or an 11th grader in America). Her dormitory room had been next to ours. I saw her often while I was at high school, but had never spoken to her before.

We were the lucky three. At the end of the "up to the mountains and down to the countryside" movement, and after the withdrawal of The Workers' Mao Tse-tung's Thought Propaganda Team, only we three students remained with our Hukou at Jiangsu Zhongzhou High. Since our high school and the Red Flag Construction Company belonged to the same district, our school conveniently assigned us to work at the Red Flag Construction Company. No Hukou transfer was involved, simply a change of address.

It was Sunday, and no one was at work. A middle-aged, short, overweight woman walked out from a door on the alley side of the courtyard and introduced herself as Mrs. Zhu. She told us that she and her husband occupied two rooms on the southeast side of the courtyard and hinted the entire courtyard complex had once belonged to them. She politely warned us to keep quiet and not disturb their life.

On the east side was a small accounting office next to Mrs. Zhu's unit. Next to the accounting office was a larger administration office for the company. A storage room and kitchen occupied the north side of the courtyard with the construction site on the west. Our attic was right above the small accounting office. In a small hallway, just in front of the entrance to the accounting office, a ladder made of bamboo hung down from the opening to the attic. Off the hallway were entrances to the accounting and administration offices. The bamboo ladder blocked the doors to both offices. We knew immediately that during office hours it would be very inconvenient for us to enter our attic. We must place the bamboo ladder sideways against the hallway wall to unblock the office doors. In the beginning, I was scared to climb up and down this bamboo ladder; the horizontal bars of the ladder seemed too far apart for me; with each step, the elasticity of the bamboo would cause the ladder to spring up and down. However, after a few months I learned to sprint up and down the ladder without fear, even when carrying a bucket of water in my hand.

With the help of Ling and Orchid, I finally moved all my stuff into the attic. Inside the attic, we were right under the ridge of the pitched roof. It was the highest point of the roof. Our hands could touch the roof without raising them all the way up. The roof was right above our heads. Ling was the tallest among us, so when she stood under the ridge of the roof her head nearly touched the roof. From the ridge, the roof sloped down, so to move around we had to bend our bodies. There was a wooden trunk under the ridge that we used as our table. Later we were told that some old accounting books were stored in the trunk. We placed our mats and bedding on the floor around the table. There was very little room to spare, but there was no complaining. We were the lucky three with a job in the city. This little attic became our home, together with a lot of rats running on the roof beams.

The next day, we got up before the office opened and placed the bamboo ladder sideways against the wall. We were told by an administration officer, Mr. Hsu, that we were hired as labor in training or 徒工 (Túgōng) with a salary of 8 Yuan ($1) per month. This was not as glamorous as described by Mr. Hua yesterday, but we didn't have high expectations. We always compared our situation to those "up to the mountains and down to the countryside" intellectual youths. We were content.

Our first job assignment was working on the construction of our future semi-conductor factory building. We carried buckets of wet cement from a mixed cement pile to the construction site. The workers were kind to us. They filled our buckets only half full. They knew we came from Jiangsu Zhongzhou High School, which was highly regarded in the community. That night our arms and shoulders were painful, but we slept soundly. Even the busy running rats couldn't wake us.

We were glad when the building was finally finished. We all became involved in painting the walls and adding the final touches to this four-story building. To my eyes, it was a very nice, sturdy-looking concrete structure. We all hoped there might be a small section allocated as our living space. Unfortunately, this dream was never realized.

After a couple of months living together, Ling, Orchid, and I, who were from totally different family backgrounds (Red, Gray and Black), formed strong bonds. We lived, cooked, and ate together as a family and were all resentful toward the Cultural Revolution. We hated all the political movements. We all despised Mao and his wife Jiang Qing, even though their names never came up in our conversations. We tacitly understood each other. We were young, and, in many ways, immature. The Cultural Revolution and the "up to the mountains and down to the countryside" movement had given us a life experience that no one in the world, other than in China, had experienced. We had formed unspoken opinions toward the world around us.

Every evening the factory held a Mao Tse-tung's Thought study or a current event discussion. It was mandatory for all workers in the company. Most people in our company were construction workers and still worked on other construction sites. Only a few were assigned to be the workers of this newly formed semi-conductor company. The newly hired high school students, like us, were all designated as workers for this new company. During the study session, the room was filled with people we hardly knew. However, the meeting was only conducted by a few people — the future leaders of this company. These people were typically the talking heads from Red worker families, or those from Gray families who were able to sail with the wind, curry favor, and play up to those in power (见风使舵, 趋

炎附势). They were the cadres of our company. Many of them were uneducated.

The three of us always kept quiet and never voluntarily opened our mouths. When push came to shove, we would say, "I one hundred percent agree with you." We were sick and tired of empty slogans and bureaucratic jargons. Coming back to our little attic, we used to mock and imitate those lengthy and empty speeches. People in the workplace called us: "niao, shi, pi" (尿屎屁), which literally means "urine, shit, fart." Since "urine, shit, fart" always happen together, this common Chinese saying was insinuating we were inseparable and always together. Unity is strength! There were some young local workers eager to be friends with us. Like flies attracted to rotten fruit, we had become popular among the younger workers. We were polite, but not ready to become true friends with anyone. Unwittingly, we had become the "unlikable" of those middle-aged, female cadres. They pointed out we were arrogant, self-important, and unwilling to swim with the tide (清高自负).

Our new company placed semi-conductor equipment orders with a state-owned, orthodox company in Yantai, Shandong Province. Our company intended to start manufacturing diode rectifiers — the simplest semi-conductor component. A large group of us were sent to Yantai to learn how to operate the new equipment we would soon be receiving. Among the group were three older, more mature former high school graduates, who would be the lead people for this effort. They were originally office workers from the Red Flag Construction Company. The three of us were also told to go with the group. We were the newly hired labor in training. We were excited by this gracious offer. Especially for me, a Black Bastard, this was the first time I hadn't been excluded from being chosen. I was overwhelmed by this unexpected grace. We understood that the company had high expectations of us, the Jiangsu Zhongzhou High School graduates. The rest of the group was composed of cadres of the company. Some of them didn't even have an elementary school education. This honorable, glorious activity surely would include them — the company's real pillars.

We took a train to Shanghai, and then boarded an ocean vessel to Yantai. No one in our group had ever seen an ocean before, even though Zhongzhou was close to the Pacific. Also, none of us had ever been on an

232

ocean vessel, so you could imagine the excitement. We were all standing on the deck watching Shanghai slowly move farther and farther away from us. As we headed out into the ocean, the waves pushed against one another. I could feel my feet move. Suddenly I felt dizzy and wanted to vomit. I hurried into the passenger cabin, which was full of small bunk beds, and climbed onto the upper bunk assigned to me. I was still seasick and afraid to move. I stayed in the bed until the following morning when the boat stopped moving. I was happy to suffer the seasickness. The opportunity and excitement of seeing the ocean and boarding an ocean vessel far outweighed the inconvenience.

Next day, we took a bus to the semi-conductor company. We toured workshops one by one where the workers wore clean, white overalls and masks. All the machines were new and unknown to me. I had no industrial work experience and had never taken a school class that involved semiconductors. I started worrying that I wouldn't be able to fulfill my task.

Ling comforted me. "Don't worry. No one in our company has been to college to learn about semi-conductors. You are good in Physics and Chemistry. You are probably the most qualified person among us."

Orchid's eyes glanced toward our cadres as she said sarcastically, "Let them worry about it. After all, they are the leaders of our company."

We were devouring all the new information regarding how to manufacture a diode rectifier. Hopefully, once we returned to Zhongzhou, we would be able to make diode rectifiers ourselves. Some of our cadre comrades became bored touring the semi-conductor company. It was all beyond their comprehension. They suggested we take the last day off and tour Yantai city.

Yantai was a seacoast city with a harbor and beach. It opened its harbor for international trading back in 1861 after the Qing Dynasty signed the Treaty of Tianjin. Near the beach we saw multi-story, Western-style townhouses and garden villas that used to be occupied by foreigners, but now had been confiscated by the Communist government. Most of the foreigners had been kicked out of China after the Communist takeover.

We walked along the beach watching seagulls fly in the overcast gray sky. We could hear the sea and feel the might of the ocean as the powerful waves broke on the shore. We took off our shoes and slowly tiptoed into the seawater. Then we leisurely strolled along its long pier and afterwards rented boats and paddled out into the bay. I handled one of the paddles and bravely maneuvered the boat. Thanks to our cadre comrades, all expenses were paid by our company. We fully enjoyed the foreign aspects of the seaport and were ready to conclude our business tour of Yantai.

On the way back to the hotel, we found that apples there were so big, so tasty, and so cheap. We learned that Yantai was famous for its apples, and so we all bought a bagful of Yantai apples. Ling, Orchid, and I wanted our family members to share a tasty Yantai apple. We boarded the sea vessel again to Shanghai, and then took the train back to Zhongzhou. Ling and Orchid didn't exit at Zhongzhou. They continued on to their homes for a few days' vacation. They both came from Wenjiang, a major city also located along the Shanghai-Beijing rail line. I also asked Mr. Hsu, our administration officer, to allow me to have a few days off. The next day after returning to Zhongzhou, I took a bus home. I hurried home so my family could enjoy the Yantai apples. Unfortunately, the apples had already started to soften. When I arrived home, it was so sad. The apples were too soft and no longer crunchy. They tasted like apple sauce! Oh well, my heart was in the right place.

Si Nai Nai (四奶奶) — My Fourth Lady

There was no peace at home. There were constant quarrels between Grandmother and Aunt Zhen. My parents had, by now, become well established in America. Father was a senior staff engineer for a defense company in Southern California. With China's closed-door policy, we had no idea of my father's status and his earnings in America, but my parents had increased compensation to Aunt Zhen to support Grandmother, my sister, and me. My father had also started allocating extra pocket money for Grandmother. Aunt Zhen became jealous of Grandmother's pocket money and worried about the future money flow from my parents as my sister and I were growing up faster than she wished. All these thoughts drove Aunt Zhen crazy.

Grandmother was a loose-hands person in terms of money. She was now 75 years old. Her teeth were almost all gone, and she could hardly eat anymore. She seldom spent money on herself, but she would buy pork and seasonally expensive food from the street markets for the children to enjoy. She also showed generosity among her old friends. Before the Liberation of China, many of the friends she played Mahjong with called her Si Nai Nai (fourth lady, my grandfather was the fourth son of the Lee family). Now they had become old and were in financial distress.

Before the Liberation of China, Si Nai Nai was well respected in Yiyang town and everyone felt honored to associate with Si Nai Nai. However, after the Liberation, our household was purged and condemned as an anti-revolutionary family, and those friends suddenly wanted nothing to do with Si Nai Nai. When Si Nai Nai visited their homes, they would ask her to hide behind their big cooking stoves to make sure no one knew that she was visiting. As the old saying goes, "people's affection is as thin as a sheet of paper." Now, the political atmosphere had changed and they again became friendly with Si Nai Nai.

Grandmother was unable to hold grudges against anyone. She was a kind, saintly person and always showed sympathy toward the needy. On the other hand, with Grandmother's advancing age, Aunt Zhen already counted Grandmother's money as her own. Every time Aunt Zhen found Grandmother giving money to her friends or to the God Pond Valley relatives, she would go into a towering rage.

She would shout at Grandmother, "You spend money like water. Don't think that money will continue to flow to you. It isn't easy for my brother-in-law to make money in a foreign land. You should save some for a rainy day. For the sake of your grandchildren, you should keep money in your own pocket instead of being a spendthrift."

She reminded Grandmother, "Your so-called friends treated you like a piece of dirt when we were in despair. They don't deserve your charity."

Sometimes she would keep a cold face and wouldn't talk to Grandmother for days. She showed no respect to Grandmother as our family elder. She sometimes complained to me, "Grandmother is too old and decrepit. She is foolish and muddleheaded and shouldn't handle money."

I was sick and tired of listening to Aunt's complaints, but I had to respect Aunt Zhen as my elder. I couldn't speak in defense of my grandmother.

When things got too bad at home, Grandmother would dash off to God Pond Valley or stay with her friends for days. Obligated as a daughter-in-law in a traditional social society, Aunt Zhen would go and visit the friend to bring Grandmother home. Often, I saw Grandmother tearful.

She bemoaned, "I am old and incapable of doing many things. Nowadays, old people have no value."

Sometimes, Grandmother begged Aunt Zhen to treat her as an elder, just for her old age sake. She would say to Aunt Zhen, "The road in front of me is much shorter than the road behind me. There aren't many years left for me. Why are you so critical of me?"

Grandmother had long ago lost her mother-in-law's status. I sensed she was fearful of Aunt Zhen. I felt very sad for Grandmother, but could do little to help. All I could do was discourage Aunt Zhen from controlling

Grandmother's pocket money. Finally, one day when Aunt Zhen was complaining to me again about Grandmother, I talked back. "I am sick and tired of you talking about Grandmother's money all the time. It is her pocket money. No one should tell her how to spend it, even if she burns her money for fun. It is her business, and no one else's."

All my incoming letters were handed to me by our company. I had told Mother that her letters should all be sent to Yiyang. Then, they would be forwarded to me using a Yiyang address. This way they wouldn't attract attention from my coworkers. Nevertheless, now I was in direct contact with my parents and had a job in Zhongzhou. My status at home had suddenly risen. Aunt Zhen hesitated to argue with me, but to escape this unceasing domestic nonsense I was ready to return to our little attic. My youthful selfishness, even today, stirs up guilt toward my grandmother.

A few months after I got my job in Zhongzhou, Xiao Mei was assigned a job as a clerk in a Chinese herbal store in a neighboring small town. Aunt Zhen told me that the day I left Yiyang for my new job in Zhongzhou, Xiao Mei screamed and cried for hours. She was questioning why all the good things happened to me, yet she got nothing. I was very happy she finally had a job. After years of suffering as a Society Youth, she deserved this job, especially since she had been very interested in herbal medicine for years.

The government had offered Xiao Mei the job without Aunt Zhen using any social connections or under-the-table bribes. It turned out that my parents had exerted influence from outside China. After I came to the US, I learned that in the late spring of 1971, after Canada and China had established resident diplomatic missions, my mother wrote to the embassy of the People's Republic of China in Canada. My mother claimed my father had a heart abnormality and that his condition was deteriorating. It was his wish to see his two daughters, and he asked for the Chinese government's help. The request was accompanied with pictures of my father in a doctor's office. To their surprise, the embassy replied (June 15, 1971) with never-before-seen courtesy asking for more information regarding my father's job status, his hospital stay in the US, and details related to his departure from China. They also asked for their two daughters' current address, so that they could work with our local government in China. Mother immediately provided all the necessary information. At this time the relationship between China and America was still sketchy. So, instead of granting us passports to leave China, they assigned Xiao Mei a job and delayed their decision.

Nixon's Visit to China

Our company was waiting for the new equipment to arrive, and so there was very little for us to do. Without any supervision from above, we didn't feel like we were working enough to earn our keep and so decided to try and contribute. We bought some books to untangle the theory of semi-conductors. The books overwhelmed us. The abstruse theory of semi-conductors was too far removed from our basic Physics knowledge. Besides, there were no driving forces to motivate us to chew over the details of a complicated scientific book. For many years, science wasn't even mentioned in the general population and especially among intellectuals. It was thought to be "academic excellence with poor political behavior" (只专不红, *Zhǐ zhuān bù hóng*). I was accused of *Zhǐ zhuān bù hóng* by Mr. Ding when I was in high school.

Our female cadres spent most of their time chit-chatting. They were uneducated housewives who had become construction workers. Gossip was their way of life. When Mr. Hua or Mr. Hsu appeared, they would flirt with and flatter their bosses. They would beguile them with seductive small-talk, simpering, pouting, and purring. Sometimes filthy and sexual words gushed out from their mouths without first passing through their brain. Apparently entertaining their bosses was their "holy responsibility." For older, married women, it was acceptable to joke using filthy and sexual words.

The middle-aged, married male cadres paid a lot of attention to us, the three young girls. While we cooked our lunch in the kitchen, the courtyard next to the kitchen would be full of middle-aged men, including Mr. Hua, the secretary of the Communist Party for our company. They offered helping hands and loved to chat with us. They relied on their married status to freely offer us their "brotherly care." Yet those unmarried young boys could only admire us from afar. They sometimes made excuses to remain longer while we were in the workshop. When they overheard that we wanted to read so-and-so book, the next day that book would be handed to us in a polite manner.

Young boys and young girls were not expected to show any affection in public. In fact, no one should show affection in public. It would be considered frivolous. Spontaneous love and dating between a young boy and a young girl were taboo in this twisted society, especially after the government announced a new policy that people were not allowed to marry until they reached the age of 25. Jealous of our youthfulness and envious of our higher education, the female cadres always kept a watchful eye on us. We answered their calls, obeyed their orders, but kept them at a respectful distance. When everybody in our newly formed semi-conductor company was idle, we became lucky loungers at ease with no qualms.

Near the end of the year, our company had received all the purchased equipment from the Yantai Semi-conductor Company. The welding furnace was placed on the third floor and the diffusion furnace on the second floor. The first floor was for testing the final products and processing silicon semi-conductor wafers. The fourth floor was the office for Mr. Hua. Ling was assigned to the testing group, Orchid helped with diffusion operation, and I was allocated to the welding workshop. The diffusion and welding operations required three shifts; the three of us would work in different workshops on different work shifts, as needed.

The wafers were cut into circular, thin pieces. They were less than 1 inch in diameter and smoothed by hand polishing. It was so primitive compared to the current semi-conductor industry. Our female cadres would take charge of this manual work. It was a privilege if you were promoted from a construction labor worker to a semi-conductor worker. Since they had very little schooling, they recognized that it was out of the question for them to operate the expensive newly purchased equipment. However, these uneducated cadres were our bosses. It was as if we were back in a traditional, feudalistic Chinese society where they were the mothers-in-law and we were the daughters-in-law. They would nitpick everything we did.

We spent our spare time reading books and listening to a short-wave radio that Ling had brought to the factory. Late one night, I was reading *Who Is to Blame* (谁之罪) by Alexander Herzen, and Orchid was reading *The Gadfly* (牛虻) by E.L. Voynich. These days we had started to tiptoe into foreign books and found they were interesting and romantic. In modern revolutionary Chinese novels of the time, heroes were heroes and villains were villains; everything was black and white. They were uninspiring. But these foreign books exploited the feelings of real human beings. Love and hate were described in the context of their intricate, complex social life. The books depicted the tragic relationships between the characters who seemed to be real, living human beings. Sometimes it struck a responsive chord with us.

Ling was listening to the short-wave radio under her padded bed quilt, even though this was prohibited. Suddenly, she jumped when the radio announced that Lin Biao's airplane had crashed in Mongolia. It was a huge shock to discover that Lin Biao had been killed. Immediately afterwards a rumor spread like wildfire suggesting that Lin Biao had attempted to assassinate Mao. Initially we were delighted that Lin Biao had been killed. We always lumped Lin Biao and Jiang Qing together and thought of them as modern-day villains. We were long tired of his continuous flattering of Mao. We hated to be forced to shout out his quotations praising Mao as God-like. I disdained him for his deification of Mao. Now I had a different opinion of him — a brave soul who unfortunately didn't succeed.

There were evening meetings every night. Our cadres repeated the government version of the Lin Biao event. They were dumbfounded too. They didn't know how to elaborate. They had to be careful using words. They showed no particular feeling toward the entire event. They didn't display any excitement, but were restrained in describing the fall of Lin Biao. All their statements were quoted from the *People's Daily*. After all, Lin Biao had been designated as Mao's official successor and Mao's "closest comrade-in-arms."

After the Lin Biao event, strangely but clearly, the political wind calmed down. I went back home for Chinese New Year celebration. Uncle Nian was home too. He was no longer blabbing about my parents coming home to contribute to our motherland. He had learned his lesson the hard way. We had our usual ancestor worship ritual. The Four Olds were reborn again and lived well. In the public eye Chairman Mao was God; but in everyone's heart, their ancestors still held commanding status. Just before I left home, there was inconceivable news. The news was especially exciting for us, a foreign connected family. It was revealed that President Nixon was visiting China. Our supreme leader, Chairman Mao, shook hands with Nixon, the President of the United States, an imperialist country, our number one enemy! Zhou Enlai seemed to have played an important role in the event.

Hope inside me was revived. The flame to get out of China had reignited again. Although I had a job, my experience in high school made me feel like a *Tong Yang Xi* (童养媳).[17] I was careful with each step I took. These days I freaked out so easily, like a frightened bird (惊弓之鸟). My family background and the rough, uneven road of my young life made me feel small and inferior to others. The intricate, complex workplace scared me. I was a nervous wreck. Unlike Ling and Orchid who dared to speak up, dared to enjoy whatever was presented to them, I always hesitated to be out-of-step with anything and always worried about stepping on other people's toes and causing trouble. As the old saying goes, "You can't please all of the people all of the time." I was living in fear.

The capricious political currents, and the female cadres — snakes in the grass — had kept the spark of leaving China alive in my heart. No one knew my thoughts, not even my best friends Ling and Orchid. Obviously, my parents were tremendously excited by Nixon's China visit. Mother's letters flowed frequently. Even Father wrote me for the first time and told me that we would see each other soon. Father had become a diehard Republican. He campaigned hard for Nixon's reelection. After I came to the US, my American-born sister told me that Father handed out campaign leaflets door-to-door during Nixon's reelection, which he had never done before in his life. While my parents had high hopes, we still lived in the dark. After Nixon's visit, no additional official news was given to the Chinese people.

Our semi-conductor company endeavor utterly failed. Not a single diode passed the test. We were waiting for the highest instructions from

---

[17] 童养媳–*Tong Yang Xi*: girl adopted into a family as a future daughter-in-law while at the same time treating her as a servant.

above. We were all idle again. It seemed I lived during a calm, quiet time. Life, like water in a creek, slowly, gently seeped onwards, but I felt an onrushing surge of emotion in my heart, a whirlpool of boiling water that had no place to vent itself. I had a hope. I hoped I could leave China and go to America. I was in fear. I feared I couldn't get out of China. And at the same time, I was fearful of leaving China. Sometimes I felt hopeless; sometimes I was lonely and felt empty inside.

The possibility of leaving China and going to America actually forced me to quit my utopian dream and wake up to reality. Anticipating a turning point in my life and facing up to the new challenges scared me. The philosophy of being disillusioned with the human world again flickered in my mind. Fame and wealth are like floating smoke and passing clouds. Why should one fight for success? Why should one struggle for a living? One should do whatever heaven says, and be cynical as one looks at today's mighty and powerful. Again, I was chewing the Won-Done Song (好了歌) from the *Dream of the Red Chamber*.

好了歌
世人都晓神仙好，只有功名忘不了！
古今将相在何方？荒冢一堆草没了！
世人都晓神仙好，只有金银忘不了！
终朝只恨聚无多，及到多时眼闭了！

Won-Done Song
(Translated by David Hawkes)

Men all know that salvation should be won.
But with ambition won't have done, have done.
Where are the famous ones of days gone by?
In grassy graves they lie now, everyone.
Men all know that salvation should be won.
But with their riches won't have done, have done.
Each day they grumble they've not made enough.
When they've enough, it's goodnight every one!

Some days, my spirit flew so high I saw the emptiness of the world beneath me. I felt I was with divine beings. I could see all and was even able to overlook life itself from above. These conflicted emotions drove me crazy. I had no one with whom to share my emotions. I started my diary again. It was March 26, 1972. I wrote:

I hope this diary can narrate my life in this modern Prospect Garden, 大观园.[18] *I want this diary to leave traces of my youth. Some day when I have grown older and wiser, I will realize how silly I was when I open my diary and read these pages. It will be like a grown person remembering their innocent childhood.*

---

[18] *Prospect Garden 大观园* is a beautiful garden described in the novel *Dream of the Red Chamber* - 紅樓夢. A group of young people lived there under the restraints and watchful eyes of feudal traditional values, which led to a tragic end.

The Epitome of My Life

Orchid was in love. Her destiny had been set by her mother and her relatives. It had been arranged for her to marry her cousin, Li Wei, who was a young factory worker in Wenjiang. After Orchid's father passed away, Li Wei was always there helping Orchid's mother. To Orchid's mother, Li Wei was like her own son. When Orchid was in high school, the two families had already tacitly consented to the marriage of Orchid and Li Wei. They had known each other since their childhood. After dismissal of our high school and the beginning of the "up to the mountains and down to the countryside" movement, when Orchid had reached the proper age, the marriage proposal was presented to the young boy and young girl. Li Wei viewed Orchid as his younger sister and always had a tender heart for her. He was happy with the arrangement. To Orchid, it was initially just an obligation and a moral commitment. Orchid was a pragmatic person. Li Wei only had a middle school education, but he was a kind and sincere person. There was no love at first sight. This wasn't a romantic attraction or pursuit. The affection was slowly built over time through mutual trust and respect after the marriage engagement. Orchid seldom mentioned Li Wei in our conversations, but we sensed her affection for her future husband. He was her personal confidante.

Ling also had a childhood sweetheart (青梅竹马), Xin. He was a military general's son. Xin's father was an old friend of Ling's parents from the revolution period in Yan'an before the Liberation of China. The two families lived in the same privileged government compound for high officials. Ling and Xin used to play happily together during their innocent childhood. Both families thought it was a suitable marriage (门当户对) with similar family backgrounds, a match made in heaven. In their parents' conversations, there was a hint of their designated future. When Ling and

Xin were old enough to understand marriage, they assumed their future together had been laid out ahead of them.

The unprecedented Cultural Revolution destroyed both families' wonderful plan. Ling's father was condemned as a capitalist-roader. In the surging and fast-changing political storm, Xin's family, for self-preservation, had to draw clear political lines between Ling's family and themselves. Xin's father ordered Xin not to contact Ling ever again. Ling's father got wind of his old friend's betrayal and was shamed into anger. In response, he ordered all his children not to associate with Xin's family. Ling had the added sorrow of realizing that Xin's love was fleeting and couldn't even stand up to this first challenge. She felt her pride had been hurt and decided she would never see him again. Sadly, the seed of love had burned before it sprouted. Now the Cultural Revolution had started to calm down a little, Xin started writing to Ling again, but Ling was determined not to return his affection. She became sad and somewhat confused.

Spontaneous dating was considered out-of-step with Chinese traditional values. "Chasing a girl" wasn't good social morality. There was a young worker, named Yan, who relied on his Red worker's family background. He began to secretly pursue Ling. In order to get closer to Ling and win her heart, Yan took any opportunity to get close to us. He offered all sorts of help to improve our daily life and ease our workload. It could be said that "he left no stone unturned" (费尽心机).

Although he was an ambitious, yet very smooth young man, Orchid and I thought he had no chance. It was like "a toad lusting for the flesh of a swan" (癞蛤蟆想吃天鹅肉). He was aiming for the moon. He only had a middle school education. He came from a typical Red, uneducated family. In contrast, Ling came from an intellectual, high official's family. Even with the recent downfall of Ling's father, a high official's family still held privileges in the eyes of all levels of society, including Orchid and me. We thought there wasn't a common language between Yan and Ling. Sometimes, we even despised Yan and thought he was a tricky, cunning man who would do anything to achieve his goal. To our surprise, Ling fell in love with Yan. Oh, well, what did we know about love? We had grown up in a traditional feudalistic society. Yan had taken advantage of Ling during her separation from Xin. As the old saying goes: "a waterfront

246

pavilion gets the moonlight first" (近水楼台先得月). Yan had conquered Ling's heart.

Dating between Ling and Yan proceeded in secrecy. Even Orchid and I were kept in the dark. Ling often disappeared from our sight without telling us where she had gone. If we asked her, she would mumble all kinds of excuses that were difficult to believe. Ling was a gentle and soft person who never lost her temper. She was our best friend. We didn't mind her little white lies.

It was a sunny day. Orchid had gone home, and Ling was in love. Ling told me that she was going to see Pearl today. Pearl was our old classmate who lived in Zhongzhou. She was one of the original Red Guards in our classroom, and was Ling's friend. She was lame, unable to walk properly, and had crossed eyes. I loathed her during our high school years. She would always take an extra step to show her loyalty to "our supreme leader, Chairman Mao." She shouted loudest during class struggles sessions and made many false accusations about the Black Bastards — people like me. She was Mr. Ding's trusted follower and submissive lackey. She was one of the chief instigators of my personal dossier during my high school days. As well as being ugly, she was also an abusive creature and ordered us, the Black Bastards, around as if she was superior to us. Although those sad, depressing days had become a memory, I still resented her. I told myself I should try to move forward. "As time passes, let the past pass and be gone with the wind."

However, I still didn't want to associate with her, such a small, low, vulgar person. So, Ling went to see Pearl alone. I was left feeling lonely and unwanted in the dim attic. I wrote in my diary.

I am like a lonely boat, floating on a vast sea toward a desolate island; no one needs me. I hope that Orchid and Ling enjoy the hot spring of love and have a happy life. Yet I don't know what love is. The only thing I know is that people wear masks and deceive each other. I will say good-bye to you soon. The lonely boat will sail to a place that even I don't know.

I was in my own world, immersed in my own pitiful life, sighing lost feelings toward the whole world. It could be said: "a young person doesn't know the true meaning of sorrow; for the sake of composing a new poem, he forces himself to be sad" (少年不知愁滋味，为赋新诗强说愁). I was a 24-year-old young woman, a lost soul, searching for the meaning of life. Looking back, I was moaning about an imaginary illness (无病呻吟).

Suddenly a call came from the downstairs courtyard. Lao Yu was looking for Ling. Lao Yu was the truck driver for our company. He had promised Ling he would give her a ride home if he had a business trip to Wenjiang. Ling knew there was a possibility that Lao Yu might look for her today. Ling went to Pearl's place in the early morning. Now it was almost lunchtime, yet she still hadn't returned. I thought it would be a good opportunity for Ling to have a free ride home and vacation for a day or two. Although I would be lonely, it would be good for Ling to see her family again.

I rode Lao Yu's truck and went to Pearl's home looking for Ling. Ling wasn't there. Pearl said Ling hadn't visited today. Ling had told me she didn't feel well yesterday and might go to the hospital to visit a doctor. I told Lao Yu to drive to our local hospital. While we were passing the Culture Palace, I suddenly realized that Ling might have lied to me. I felt insulted and betrayed. *For Pete's sake, I am your best friend. Why do you lie to me?* I told Lao Yu to stop looking for her and go back home. Later Ling returned and, after my questioning, told me the truth. She had been with Yan all day. I was annoyed, but I had to help her cover up. I told Lao Yu and others that I had been mixed up and that Ling was actually visiting another friend. I felt the whole episode had been so silly and laughable.

While I was with my close friends, I would often discuss current events, and expound upon the dynasties of Chinese history. I would keep up a torrential flow of words brimming with wit and humor. Yet in front of others, I had always been viewed as aloof. I was quiet and said nothing. I would keep my distance. I was nervous and afraid of upsetting people. As people say, "Even if you don't have an ugly nose, people still gossip about you." If you are nice, people think you are tricky; if you are straightforward, people criticize you for being nasty; if you are kind and pure, people say you must be stupid. People like to gossip.

Some of my older coworkers praised me for being educated, reasonable, and refined, but a few criticized me as arrogant, self-important, and tricky. Many people treated me differently from Orchid and Ling simply because my parents resided in the US. They were cold toward me. I became a crazy person afraid of everything. I wasn't the type to flatter or change direction with the wind and attach myself to powerful and influential people. By nature, I was a straightforward, upright person. Such a person cannot survive in this society. After I heard these rumors and falsehoods, I became apprehensive. It was a jungle there. During those times, I wanted to leave that twisted place and immediately go to America where I would explore and start a new life. I could pursue my "land of eternal peace far from the madding crowd" (世外桃源), even though I didn't have the faintest idea of life in America.

At night, I expressed my feelings to Ling. Ling encouraged me to be daring, not a softy. She said, "As the old saying goes, 'People are afraid of ferocity, ghosts are afraid of evil' (人怕凶鬼怕恶). Let them know you are not so easygoing and cannot be taken for granted."

Ling said we all should learn from Orchid. Orchid was frank and open in nature. She possessed a straightforward temperament combined with a hint of shrewdness. But my upbringing, my Black family background, would not allow me to be like her. I smiled at Ling and tears welled up in my eyes.

I said, "I can't be her. Worry and fear will always be part of my life."

Ling blamed me. "You always worry about this, worry about that. You would rather crawl into your coffin early and rest in peace than live your life."

Ling was right. Why should I treat everything so seriously? I should take one day at a time, live for today. Ling and I kept talking until the middle of the night.

The next day, we woke up late. The night before, Ling and I had agreed that we should get up early and go to Pearl's house to borrow her scissors and sewing stuff. I was planning to make a shirt for myself. Afterwards, we planned to go to the market and buy fresh vegetables for lunch. Oh, well, we were a lazy bunch. We were too late. We started teasing each other as we lay in bed.

I said, "Yan is calling you."

"How come I didn't hear it?" Ling tried to listen to the call from downstairs.

I was giggling. "I am just kidding!"

Ling opened my mosquito net and threatened me. "Let me teach you a lesson for teasing me."

Right away, I covered my head with the bed quilt, leaving a slit open to look at Ling. I was laughing. "I am a little bunny in a cave."

Ling shouted, "Little frightened bunny carefully examining its surroundings! A slight movement of grass in a light wind would make her jump with fear." She was making fun about our chat last night.

I lamented, "That is the epitome of my life."

Ling was also feeling despondent. She had lost a lot of weight recently. She told me love wasn't as sweet as it should be. Sometimes it frightened her; she felt uneasy, unsettled.

She said, "in the eye of the beholder he is always perfect" (情人眼里出西施), but this was only half true. I can see all the faults in Yan. But in the end, the mystery of love has wiped away all his faults."

Ling was the nicest person I had ever known. She was gentle and kind toward me. If I had been born a man, I would have been a competitor of Yan. She was often carried away by her emotions, but she was also sometimes light-hearted. As her stepbrother once said, Ling was the "odd, abnormal child" of their family and this society. She came from a bright Red family, yet she was the ugly stepchild.

I worried for Ling. I hoped no one would take advantage of Ling's weaknesses. I didn't want her sprouting love to end in tragedy, or follow in the footsteps of her aunt (her biological mother). At the same time, I admired Ling's courage. She dared to break out from social restraints — those hypocritical etiquettes and feudal codes. People should choose their own lifestyle, their own road through life by following their own beliefs and their own likes. Sadly, in this twisted, "modern communist, yet thousands-of-years-old feudal" society, we were not allowed to do what we liked. We were doomed to suffer. I wanted to believe that people like Ling, a happy soul, would not meet with misfortune. God willing, let her be happy. Bless all of us with love.

In the end we did go to Pearl's place. During the afternoon, I cut the fabric for my new shirt and did some chores. Night was approaching, and the misty evening evoked strange, mysterious feelings. Ling had gone out with Yan again. Yan had taken away my only companion. I secretly protested, but was powerless. They were immersed in a raging love. They had been carried away by a mighty torrent of emotion that nothing could stop.

After receiving my father's letter, the possibility of stepping into a different life had increased for me, at least I hoped so. Thinking of parting with my best friends Ling and Orchid made me sad. I contemplated a song:

当我离开可爱的故乡，
你想不到我是多么悲伤。
我象鸽子一样，四处飞翔.

When I left my lovely hometown,
You couldn't imagine how sad I was;
I was like a dove, flying around alone.

My mind was drifting, floating everywhere. I wrote,

Someday, I might leave my hometown to a far, far away place. I would drift and wander in a foreign land like a rolling stone. I worry about my future; I am afraid of loneliness. Sorrow, anxiety, and hope are bottled up inside me; but I want to believe my future will be bright. Even if the future is not so beautiful, I would rather live in a dreamland; it is tough to live in reality. Even if I live at the other end of the world, I will dare to experience it. I will not seek success, but will look forward to taste 'life and death,' 'war and peace,' all kinds of life in a foreign land.

I tried to encourage myself. I forced myself to study English, but I possessed so little. The only thing I remembered from my English class was: "Long Live Chairman Mao," "Long Live the Communist Party." Nevertheless, I couldn't focus on anything. I hated myself for being absent-minded all the time. I wished I could remain calm and not become tangled in these boundless, endless, yet unhelpful thoughts. Orchid once said that since she left high school, she hadn't been able to spend one minute focused on studying. Orchid and I promised each other to revisit the subject of English. She blamed our lack of focus on all the disturbances in our life. I felt we had evolved from innocent high school students into complicated human beings entangled in a self-weaved web.

As I became more and more immersed in self-pity, Ling and Yan suddenly arrived in our little attic. The unexpected appearance of Yan made me feel awkward. I quickly hid my diary under my pillow and politely welcomed him. Shortly after, another young worker, Hai, called us as he was climbing up the bamboo ladder. Hai was, like us, a young high school graduate. He was a shy, bookworm-like young man. He was about our age and wore a pair of eyeglasses. He seemed to always be trying to be friends with us. He told us he had come to borrow a book. When he saw Yan, he left after a short stay. Yan was very pleasant. All we talked about was sheer nonsense, of no importance, but he made sure nothing he said offended me. It was 9 o'clock and we went to the train station to meet Orchid. Orchid didn't show up. She had probably been reluctant to leave her fiancé.

Play Safe, Seek Only to Avoid Blame

明哲保身 但求无过

The next day we again had nothing to do at our workplace. Feeling worried and guilty, I said to Ling, "We are getting paid for doing nothing. It might cause gossip among those malicious mouths."

Ling exclaimed, "We are not to blame. It is God given. Let's enjoy as much as we can."

I felt somewhat overwhelmed by this "gracious favor" from God. Chang Gong, a middle-aged married man, was in charge of the company's purchases. He came from a Gray family. He was also bothered by a guilty conscience. He said, "Let's clean up this place." In the morning we spent most of our time cleaning the windows, mopping the floor, and wiping tables and chairs. Chang Gong was a very smooth person who joked around and tried to please everyone. Once I recited a couplet to him:

摩擦系数零点零零, 滑得要死.
So smooth; friction coefficient is 0.00

曲率半径处处相等, 圆得要命.
So round; the radius of curvature is equal everywhere.

He laughed and hinted that we should all try to be this kind of person.

Two weeks earlier, my sister Xiao Mei had visited me at my work. I had been assigned to the second shift and was thinking to take Xiao Mei sightseeing to Plum Flower Park. However, Xiao Mei wanted to see my workplace. That morning, I took her to tour the welding workshop on the third floor, where I normally worked. Mrs. Fong was there. She was on the first shift. Mrs. Fong was a former high school graduate and an original office worker for the company. She possessed years of seniority over us. She was the leader of our welding group and my unofficial mentor. Mrs. Fong welcomed Xiao Mei and seemed very happy to see her. She showed genuine concern regarding my sister's stay in Zhongzhou. I always had reservations about Mrs. Fong, but after seeing her being so nice to my sister, I blamed myself for being too suspicious. Xiao Mei only stayed two days, and then returned home.

Afterwards, to my surprise, Mr. Hua called me to his office and told me that it was improper to bring an outside person to our workshop. I couldn't believe it. Mrs. Fong had stabbed me in the back. She could have told me not to bring anyone to the workshop while my sister was visiting. She was so vindictive, a "witch on wheels." When Mrs. Fong and I met again in the workshop, she was all smiles and asked whether my sister had liked my workplace. I was sick of this two-faced, deceitful person. I was cold to her and refused to speak.

Chang Gong was there, and later he asked me what had happened between Mrs. Fong and me. I told Chang Gong that, behind my back, Mrs. Fong reported to Mr. Hua that my sister had visited the workshop. I told him that I didn't understand why she treated me so poorly. I had always respected her and never wronged her. Why couldn't she be a little kinder to people?

He advised me to be a little bit "round" and said, "When you meet any person, enemy or a friend, you should always greet them with a 'Hi,' and flatter them with a few kind words." He continued, "Harbor no ill intentions against others, but never relax vigilance against evildoers" (害人之心不可有，防人之心不可无). To her face you should enshrine Mrs. Fong like a Buddha, but behind her back guard against her as if she was a thief." He added, "When you have been wronged, you should give up your hatred because it just destroys you inside. You say okay, no problem."

I laughed. "What an Ah-Q spirit!"

Chang Gong was a wise man. Nowadays, there were many wise men around. A lot of people held the philosophy of "be worldly-wise: play safe and seek only to avoid blame" (明哲保身 但求无过). It was a product of the Cultural Revolution. I found it difficult to be a person you weren't, but, in this dynasty, you must grind yourself to be round.

After the cleanup, I stayed alone in the workshop on the third floor reading a book. Hai came up with a book in hand and asked me whether he could read it in my workshop. I said, "Of course." What could I say? It was not my private room. It was a workshop. We sat quietly, many feet apart, reading our books. I sensed his unspoken motive. I made an excuse and went downstairs to Ling's testing workshop. I shouldn't encourage his wishful thinking. I also couldn't afford to upset anyone. Under all the watchful eyes, any little innocent encounter between a young man and a young woman would stir up gossip and criticism. I continued to loaf around in the testing workshop until morning had passed.

When lunchtime came, Orchid returned from Wenjiang. Ling and I were excited and happy to see her. Orchid claimed she brought the radiance and charm of spring to our little attic. She carried her youthful vigor with her. She warned Ling and me that we were an aging, feeble, emotional, pessimistic pair. We all laughed heartily.

In the afternoon a company meeting was called, as we faced an urgent problem: the failure of our product! We all joined the discussion and gave our opinions and suggestions. However, at the end of the meeting, the problem remained unsolved. Making a simple diode was too much of a stretch for our newly formed Red Flag Semi-conductor Company. Mr. Hua was contemplating sending out a team for further training.

After the meeting, there was nothing for us to do, so we snuck off to the market to buy some rice. Unfortunately, we were caught by one of our female cadres, Mrs. Yang. From her facial expression, she wasn't very happy with us, but didn't scold us. She told us to hurry up so that we could go to a district meeting. The meeting was to expose and denounce the "516 elements — the new class enemies" (五一六分子). By this time, we had become accustomed to these class struggle sessions. These so-called 516 class enemies were irrelevant and disconnected from us. At this time, the atmosphere wasn't as fierce or brutal as it had been during the beginning of the Cultural Revolution. We slept through the meeting. On the political stage, we had become "the backward elements" (落后分子).

The Forbidden Love

These days, Ling had become so confused. Xin requested to meet Ling on April 5th to have a heart-to-heart talk. Xin was now a young military officer in Shanghai. He was planning to take a train to Zhongzhou just to meet with Ling. Ling didn't know what to do. She showed his letter to me. I felt very sorry for Xin. I used to despise those military generals' sons and thought them to be arrogant, spoiled brats. From Xin's letter, he seemed to be a gentle, nice person. He was deeply in love with Ling. It was so regrettable. Such an innocent, pure love had been destroyed by the Cultural Revolution and their stale, backward parents.

Ling blamed the whole thing on Xin. Ling's feeling toward Xin had faded away. Lured by daily sweet talk, Ling was now falling in love with Yan, who was always so close. I teased Ling, that she was "forsaking the old for the new" (弃旧图新). Ling didn't like my comment. She was angry with me. She told me I was playing games with her, while she considered me her confidant. She was angry that I insulted her morals. Oh, well, she was in a bad mood, so I decided to be careful what I said in the future.

While we were talking, Ling's sister called to let her know that her father was sick and needed Ling home at once. Ling told us in secrecy that tomorrow was her father's sixtieth birthday. Her family planned to celebrate her father's birthday together. As I grew up in China, I didn't even know my exact birthdate. I only knew I had been born during the Pig Year of 1947. My age was determined by the Chinese calendar. After each Chinese New Year, I became one year older. After I arrived in America, my parents told me my exact birth date. In our family in China we never celebrated anyone's birthday, even for Grandmother. Celebration of a birthday was only for the very few in China. That night Orchid and I went to the train station to see Ling off. The three of us were inseparable. The train station was only a half mile away, so we always walked each other to the train or bus stations.

On the way back, Orchid asked me, "Now that only you are left, any thoughts? Li Wei once told me that marriage isn't just seeking a husband or wife. In this society, we all need a confidant, someone to lean on. Living alone in this society will be tough and lonely."

She was hinting at my prospects for future marriage. I said, "I never think of this."

I pondered, *How can I think about where my life voyage will take me? I don't even know where I will land. Will I remain on this side of the Pacific Ocean or cross to the other?*

I had always looked down on marriage and viewed it as a major turning point for a woman from a broad road to a narrow alley, a self-destructive process and the first step toward mundanity. Of course, I couldn't tell Orchid everything I was thinking about marriage. They would snigger at me and accuse me of being an impractical and overly ambitious person. I preferred to experience life alone until my nose had been flattened by all the obstacles, or there was no road left to follow, then I could let fate decide where I really belonged. I might end up being single, remaining in my boudoir all my life.

I had never really known my grandfather. Uncle Nian had only stayed home a couple of weeks a year. Grandmother and Aunt Zhen had lived without husbands most of their lives. Mr. Chang, an elementary school teacher who lived across from us in Yiyang, had not spoken to his wife since the anti-rightist movement. During the anti-rightist movement, he was falsely accused of having an affair with Wu Mei's aunt, who was also a schoolteacher. His wife made a huge fuss about it. I remember when we moved to Dayin Lane, they were a loving couple. Sometimes, I had seen him comb his wife's hair. They had five children together. After the anti-rightist movement, even though he was cleared of the marital affair, he never put an eye on his wife again. They still lived under same roof, but he couldn't forgive his wife for her betrayal. I didn't see the sweetness of marriage.

Ling once told me, "Love is a dirty word. Marriage is a forbidden topic for us young girls. Until you meet a man who becomes your only comfort and reliance; a person you can trust without limit such that you become inseparable; until that time, all this celibate talk is meaningless." I had no reason to deny Ling. She might well be right. How did I know?

Ling had told us she would stay home for only one day and would return the following evening at 8 o'clock via the number 303 train. We went to the station to greet Ling. The number 303 train arrived without her. We wondered if she had missed the train. Late that night, Ling eventually showed up. She had told us a white lie. The train had arrived later than 8 o'clock. We guessed that Yan greeted her at the train station and they had snuck away together. Since then, Ling always returned around 10 o'clock at night. The people at our company had seen Yan and Ling together walking on the street. Some had become suspicious that they were dating. During the workshop meeting, Yan's boss asked Yan directly. Yan totally denied any interaction besides the normal coworker relationship. He stated there was nothing going on between them. But Ling's heart already belonged to Yan.

April 5th was the Qingming Festival day. Branches of tender, green willow were hung on every family's door. It was the ghosts' holiday. It was overcast and drizzling.

I couldn't help asking, "Why is it always raining on Qingming Festival day?"

Orchid said, "Today is the ghosts' holiday. It is not a day for humans to be happy. We humans, in memory of the dead, are supposed to be sad. This is why heaven is crying."

I argued, "Not everyone is sad today. Some are sad, but some are happy."

"Maybe it is due to the seasonal climate," Orchid replied.

While Orchid and I were chatting, we noted that Ling was very quiet. She seemed sad and preoccupied. Orchid and I started a new topic: *Dreams*. We hoped Ling would join the conversation.

Orchid said, "If you have a terrible day, then you will have a good dream during the night; but if you have a happy day, then you will have a horrible dream that night."

I laughed. "You are so naive. God will not be so kind to equalize everything for you. Good and bad can't be perfectly balanced. Everyone has his or her own standard of *happy* or *not happy*. For example, if you are content with what you have, then you will be happy. On the other hand, if you are never satisfied with what you possess, then you will never be happy. God always gives more to those who have everything, but takes away from those who have nothing. So, I think people whose life is loving and comfortable will have sweet dreams. Conversely, if you have had a rough day, you probably will have a bad dream that night. As the old saying goes, "What you think about in the day, you will dream of at night" (日有 所思，夜有所梦).

After saying all these things, Orchid and I looked at each other and suddenly burst into laughter. What silly talk, sheer nonsense! During all of this, Ling never said a word. Orchid and I looked at each other and wondered what was going on in Ling's head. Soon after, our gatekeeper called Ling from downstairs and informed her that a young man was asking for her. Xin was waiting at the gate.

"No wonder Ling was preoccupied," Orchid and I said to ourselves suddenly realizing the reason for her silence.

Today was April 5th. Xin had told Ling in his letter he would come to see her today. After less than half an hour, Ling returned with tears welling up in her eyes. She had just rejected Xin and was sad and conflicted. Love hurt. It's like a bottle of mixed spices — sour, sweet, bitter, and hot. Ling declared she was perfectly happy without Xin. For Yan, it was like drinking a glass of wine. Regardless of whether sweet or bitter, she must drink it all to the last drop.

Xin had bought a small pocket radio for Ling who refused to accept it. Xin left the small radio with the gatekeeper, asking him to give it to Ling. Only military officers were typically allowed to own a small pocket radio. Luckily for Orchid and me, this allowed us to take English lessons and listen to the Model Operas such as *The Legend of the Red Lantern* and *Red Detachment of Women*.

Ling and Yan used to often sneak into Plum Flower Park for their quiet, romantic times together. To avoid the eyes of coworkers, they normally walked through the alleys and roads behind Plum Flower Park. Lately they had become braver and sometimes even ventured onto the main roads.

Orchid and I always loved to second-guess Yan, but Ling seemed to always trust and accommodate him. While we both appreciated Ling's soft temperament and unlimited patience, we were worried she was making unnecessary sacrifices. Orchid and I agreed that Ling would be a wonderful wife, but she would be like a candle — brightening others yet destroying herself.

I commented, "Even between husband and wife, if the east wind does not suppress the west wind, then the west wind must suppress the east wind."

Orchid disagreed. "I would never climb above someone, but also I would never allow anyone to control me. Even between husband and wife, we should have mutual respect."

"Mutual respect should start with self-respect," I replied.

Even Orchid and I, Ling's best friends, started talking behind her back. Afterwards we self-confessed that we belonged to the ancient, feudal 18th century. Who were we to judge others? The people around us were not so kind and forgiving. Rumors and slanders were spreading and flying among our coworkers. Criticisms started with our female cadres, who seemed to place the blame solely on Ling. "A daughter of a high official should have a bright future ahead of her, yet she is acting frivolously and vainly. A young lady who follows a man all over the place. What a scandal! Whatever next?"

One of the young girls, Xiang, informed us about the situation and suggested we talk some sense into Ling. Orchid and I were initially angry with all these nosy, gossiping female cadres. "What a bunch of evil, insidious, vicious witches! Very soon Ling will be 25 years old, the government-sanctioned age for marriage. Ling and Yan just walked together. They didn't even touch hands. What's wrong with these good-for-nothing cadre comrades?"

We were sympathetic toward Ling and angry with the female cadres. Mostly we felt a bitter hatred toward these stale, backward, so-called bosses, who used double-standards to judge people. "The fox mourns over the death of the hare; all beings grieve their fellow beings" (兔死狐悲 物伤其类). We were worried for Ling. We wanted to warn her, but were afraid we might hurt her feelings. Ling was already annoyed with me for my earlier comment, "forsaking the old for the new" (弃旧图新). That night, Ling came home late again. Orchid and I had already gone to bed before she came home.

Feeling perplexed, I drifted to sleep and started to dream. The three of us were standing on the lawn in front of our third-grade classroom building. We were students in our high school again. We were taking pictures. While I was taking a picture of Ling and Orchid, a ray of light shone onto their faces. I was trying to adjust the lens, when suddenly someone grabbed the camera from me and said, "Let me take the picture of them." It was Yan, but he seemed to look like Hai. Then we returned to our classroom. Ling was sitting in front of me and said, "A person hanged herself right where you are sitting." Not knowing why, the place suddenly became our little attic! I became very scared. In front of me it was all dark and a ghostly chill went down my spine. My heart was thumping.

Suddenly, I awoke from the nightmare. I was scared and still afraid to open my eyes in case the ghost might be standing before me. I covered my head with a quilt. I was on tenterhooks and dazed until a wisp of the morning sun shone in from the skylight. I got up and told Orchid I had just had a bad dream. I heard that if you tell people about your dream, then the dream will never become real.

Orchid said to me, "I don't know why, but I had a terrible dream too."

She continued, "Seemingly, a Cossack couple was lying in a wagon. The wife was sleeping. The bright moon shone brightly in the chilly sky. A horse was pulling the wagon quietly along."

I interrupted her and exclaimed, "You must have read *Quietly Flows the Don* (静静的顿河)!"

Orchid said, "You are right indeed."

She continued with her dream. "The wife awoke and discovered her husband was no longer with her. She became worried and anxious. She got up and was surrounded by a scene of utter desolation. The moon had faded, and all was in fearful darkness. Suddenly, three wolves jumped out from nowhere. She was scared and jumped up onto a large stone. At that moment, it seemed I became a spectator. I was flustered and felt nervous for her. She thought, maybe I was thinking, if I throw coins toward the wolves, the wolves won't climb up. She kept throwing coins to the wolves, but the wolves were throwing the coins back."

Orchid continued. "Somehow, we three suddenly replaced the Cossack wife. So much money had been thrown toward us. Throwing and receiving, now in my dream the coins became books. The wolves suddenly disappeared, and Mrs. Yang was standing in front of me asking for my books. Right away, I hid my books under my coat and ran up to our attic. 'They might search our attic!' I hurried to hide my books in Ling's big book-bag. There was a lot of noise, and hurried footsteps were approaching from downstairs. You were both sleeping. I, with all my might, drew the ladder up into our attic, then I placed the ladder through the skylight. I carried the book-bag and climbed up through the skylight and jumped down onto the street below. I was running. Seemingly, I was running on Chong Hua Road in Wenjiang. I heard coworkers enter our attic and question you about my whereabouts. You were both quiet. I was anxious. Why don't they cover up for me? At least that would slow them down a little. They discovered I had escaped and ran down the stairs chasing after me. I was running and running. Somehow, my two legs were getting weaker so that I couldn't move anymore. Suddenly, I woke up short of breath with one of my hands pressed against my chest."

Orchid, like me, had tossed and turned throughout the night and hadn't slept well at all. She said, "I couldn't believe I had such a dream. The dream is still so clear to me. It remains fresh in my mind."

I replied, "Maybe it was too hot last night."

The next morning, Orchid woke up, smiled at me, and said, "Mrs. Yang was a good person in my dream last night. Mrs. Yang and we were underground workers for the Communist Party before the Liberation of China. Mrs. Fong was a spy. All night we were playing hide and seek with Mrs. Fong, avoiding her, guarding ourselves against her."

I laughed loudly. "One will dream what one thinks during the day" (日有所思, 夜有所梦).

It was so ridiculous and absurd, talking about dreams all the time! Orchid and I kept having strange dreams, while Ling went on with her routine life. But rumors of Ling and Yan continued to run sky high. They became the main talking point among the middle-aged female workers. Even the middle-aged men started making inquiries about Ling and Yan. We became alarmed. Finally, we told Ling what Xiang had told us a few days before. Ling felt wronged and humiliated. She burst into tears from sheer helplessness. Tears ran down her cheeks. She was a Red high official's daughter and had never been insulted like this before.

263

The spring rain pattered down for days, and the cold air depressed me. In this Yangtze River Delta, a land of plenty, sunny days far exceeded rainy days. We were so used to bright sunny days that these rainy days seemed too long. I thought, *No wonder people say the sweet, calm, good, and exciting days pass unwittingly, yet during harsh, suffering days, even one day seems equivalent to a year.*

The three of us were stuck in our attic chatting. The dusky, gloomy evening came down early. Ling went down to fetch some water.

She came back and exclaimed, "Unbelievable! It is snowing. Lumps and lumps of goose feather snow are falling."

I reflected, saying, "Yesterday, I made a claim in the workshop. 'It is so cold, it might even snow tomorrow.' Chang Gong doubted my claim saying, 'Will there be **June Snow**[19]?' It turns out, I was right."

Orchid said, "For the last few years, the weather has been very abnormal and unpredictable. People get sick during this type of weather."

Ling commented, "Just as storms gather without warning in nature, people's luck can change instantly! (天有不测风云，人有旦夕祸福). These days nobody can predict anything. For example, who could have foreseen the ferry capsizing and killing many in front of the Third Textile Factory? Also, who could have imagined the collapse of the bridge in Qiyan a few days ago?"

I sighed. "Nobody can predict their own today or tomorrow. A few days ago, a man was killed by a truck. He probably never thought he would suddenly die on the street without even being able to have lunch with his family. As people say, 'Today people talk about the short-lives of others; tomorrow it could be they who die on the street.' (今日笑人寿命短，明日自己街头亡). People should be content with what they have today and enjoy

---

[19] **June Snow** is a reference to a play - 《窦娥冤》or《六月雪》. It tells of a woman, Dou, who is falsely accused and framed of murder. The officials decide to execute her, but on the day of her execution she exclaims, 'I was falsely accused; to prove this injustice, snow will fall today from heaven'. After her execution, snow did indeed fall; it was in June. June snow is such a strange phenomenon that heaven appeared to be confirming her innocence. Since then, June snow is described as an impossible phenomenon.

their lives. No need to be 'geese and chickens fighting each other' (鸡争鹅斗) for a lifetime asking for trouble."

The conversation jumped from one thing to another, but we all sighed as if we were worldly wise old men who knew it all.

A ray of bright sunlight suddenly burst through our skylight. The overnight snow had finally given way to the long-missed sun. We were suddenly in high spirits and were feeling happy and gay. Since the day when we mentioned the rumors to Ling, Yan and she hadn't spent time alone together. That morning, Orchid and I were in my workshop chatting.

Yan came up and smiled, "Looks like you guys have nothing to do. Bored? I am going to the storage house to fetch wafers. Do you want to come with me?"

"Sure!" We accepted the invitation.

We also sensed that Yan hoped we would also invite Ling to come along, but we didn't. We acted as if we were two dimwits — dumb and insensible.

On the way back, Yan said to me, "I have heard you would like to learn to ride a bike. This evening I will leave my bike here for you to use tomorrow. Plum Flower Park has lots of broad, paved roads. It is a good place to learn to ride."

Before I said a word, Orchid enthusiastically answered for me, "Tomorrow should be a nice day. I will teach you."

The next day was a bright spring day. It was Sunday, our off-day. All three of us got up early. For many days we had been stuck in our suffocating, small, no-room-to-turn-around attic. Walking in Plum Flower Park, we realized that spring had already arrived: the pink peach blossoms were shadowed by the tender green swaying willows. The fragrance of all the blooming flowers was accompanied by the spring birds happily singing. There was more red than green in the park. Spring was in the air and in front of our eyes.

Although Tianyun Temple and Plum Flower Park were totally destroyed during the "destroy the four olds" movement and the pavilions and the Wenbi Pagoda were still in shambles, nature had risen up to embellish the park. Plum Flower Park was a garden permeated with the charms of springtime. In between the woods and the lakeside, old men could be seen practicing Tai Chi and doing their morning exercises.

Suddenly the world of noise, the worries in people's daily life seemed to have disappeared with the wind. The calm and tranquility made me feel like I was flying in a heavenly scene.

Love couples were immersed in their romantic moments. Their heads lowered; their eyes fixed on the pavement; they quietly expressed their love for one another. Even this "words-only" dating was unacceptable to their parents and to society. However, on this beautiful spring morning in Plum Flower Park, nobody seemed bothered by what others were doing.

Soon, as Orchid and I anticipated, Yan appeared. I sensed Ling and Yan wanted to spend some time alone together. I was tactful and said, with a meaningful glance to Orchid, "Could you teach me to ride?"

Orchid understood me perfectly and replied, "Of course!"

Orchid pushed the bike, and together we walked ahead, leaving Ling and Yan far behind. Orchid and I smiled to each other, "Let these two love-birds be carried away together!"

I was utterly useless regarding any physical exercise. I was so clumsy and continuously fell from the bike. Orchid kept helping to balance the bike, yet I kept falling off! I lost all confidence and, by 10 o'clock, became very tired and suddenly felt really hungry. I suggested to Orchid, "Let's go to the park cafe, and have some food."

We pushed the bike to the cafe. As we sat in the cafe eating, Ling and Yan soon arrived. After we finished eating, Yan rode his bike home and we leisurely walked back toward the Red Flag Semi-conductor Company. During the evening, Ling went out alone. I was so tired, and my two legs ached after my bike-riding attempts. It was an exceptionally quiet spring evening, and Orchid and I went to bed early.

I Want to Live According to My Own Ability!

The news that we remained in Zhongzhou and were working at the Red Flag Semi-conductor Company had spread among our classmates. One morning, to my surprise, Mei Qin visited us. Mei Qin was my sworn enemy during my high school years, but she didn't realize I held such negative feelings toward her. In our high school, it was a one-way street. Only the Reds — people like Mei Qin — were allowed to abuse the Blacks. The Blacks didn't dare show any resentment toward the Reds. Even though you clenched your teeth and loathed them, you still had to bite your lip, bow your head, and abide the insults. In her eyes, we, the Blacks, shouldn't have any feelings. Mei Qin's visit reminded me of those horrors and those sad days. The wound in my heart still hadn't fully recovered; it only needed a little poke and it would bleed again. I tried to tell myself to let bygones be bygones. Abiding by traditional Chinese morals, even if it was a vendetta, I should still tread the beaten track and greet her with civility.

We politely invited Mei Qin inside but with little enthusiasm. She was tanned, and her wrinkled face showed the effects of the heavy physical labor she had endured. She looked much older. Obviously, she was a little jealous of us staying in Zhongzhou, having a city job and a city Hukou. It was her dream life — a city Hukou. But fortune had rotated, her dream had been completely destroyed and she had suffered a steep decline. I started to feel sorry for her. After a short stay, Ling managed to push her out. We breathed a sigh of relief.

Soon, another classmate visited named Wong Bing, a military general's son. After hearing Yan shout out to us, "Wong Bing has come to see you," I tried to escape. Unfortunately, I ran into him, face-to-face, at the front door of our building. Wong Bing was an original Red Guard in my high school. He was a quiet, gentle person and never exerted his Red power over us. I used to admire him as he could play the flute beautifully, whereas I was desperate to learn. During the evening, before the self-study period, he sometimes played *Spring River* (春江花月夜), and I secretly wished it was me playing.

Nevertheless, now I was unwilling to deal with people like him. There wasn't a common language, only small talk. He came here to tell us he was going to university: Nanjing Educational University. After school ended, he was sent to military training, and then was assigned a teaching job. During the same period, he also attended Five-seven (五七) cadre training school and became a leader of the Communist Youth League. Lucky for him, he had it all! He was tirelessly bragging his success. It spared us the necessity to speak. Obviously, we couldn't be mentioned in the same breath. Vanity and vulgarity had carried him far above his head, and he was walking on air. I couldn't believe that such a nice boy had become such a fortune-grabbing fool, full of philistine points of view. I almost said, "Be careful! The bigger you are, the harder you fall."

Soon we were surrounded by a throng of people. Our coworkers had come out to watch the fun — a handsome young man, wearing a military uniform, visiting us. We made an excuse that we had to go back to work and finally sent this uninvited classmate on his way.

The Red Flag Semi-conductor Company was idle. We had no assignment from our bosses, and yet we had to continue our shifts and act as if we were working. We were bored to tears. Chang Gong teased us, "You guys are living a monastic life — three meals a day, a good sleep at night, a vapid life." We were wasting our lives here. We wondered what our cadres were thinking. Are we going to stay in business? I worried.

Seeing us, the younger workers, loafing around, Mr. Hua told us he was planning to send a team to Laiyang in Shandong Province for further training. Laiyang Semi-conductor Company was run by the military. As I assessed my own Black family background, it seemed very possible that I would not be chosen this time. Vanity gripped my young, eager heart. If I wasn't selected, people would look down on me. People had already distinguished between me, Ling, and Orchid. Living here would become more difficult. I worried my pride would be hurt. At the same time, I blamed myself for being so vain. Vanity and pride were imaginary and illusory things, not worth holding on to.

On the other hand, Mother wrote and asked why she couldn't send mail directly to my workplace, since the relationship between the US and China was on the mend. I couldn't tell Mother the truth. In China, the political wind could still easily change direction. Whether I would be able to eventually leave China was, in fact, far from certain. If I couldn't leave China, the consequence of receiving letters from America, an imperialist country, would be huge. My coworkers could use this to condemn me in the future. Who knows, anything could happen in this unpredictable society. Why should I remind people, "I am an American daughter"? However, from Mother's letters, things were progressing for the better. She mentioned that she had sent a letter to my hometown local Public Security Bureau to request permission for Xiao Mei and I to go to America. I didn't want to leave Zhongzhou at this time, in case something might happen regarding America. I was being swayed by considerations of gain and loss, and I agonized over my dilemma. The trip to Laiyang was still an ongoing topic. Nothing was certain yet.

The next day, our cadres held a meeting on the third floor of my workshop to discuss a document recently sent down from the central government. It indicated that all the economic sectors of China had to be reformed. It emphasized, for the first time, that our socialist system now followed "from each according to his ability, to each according to his contribution" (各尽所能，按劳取酬), instead of "from each according to his ability, to each according to his need" (各尽所能，按需分配).[20] I loafed around and finally went to Ling's testing workshop. Chang Gong was there too. From rumors, he had learned that Laiyang Semi-conductor Company was only planning to allow seven people to attend the training. This time Mr. Hua himself would lead the team. It seemed Orchid and I would go, but strangely not Ling. That night, I was torn apart and was brooding over what I should do. I oscillated between going and not going to Laiyang. I was listening to *Sha-jia Village, a modern opera* (沙家浜), and I wrote in my

---

[20] "From each according to his ability, to each according to his needs" is a slogan popularized by Karl Marx in his 1875 *Critique of the Gotha Program*. Source: Wikipedia

diary, "at this moment, I am in a dilemma" (事到如今好为难) – an aria in Sha-jia Village.

The next morning during our political study assembly, Mrs. Yang declared that today would be a cleaning day. All the workshops would be cleaned. Orchid and I were assigned to clean up the third-floor workshop. The third-floor workshop was a pigsty. Our cadres had a meeting there yesterday. Cigarette butts, peanut shells, waste paper were all over the floor. Orchid and I spent more than two hours cleaning the windows and sweeping and mopping the floor. When we had almost finished cleaning, Mr. Hua came and told us to prepare for the Laiyang trip.

"Mr. Hua, you know my family background isn't good. People may be upset when they find out you have chosen me instead of them. I don't mind letting others have this opportunity," I said to Mr. Hua without thinking carefully.

Orchid looked at me, shocked and worried. Her eyes seemed to shout out at me, "Are you nuts? Why are you doing this? You are asking for trouble!"

Luckily, Mr. Hua was in a good mood. Mr. Hua had always been extra kind to us. He didn't put on bureaucratic airs.

He said with a smile, "I know you don't want to be involved with political affairs. You don't care to judge others. You refuse to say 'yes' or 'no' on any matter and are indifferent to everything. You just want to be a nice person and not upset anyone. Everyone here has told me you are a nice person, but that isn't good enough for me."

Then he smiled again and continued, "My military commander was a goody-goody person. We used to be fond of him."

Mr. Hua loved talking about his military life. He indicated to us he was also that type of goody-goody person. We got the hint that he had been extremely nice to us. We listened to his story respectfully. In the end, he agreed with me and thought I made a good point. He said he would think about it and might let Ling go to Laiyang. Orchid wanted me to go. She didn't understand that there was a hidden reason behind my request. She insisted that I was the most suitable one for the trip.

Orchid said to me, "Be careful what you wish for."

In the evening, we had a company meeting to pass on the essence of the central government's five-year plan. Mr. Hua mentioned the names of many company cadres. To our surprise, he pointed out there was room for improvement from these cadres. Wow, Mr. Hua wasn't a goody-goody person after all.

Over the last few days, I had developed a toothache and it was getting worse. In the morning, while I was at my workshop, it was so painful. I returned to our attic, took two pain pills and went to bed. Around 1 o'clock I became drowsy.

Orchid came back and told me, "Mr. Hua has made his decision and Ling will go to Laiyang. He has assigned you to the testing workshop." I would take over Ling's current task and would start my training as a member of the testing workshop right away.

Orchid said gloomily, "That is what you asked for; the testing group people are not easy to deal with."

I started having second thoughts. Ling had told us there were all sorts of people in the testing workshop. It teemed with contradictions; it was a snake pit and people there were difficult to get along with. However, it was done, the decision had been made. I wondered, "Are people there going to disdain me?"

It would remind people that I am an American daughter and for that reason hadn't been chosen this time. I hated myself for always worrying about what other people thought of me. Tomorrow I would work at the testing workshop. I told myself to follow Chairman Mao's famous quotation: "be modest and prudent; guard against arrogance and rashness" (谦虚，谨慎，戒骄，戒躁). I told myself to do more and say less, never argue with others unnecessarily. I wanted to be a "worldly-wise man," who remained reticent about other people's affairs and refuse to make any comment on matters that didn't concern me.

I was preparing for a battle of self-preservation. I would rather be a blockhead than climb the rankings. I had lost all the innocence of a young person. I had become a good apprentice of Chang Gong. I tried to grind myself into a round person. I thought Ling would be happy to go to Laiyang. She once told me that she would love to sightsee in Shandong. It turned out that Ling wasn't interested for the obvious reason — Yan!

I started my job training. I was depressed, but had to act like I enjoyed everything that was presented to me. The weather seemed to have the same dim mood. It started drizzling. There was a stone stuck in my heart, and my heart was heavy. It was the first time I asked God, "I came to this world the same as everyone else. Why are you so unfair to me?"

Incredibly, I actually dared to write in my diary. In this "Greatest Communist Country," writing complaints about your life was a big taboo, especially during this turbulent era. I wrote:

> *God, please let me breathe the free air; help me get rid of the bloodline that has shackled me since the day I was born. I so much want to free myself from these bindings that have already sucked away my youth. These bindings are solely because of my family background and not a consequence of anything I have done. I want to live according to my own ability!*

Ling and Orchid were busy preparing for their Laiyang trip. They had a meeting today. They went as a group to purchase the train tickets. Orchid invited me to go along with them to the train station, but I politely refused. I didn't belong to the group. I suddenly realized I would be alone. I would live in this dim attic by myself for more than 30 days. The three of us had been inseparable. If any one of us left, we would miss her. We were like a happy family. We spoke our mind freely to each other. We chatted cheerfully and were carefree. We didn't need to pretend, or to act. I had been so spoiled by Ling and Orchid. They shielded me from all the political affairs surrounding our workplace.

Now I had to deal with everything myself. It was scary. I decided to embroider pillowcases to pass my lonely time. After work I went to the department store to buy some fabric. Xiang offered to come with me. Xiang was a few years younger than me, but she was a sensible girl. She noted my miserable mood and offered to stay overnight after Ling and Orchid had left. I accepted her gracious offer and thanked her for her kindness.

Besides me, there was someone else also feeling sad. Yan visited us every evening. I teased him, "Since ancient times, lovers have been distressed with parting sorrows" (多情自古伤离别). Yan had thick skin. No matter how much Orchid and I teased him, he was unaffected and kept smiling. The evening before their parting day, Yan suggested we all go for a walk together. Orchid and I understood that Yan and Ling wanted to have some alone-time together, but they needed Orchid and I to escort them.

It was a comfortable spring evening. Not too cold, not too hot. It was a moonless night. A gentle, spring breeze caused our hair to sway and touch our faces. Yet we were all unhappy and unable to enjoy the walk. We slowly strolled toward the train station, and then along Guanhe Road next to the river. Guanhe Road was dark with very few street lights and people around. When we reached Guanhe Road, Orchid and I went ahead, intentionally leaving Ling and Yan to stroll together. After a while we turned away from the river along Bo Ai Road — another small, quiet street. Ling and Yan were now inseparable in their hearts. It would be really tough for them to be apart, even for a month. When we reached the intersection of Bo Ai Road and Xinghe Road, Yan went ahead alone; then Ling, Orchid, and I slowly returned to our attic. We made sure that people saw the three of us together without Yan.

Early the next morning before dawn, Ling and Orchid left for Laiyang. During the entire day, it seemed my spirit was following Ling and Orchid. They must be on the ocean vessel by now. Did Ling become seasick? I wished deep in my heart that they had smooth sailing to Laiyang.

I pondered a verse by Li Bai. *"I am sending my sad heart to accompany you together with tonight's bright moon, all the way following you to Yelang West"* (我寄愁心与明月，随君直到夜郎西).

They had just left, and I was already looking forward to their return. It was the first night I would be alone here. Xiang told me she would move in tomorrow night. Tomorrow was Sunday so she could more easily prepare to move in with me. I locked the door, turned the light off, and went to sleep pretty quickly. I had been busy in the testing workshop all day and was tired. Unfortunately, for some reason, the rats were running everywhere and were continuously making *"Zi, Zi"* sounds. They woke me up. They must have sensed that I was alone. I couldn't go back to sleep no matter how hard I tried. As I lay awake, I suddenly remembered my bad dream, when I was told a person had previously been hanged here in our attic. I was afraid and turned the light on. All night my eyes were wide open. I was afraid to go back to sleep again.

At 5 o'clock in the early morning, I got up. I mopped the attic floor and even waxed it. I washed my bedding and cleaned and tidied up our little attic. Since the day we moved in, we had never cleaned our attic so thoroughly. I was busy all day. I was sweating like it was the middle of summer. After a quick bath, Xiang arrived. I was glad that tonight I wouldn't be so scared and could, hopefully, have a good night's sleep.

People in the testing workshop seemed very nice and polite to me. Every day we had early morning assembly and political announcements. There were also political discussion meetings in the evening. During one evening meeting, Mrs. Yang said, "In our group, people like me, who have no education, must give a speech, yet those who are educated don't want to open their mouths one bit or say even one word." We, the young "labor in training," sensed her hint. We hung our heads and looked down at the floor and said nothing.

The testing coupled with the meetings kept me busy. During my spare time, I embroidered pillowcases. Gradually, my time seemed to pass faster. The testing group people seemed more interested in Ling than caring about my training or performance. Mrs. Gao was the unofficial mentor of Ling, and she kept inquiring about Ling and Yan. I couldn't believe that a high school graduate could be so nosy, so suspicious. She seemed to love to gossip. She asked me directly whether I knew anything about dating between Ling and Yan. I denied flatly, "No, I wasn't aware of anything of this kind. It must be a rumor."

Mrs. Gao believed I was an innocent bystander, and so described what they had discovered regarding Ling and Yan's love story. They had seen them walking together at night on the street. They knew they had gone to Plum Flower Park together, and so on. She sighed that Ling was too young. It was too bad Ling was dating Yan. He was really beneath her. She asked me to talk to Ling and make her aware. She acted as if she was a nice person who cared about Ling. However, in between her words, I sensed a hostility and dislike of Ling. It seemed she was jealous of Ling's Red bloodline. She even disdained Ling for her gentle disposition. I remained quiet as she revealed all these things to me. I didn't know what to say. The good thing was I had always been quiet in front of her, so she didn't suspect my resentment.

During the shift exchange period, Mrs. Yang came to the workshop to arrange personnel for the next shift. Yan happened to walk in.

Mrs. Yang said sarcastically to Yan, "Yan, these last few days, you look like you've lost a lot of weight!"

"No, it is not true. In fact, I have gained a few pounds," Yan replied carefully.

Mrs. Gao gave Yan a knowing smile. "Yan, you have lost weight so fast. It seems very strange."

Although all these slanders were nothing to do with me, I was worried for Ling. If these people thought dating was wrong, I couldn't understand why they didn't just talk to Ling. All these behind-the-scène maneuvers disturbed me. Open attacks are easier to deal with than all these hidden innuendoes. I started to blame Ling for her carelessness. Ling had grown up in a bright Red family and hadn't learned how to guard against others.

Mr. Chen was the second highest ranked official in our company and was a Communist Party member. In a morning assembly, he led the political study session. Near the end of the assembly, he suddenly declared in a serious manner, "Some people in our company think that just because they have many Communist Party members in their family, they can be arrogant and ignore all the rules."

He added, "You, young people, need to change your thinking and reform. There are many cultural contaminations around here. We need to get rid of these unhealthy tendencies."

I had a feeling he was alluding to Ling even though she was not there. After all, who else in our company had so many Communist Party members in their family? From my conversations with the top cadres, I sensed that they had an unfavorable opinion of Ling. I also suspected that our cadres thought the three of us, even though we professionally excelled, were all politically "backward elements." I became alarmed. I didn't mind being viewed as a politically "backward element"; after all people such as me could never be viewed as a "progressive element." However, I realized I had to be careful and couldn't afford to make any mistakes.

After Ling and Orchid left, Yan started to spend more time with me. Ling might have asked him to take care of me while she was away. Although Ling was kind, I was afraid of gossip and became sick and tired of him being around me all the time. Mostly I was fearful of those watchful eyes. He was Ling's boyfriend, so I had to be polite toward him. I didn't know how to tell him: "Get out of my life!" There were also other young men that visited the testing workshop while I was working. They made excuses to chat and spend time with me. Although Yan was in trouble because he was dating Ling, this also gave these young men hope that they might pursue and win my heart. However, I had no intention to get married. During those days, secret dating between young people was a sign of future marriage (许下终身). It wasn't like today where dating is driven initially by sexual attraction and viewed as a fun thing. I was paranoid about those snakes in the grass, those poisonous mouths. I reminded myself that I couldn't afford to make a mistake.

One of the young men was very daring and acted like a bully. I found him disgusting and was already cold to him. However, he wasn't the sharpest knife in the drawer and insisted on continuously visiting my workshop. If I offended him badly, I would create a future enemy, and I couldn't afford this type of enemy.

As the old saying goes, "Watch whose toes you step on, because they may belong to the person whose butt you'll need to kiss in the future."

In Chinese society, people give more leeway to boys. It was "understandable" that boys were attracted to girls. Yet for a girl, it was always viewed as her responsibility to behave like a lady. If a boy was attracted toward you because you were *frivolous*, you had behaved improperly. The girl was to blame. If there was a premarital affair, the boy could still have a bright future, be married again, and have a good family life; but the girl would be scarred and condemned as a "broken shoe" (破鞋) for life. For a girl, as the old saying goes, "a moment's error can bring a lifetime of regret" (一失足成千古恨). I was walking on a thorny path and wished Ling and Orchid were here.

I finally received a letter from Ling and Orchid. It had taken them many days to reach the military semi-conductor company. Ling said the soldiers were very nice and had been very willing to teach them all about the technology they possessed. Ling pointed out that it would benefit our mentors to adopt the style and spirit displayed by the soldiers, instead of resorting to all sorts of deceptions and innuendoes. In the letter, Orchid mentioned that during their trip, Mrs. Fong, my unofficial mentor, often praised my professional excellence, but also exhibited plenty of jealousy toward me. Orchid warned that it was easy to dodge an incoming spear, but difficult to guard against the hidden sniper. I sighed deeply, and in my reply letter, I referred to a literary quotation. "A tree that grows above the forest will be hit by the wind; mounds that are prominent at the shore will be scoured by the water flow; a person with a nobler character than others will be discredited by everyone" (木秀于林，风必摧之；堆出于岸，流必湍之；行高于人，众必非之).

I continued my letter. "I prefer to be a small tree hidden in a forest protected from the wind. Let others be the mainstay, the chief cornerstone. Let others climb the ranks. I only want to be a stone buried at the bottom of the ocean. Although I wouldn't be able to enjoy the beautiful scenery at the ocean surface, I also wouldn't be punched by the stormy waves and smashed by the hurricanes. I would rather live quietly where no one even notices my existence. True beauty comes from within."

I wrote four long pages, spouting a stream of pessimistic, philosophical feelings. I wished to escape the conflicts of this human society. I must have read too much from *Dream of the Red Chamber*. I ended the letter by citing a Tang five-character-quatrain:

一度风雨夕，几时话离别.
尺素千里去，魂魄一梦来.
A night of wind and rain, when can we be together chatting this parting?
This letter will travel thousands of miles to reach you; I am thinking of you tonight.

Ling criticized my "stand aloof from worldly strife" (与世无争) philosophy. She wrote back, "This world will not allow you to exist with this retiring, passive attitude. You shouldn't be so afraid to open your eyes and glance at the sun. Even though you don't want to confront people, you shouldn't let yourself become such a softy with the Ah-Q spirit. If someone smacks your right face, then you offer your left face. If someone snatches your coat, you also hand over your underwear."

She added, "I don't care about all the gossip and slanders. All these do not hurt me one tiny bit, not even a wisp of my hair."

She encouraged me to be strong and fight for my rights. Ling sighed, "You and I both cling too much to our feelings, yet you like to hide your feelings. There is also a touch of aloofness in you."

My friends knew me best. I had to admit that Ling's assessment of me was absolutely correct. I used to be an innocent, lively child. I was once brimming with youthful vigor. The Black bloodline had dragged me down. People say a person's temperament is inborn, but my life story proclaims otherwise: my character has evolved because of society and the environment I endured throughout my life.

Orchid indicated that I worried too much. She emphasized, "We should not be constrained by all the hypocritical etiquettes. Once you dare to do whatever you want and are ready to pay the price, then they can't do much to hurt you. They will even be afraid of you. One needs to be assertive and forceful."

Orchid added, "Don't hesitate. Hesitation will lead to nothing."

Orchid was a strong, yet steady person. Her actions were always quick, decisive, and resolute, the opposite of Ling and me who were too emotional. My best friends had sent me their most precious gifts — consolation and soulful encouragement. It was God's love, letting us live together. Please let this part of our life leave a forever indelible impression on all of us! They ended their letter with a Tang seven-character-quatrain:

君问归期未有期，
巴山夜雨涨秋池。
何当共剪西窗烛，
却话巴山夜雨时。

You asked me when I will be back, I have not yet scheduled a return date;
Tonight, Bashan is under heavy rain, autumn rains swell the pond.
When you and I are together again, trimming the wick of the western window candle;
Then I will tell you about my night at Bashan in the autumn rain.

By now I was already used to my "Robinson Island," affectionless life. Xiang was nice. We cooked together. Sometimes, she brought homemade dumplings for us to share. She treated me like her big sister. It wasn't the same as the friendship between Ling, Orchid, and me. There wasn't any poetic chemistry with Xiang. She was too young and too innocent to have these complicated feelings. It was better for her not to have those "bourgeois, intellectual" sentiments.

After Mr. Hua left for Laiyang, Mr. Chen, our second-ranked commander, had kept me busy. I was not only performing testing for my workshop; Mr. Chen also often ordered me to sort out his political documents and sometimes to write the Big Character poster for him. Mr. Chen reminded me of my high school teacher Mr. Ding. He loved to self-praise his loyalty of political movements. He bragged that he studied the thoughts of Marx and Lenin every day late at night before bed. Therefore, he left many things that were his duty for me to finish.

One day, during morning assembly, he claimed that he had seen two "labor in training" people walking together on the street at 11 o'clock last night. I guessed he hadn't been studying the thoughts of Marx and Lenin last night. I wondered what he himself was doing out late at night on the street, but no one dared ask him. As he described these two unfortunate "labor in training" people, he was so excited. Out of his mouth, it became so vivid and colorful. He held poses and imitated sounds. To my surprise, it turned out he was a comedian! He was putting on a drama show.

Afterward, people in my workshop said, these two "labor in training" could be in trouble. People commented, "If they needed to talk to each other, they could talk during the daytime. Why did they have to meet at night?"

I couldn't help asking myself inside, "During the daytime, under watchful eyes, do young boys and girls have the freedom to talk to each other?"

I didn't understand. The government allows young people to get married at 25 years of age. Many of us, the "labor in training," were at or close to 25 years of age, yet our middle-aged cadres and coworkers discouraged us from dating. I could only guess that those middle-aged men and women must have seen that their own youth had passed and were worried that their days were shortening and approaching sunset. They were jealous of the youth. They had never had freedom to date. Their own marriages were arranged. They felt that they had to force us to follow in their footsteps. They set the antiquated rules. Let those worn-out concepts follow those stale, middle-aged men and women to their graves. Let new, youthful vigor replace the old, feudalistic dark forces. History can't turn backward. Internally, I declared a war against those middle-aged coworkers. I could only think about it, though. I could never speak up. I worried about Ling. What would be the end of her love story?

The Lost Generation

During the absence of Ling and Orchid, I once met my high school classmate Chen Ming in front of the department store. I went to the store for some fabric to make a new pair of pants. To my surprise, Chen Ming was there with Xuan and Green. Chen Ming now worked for the Hujin Construction Company. Just like us, he was a "labor in training." His work involved heavy labor, but he was content. He was grateful to have a job instead of being a peasant. Chen Ming was a highly moral, kind young man. If I had been allowed to have a male friend, he would have been one of my most trusted. Xuan and Green were second graders in our high school, and they were Lin Da's friends. During our high school years, they all joined the radical "501" Rebel Group as the Cultural Revolution evolved.

After school was dismissed, Lin Da had returned to her village where her adopted parents arranged for her to marry a village official. A year ago, I visited her and she had just given birth to a baby. She was changing the baby's diaper. I didn't know what to say to her. Married life and taking care of a baby were still uncharted territory for me. I didn't know if I should congratulate her or not. Lin Da seemed to also be a little embarrassed by my visit.

Xuan and Green were sent "down to the countryside." Xuan was assigned to a village near Yiyang. She had stayed at my home twice while she traveled from Zhongzhou to her village. She had described "our dilapidated home" to Lin Da and had sneered at our poor living conditions. She complained she had to sleep on our kitchen floor while she stayed with us. After hearing these things from Lin Da, I became annoyed with Xuan and thought how ungrateful she was.

Now she had sneaked back to Zhongzhou, yet her Hukou remained in the village. I sensed the jealousy in her eyes. She inspected me from top to bottom. I dressed fancier than when I was in high school and even wore a pair of store-purchased leather shoes. When I greeted her, she didn't say a word back. She rolled her eyes and stared into the sky. She must have been asking why people such as me should receive such favorable treatment. To me, I couldn't believe how such a famous, bold general of 501 could be so childish? I smiled. It was as if I was seeing a temperamental child. I gave her a cold smile. Chen Ming later told Ling that after I went, Xuan poured out a torrent of acid rain. I sighed. I had nothing to do with her misfortune. I didn't even know her very well and didn't understand why she vented her grievances on me.

In the turmoil of the "up to the mountains and down to the countryside" movement, the parents of my friend YeYe had been placed under daily pressure from Mr. Yin's work unit and their neighborhood residential committee. They had become panic-stricken. At the same time, one of Mr. Yin's fellow workers told him that there was a young man in his neighborhood urgently searching for a wife. The young man, Mr. Zhao, was a worker in a Zhongzhou factory. The government was preparing to build a weapon defense industry in the Da Bie Mountainous region in Anhui Province. Mr. Zhao had been chosen by his factory to relocate to the Da Bie Mountainous region.

To entice workers to move from Zhongzhou city to the bleak and desolate mountainous region, the government promised a job in the same factory for the workers' wife. For unmarried young workers, like Mr. Zhao, it was obvious that finding a suitable wife in the mountainous region was not practical. In the rush of the moment, Mr. Yin decided to allow YeYe to marry Mr. Zhao. Although Da Bie Mountainous region was far from home, it was far better than letting YeYe become a hard labored, poor peasant. In the Da Bie Mountainous region, YeYe would still be entitled to government rations. In addition, the government promised her a job in the same factory as her future husband. Within a couple of weeks, YeYe had married Mr. Zhao and moved to the Da Bie Mountainous region.

Although YeYe had moved to the Da Bie Mountainous region where she had established her own life, I still maintained contact with her parents. I had tremendous respect for Mr. Yin. I sometimes brought gifts to him, such as bunches of expensive bananas. I seldom indulged in such highly priced food. Mr. and Mrs. Yin would often return the favor by sending me some home-cooked food. One day, YeYe's younger brother, KeKe, brought over a box of fried dumplings. He told me that to celebrate May Labor Day, Huayi had returned home from her village.

Huayi was YeYe's neighbor and was our friend during our high school time. During those chaotic days, we often chatted in Huayi's bedroom until the middle of the night expressing our youthful anger. She had now been sent "down to the countryside." I decided to see her. YeYe always teased Huayi that she had a round, cute, and happy face. YeYe used to claim that, because of this face, Huayi would always be happy in her future.

Unfortunately, fate had treated her harshly; at least her fortune hadn't arrived yet. Huayi looked much older. After years of working in the sun and wind, her face was dark and wrinkled. She used to be a Chatty Cathy talker with a silver tongue. She was humorous and witty. YeYe and I really enjoyed those evening talks with her. We laughed together and poured over our doubts about the chaotic Cultural Revolution. Now Huayi had changed. After her harsh life as a peasant, she had gained experience and become a prudent person. Such a loving, lively person had been worn down over time and turned into a lifeless, apathetic young woman. Chang Gong always said we should grind ourselves from "square" to "round," but this young girl had been ground into pieces by this society.

Huayi told me that her village official had arranged for her to marry a village teacher. She didn't know what to do. She mulled, "I am getting older and should marry soon. If I get married, my Hukou would forever stay with the village and there would be no chance to move back to the city. Is there really any possibility for me to return to the city?"

The future was murky and dim. She was confused and conflicted. She asked me, "Do I look much older now?"

I answered, "No, you look just like the day when we parted."

I lied to her and deceived my own conscience. She smiled a bitter, I-don't-believe-you smile. I felt I had no choice but to lie. I thought my answer was better than the truth. She asked me about my prospects for future marriage. I told her that I hoped someday to leave China for America. Marriage wasn't on my horizon at this moment. She wondered why I didn't go back home on May Labor Day. I said there wasn't any peace in my home. There were lots of family conflicts playing out. Although my family treated me well, I had many things on my mind. I didn't want to be burdened by trivial domestic matters. I admitted in front of her that I was a selfish person.

I felt so sorry for Huayi. Millions of "up to the mountain and down to the countryside" intellectual youths were suffering. I was sad and sympathetic for all my "down to the countryside" schoolmates, including Xuan, even though she felt I didn't deserve to stay in the city since I was an American daughter. All those forced "down to the countryside" intellectual youths were hopelessly seeking a better future, yet a better future seemed out of reach. I hoped that one day good fortune would shine on Huayi, and all the suffering youths could return to the city.

My Wish May Become True

Those days, my status at home had been raised. Everything about my family revolved around money. Aunt Zhen wrote to me complaining Grandmother was wasting her money. Uncle Nian had moved in with Grandma Chow in Shanghai. He had suddenly realized that Grandma Chow was using him as bait to lure more money from my parents. He asked me to write to my parents and tell them not to send money to Grandma Chow. Mother also wrote to me. Mother was angry with Grandmother. Grandmother had written to my father complaining that Aunt Zhen mistreated her and showed her no respect. Sadly, Mother had supported Aunt Zhen. She credited all our upbringing to Aunt Zhen, and I sensed Mother had an unfavorable opinion of Grandmother.

I felt it was so unfair. Grandmother had always been there for me. Grandmother was the only person who had really loved me and Xiao Mei. When we were young, she fed us and cleaned us. Even when a friend gave her a piece of candy, she was unwilling to indulge herself and always let us, the children, enjoy. To me, Grandmother was my mother. She would do anything for me, even beyond what a mother would do. As Grandmother got older and became unable to handle the household chores, Xiao Mei, San Mei, and I took over the cooking and washing. Aunt Zhen spent most of her time on her sewing machine and chatting with the neighbors. She did make a few new clothes for me and Xiao Mei. She seldom scolded Xiao Mei and me, but any affection towards us was simulated. I never felt she was truly concerned about us. The only thing she cared about was how much she could accumulate for her own cash pile.

Tears welled up in my eyes and streamed silently down my face. I began reminiscing my youth. I was thinking to write Mother and speak in defense of Grandmother. As I started holding the pen, I suddenly stopped and thought it was better not to offend Mother. In Mother's letters, reading between the lines, I never felt any love for me. To me, she was my authority. At one time I used to dream of being united with my parents and enjoying family happiness. I was so much longing for a mother's love. It seemed my innocent desire wouldn't become true. In her letters, I sensed Mother hesitated to become reunited with her two already grown-up daughters. I realized a mother's love grew gradually over the long time nurturing and caring for her young. I had no high expectations or fantasies about my mother. I anticipated there would always be a gap between us. It bothered me, but one thing stood firm. I had to leave China, no matter what.

The next day would be Sunday. Xiang would spend Sunday at her home. After the morning shift, I was off from work. I had gotten everything arranged in perfect order and, hopefully I would have a quiet, peaceful Sunday all alone. Suddenly the sound of the moving bamboo ladder disturbed me.

"Who is coming at this time?" I wondered.

It was Yan. As he climbed the ladder, he said, "I have come to give you something. It might upset you."

I was mystified and wondered what it was all about.

He handed me a telegram. *Grandmother sick; come home at once.*

I was perplexed, but not sad at first. I wasn't thinking clearly. I was numb. My thoughts frozen. When I realized Yan was still there, I politely smiled, yet inside I felt sadness start to overwhelm me.

"Are you okay?" Yan asked.

"I am fine, thank you," I answered firmly.

Yan went away. When I was alone, I couldn't stop tears from streaming down my face. I began to cry louder and louder. I cried with sorrow. I had never cried so uncontrollably. I felt so sorry for Grandmother. Guilty feelings toward Grandmother were torturing me. Aunt Zhen always said that Grandmother had such good fortune living with so many wonderful grandchildren. Aunt Zhen was a little jealous of Grandmother because she was so popular with her grandchildren. Even her own three sons were closer to Grandmother than their own mother.

I always believed Grandmother had suffered for many years. During the Japanese and Chinese war, my father, Aunt Ermay, and Uncle Nian had all left home and gone to Sichuan Province for a long eight years. After the war, Grandmother was hoping that the kids would return home, so the family could enjoy a happy-go-lucky life together. Sadly, very soon, the civil war started, and then afterwards the Communist Party took over. My father left for America and Aunt Ermay escaped to Hong Kong as a refugee. Since then, Grandmother hadn't been able to even have a fleeting glimpse of them. They were always so near to her heart, yet so far away and out of reach. When she was only in her early fifties, her husband escaped to Hong Kong and suddenly left her without warning. She often had dreams of Grandfather. She quietly endured the loneliness, hopelessly thinking about his return.

In our family, I was the one closest to her and sensed her deeply buried lonely feelings. She often mistakenly called me Ermay. She was thinking about Aunt Ermay, her oldest daughter, all the time. After more than 20 years of separation, was there any chance her daughter would return to her? She had now decided to put all her energy and hope on the next generation, her grandchildren. She cared for us. She raised us. She was the greatest, most unselfish grandmother to me.

She was getting older and unable to do physical work. As she always sighed lately: "Old age comes all too soon." Now, she lived with her old age and watched Aunt Zhen's cold face day-by-day. I was so sorry that she was quietly leaving this world with such a lonely heart. We all couldn't follow her. We all had a Godly duty to live on. We were like little birds nurtured by her. Now our wings had grown strong, and we were ready to fly. Yet we couldn't do anything to help her. We couldn't even bring her a little comfort. *I must go home at once. I must take care of her while she is on her sick bed. I owe her so much, and I must repay her for raising me.* Thousands of thoughts went through my mind. There were regrets; there were sorrows; there were sweet memories.

With two red and swollen eyes, I went to Mrs. Yang and asked for permission to take a few days off. Heaven was crying too. It sent down pouring rain. In the heavy rain, I went to buy the ticket for the next bus to Yiyang. There was only one bus per day, and the next bus was scheduled to leave the following day. I went to the department store to buy many bottles of preserved fruits. They were expensive, and I had never eaten bottled fruit. I assumed they would be good for Grandmother. Bottled fruits were only for the few very rich in China. I wanted Grandmother to have something she had never previously tasted. Grandmother had only a few teeth left and was sick. The sweet and juicy fruits might bring her appetite back. I was randomly processing all these tasks.

The next day, on the bus, I felt terribly sick. I wanted to vomit. I wanted so much to lie down. Finally, the bus stopped at Yiyang station. By that time, I had no energy left in my body. My two legs were so soft and weak. I started to slowly walk toward home. Then I remembered what I had come home for. I sped up and rushed to see Grandmother.

When I stepped inside the door, I suddenly realized the whole thing had been a fabrication! Grandmother was there eating her dinner, and she welcomed me with a loud laugh, grinning from ear to ear. "I knew you would come home soon!"

I was so exhausted and went to the bedroom to lie down. Xiao Mei followed me into the bedroom and told me: "The Public Security Bureau has agreed to let us go to America. They have given us an application form to complete."

She showed me the form. Going to America had been my wish for so many years, but somehow the sudden news didn't excite me. I wasn't happy. Years of waiting for my dream to come true, and now it seemed it had, yet I was at sea and apathetic. I was tired and went to bed. Grandmother and Aunt Zhen all came to my bedroom and offered me some food, but I had no appetite. The sudden, huge news disturbed and worried me. I would now face a new starting point and a new life. I didn't know whether that new life would be sweet or bitter. I was scared to step into the unknown. It was my own decision to pursue leaving China. Since the start of the Cultural Revolution, going to America had been my only hope. It had sustained me through the years. Like Ling, I had to drink this self-fermented cup of wine, "bottoms up," regardless of whether it would be sweet or bitter.

The next morning, I went to the photo shop to have my picture taken. The application form required a 2-inch x 2-inch picture. On the way, I couldn't help but think about the Red Flag Semi-conductor Company. The female cadres, whom I used to hate, seemed not so nasty anymore. Today, for some reason, I only remembered the good people, the happy events. I couldn't understand why I had such a conflicted and split personality. I felt like a dying person. Everything in this world became so precious and sentimental. A dying person is reluctant to leave. I knew that, in fact, I was entering my second life.

I was thinking of Ling and Orchid. At this moment, there was so much worry and anxiety entangling me. I badly needed them to untie me. Life in that small, dim, full-of-rats attic seemed so sweet, and our friendship became so important to me. I hated to leave them. I was like a young girl in love. I was thinking about them all the time and hoped they would come to me soon. I needed their encouragement, their enlightenment. They were the only people who could spur me forward.

My cousins were excited. Da Di and Xiao Di were both home. During the evening, Xiao Di was playing a *Hugin* and Da Di was blowing a flute. Da Di couldn't play the flute very well. I grabbed the flute and started to play. I hadn't played the flute since high school. I was reminiscing about my high school life and wished I could have left this country much earlier, when I was a young, vigorous girl. At that age, I might have been able to achieve some goals while I was abroad. Now at age 25, I felt I was too old. I had forgotten what I learned in high school. I probably wouldn't be able to accomplish anything. In America, I would be a chicken among the phoenixes — unmatched. Worry grabbed my heart again.

Little Tiger, my youngest cousin, was extremely excited. He wanted to play the *Hugin*, but Xiao Di didn't let him. He asked me for the flute, but I wouldn't give it to him. He finally found a bamboo tube. He pasted some waxed paper on one end of the bamboo tube and started blowing into the tube. He made a loud and funny noise. He was so cute and lovable. Suddenly, the whole family bustled with excitement and was full of joy. If it wasn't for the unceasing quarrels between Grandmother and Aunt Zhen, it would be such a happy and wonderful family. Grandmother and Aunt Zhen both came to me complaining about each other. All the complaints were focused on money. It seemed Aunt Zhen never had enough money. Suddenly, I felt sick and tired of all this nonsense again.

The photo shop delivered the pictures to us. Xiao Mei and I went to the Public Security Bureau right away. The head of the Public Security Bureau received us. It was the first time for us to have a formal talk with such an important government official. He was extremely polite.

He said, "Our local government has decided to let you go abroad. We will send your application to the central government. We don't know whether the central government will approve or not. We also don't know when the central government will make a decision."

However, I felt he was acting out a drama. Letting us go abroad was a decision made from the top down. The local government wouldn't dare to take the initiative on such a decision.

He continued. "I hope you both will not be upset by this process and will prepare yourselves for whatever the outcome. You should continue your good work for your companies."

He repeatedly explained why the government discriminated against people who had foreign connections. "It is good for our country. We should all take the general public interest into account. I hope you understand the government situation. You should be a good citizen when you live in our motherland, and also, you should be an overseas Chinese who loves her motherland when you live abroad."

Anyway, he had said what the head of the Public Security Bureau was supposed to say. He reconfirmed the information on our application form. He also asked for another two pictures from us. He walked us to the door with unusual courtesy.

We went to the photo shop again to take another picture. The photo shop was busy. After a lot of persuasion and begging, the photo shop finally agreed they would get the photos ready after another week. Afterward, Xiao Mei returned to her workplace. I wrote a letter to Mother explaining what had happened. I also wrote to Mother's cousin, Mr. Lou, who lived at Hangzhou. Mr. Lou had written to Mother explaining that Mother's 16 ounces (9 *liang*) of gold under his care had been confiscated by the government during the "Destroy the Four Olds" movement. After Nixon's China visit, it was agreed that if any confiscated property belonged to overseas Chinese, then the overseas Chinese could reclaim the property. Mother wanted us to bring the gold to her when we came to America. I wrote to Mr. Lou about Mother's desire and the possibility that we might leave China for America. I arranged for Aunt Zhen to pick up our pictures and deliver them to the Public Security Bureau. I had sorted out all the necessary things, and so was ready to return to Zhongzhou. I was hoping that Ling and Orchid would also be back in Zhongzhou, because I wanted

290

to urgently talk to them. I had missed them so much. I purchased a bus ticket for the next day.

Grandmother became so quiet when she heard I was leaving. Grandmother seldom showed her sad feelings, but every time when I left her for school or work, she was always so quiet. She spoke to no one. Sometimes I noted she was looking at me and wiping her tears. A deep sense of sorrow and guilt grabbed me. We both hid our complicated feelings toward each other. When I was young, Grandmother used to call me "my sweetheart" (心肝宝贝). Now we both avoided expressing our love for each other. I had thousands of words to say to Grandmother, yet I refused to say a word. I swallowed the bitter water quietly.

Grandmother had decided a long time ago that, at her age, she would rather stay in China than go with us. She would rather die in China and be buried in Lee's graveyard than travel to a foreign land. I also sensed that Grandmother didn't wish to live with my mother, and I suspect my mother had a similar thought.

I should be a dutiful granddaughter, yet I couldn't sacrifice my future for Grandmother. Our parting was inevitable now. As I thought about separating from Grandmother, I realized that it was very likely parting forever. In 1972, no one thought that, after leaving China, you would ever return again. It was like escaping from a tiger's den. The guilty feeling toward Grandmother speared my heart; my heart was bleeding.

I was so selfish; to escape Aunt Zhen's unceasing complaints about money, to avoid seeing Grandmother's sorrowful tears, I ran away from my home, my hometown. That home, that hometown brought me up for more than 20 years, yet I would leave all behind. The next day, I took the bus back to Zhongzhou. Aunt Zhen offered to walk me to the bus station. She never used to walk me to the bus station. I refused politely and firmly. Once I got outside Yiyang town, I breathed deeply. It seemed to be my last gasp. I inhaled a lungful. I looked around. It seemed my last glance.

Finally, I Reveal My Secret

Back at my workplace, I wanted myself to be laser focused on studying English. I couldn't calm down. My butt wouldn't stick to the chair for one minute. I was preoccupied with so many things. I continued to embroider pillowcases instead of studying English. I was looking forward to the return of Ling and Orchid. I was itching to tell them I might leave China for America soon. They were my best friends and confidants, yet I had kept a big secret from them. At that time, pursuing travel abroad was a big taboo. Now was the time for me to share the news and excitement. Although I wasn't a hundred percent certain that I would get permission, I was dying to tell them.

The people that went to Laiyang returned. They told me that Ling and Orchid had gone home to Wenjiang and would be back by Monday or Tuesday. I was so happy anticipating their return. Monday came, and Ling and Orchid still didn't show up. Yan informed me that Ling might go to Beijing. I hoped Ling wouldn't go to Beijing, as the days of us living together were numbered.

Tonight, we would have a companywide meeting, and so I assumed the afternoon political study in our workshop had been cancelled. I was on the second shift and at 2:30 I headed for work. I found everybody was already there, and political study was still being held. Mrs. Yang wasn't happy with me. She said in front of my coworkers: "Even if you are assigned to the second shift, you are still required to come early and participate in the political study. Don't try to take advantage."

My coworkers tried to help me out and gave her the excuse that I didn't know there was an afternoon study session. It was sad to live in China. People ordered you around and shouted at you like you were their slaves. I had to bite my lip and bury the anger inside.

It looked as if the political winds were blowing again. Mr. Chen gave a lengthy speech. Unfortunately for him, his "enthusiastic and earnest" words were in vain. People were only half listening to his empty talk. Their hearts were not there. To him, any little misconduct was an act against the Communist Party. If he was in charge of the law enforcement agency, 80% of the Chinese people would be found guilty for doing nothing. Millions would be sent to the execution ground. In fact, he was the one doing nothing for the country besides speaking empty words, yet he yelled at us and accused us of being lazy. What a world we were living in!

After the meeting, matters got worse. Mr. Chen asked me to write a report on "Criticize only pursuing professional excellence and ignoring political study" (只专不红, *Zhǐ zhuān bù hóng*). I sensed his intention. I had been targeted again. I was already sick of this political clown. I bravely refused his task. I gave vent to my anger, gambling that I would be leaving soon. It was a dangerous move.

That evening, Ling and Orchid returned. We were so excited. We went to the evening companywide meeting together. We had so much to pour out to each other. We couldn't wait until the end of the meeting. That night, we chatted until 3 o'clock in the morning. I couldn't believe we had so much to say to each other.

Ling and Orchid were happy that I might have an opportunity to go abroad. They suggested that I should pursue a university education, which had been my dream since middle school. I hoped there would be a university opportunity for me in America. I thought a university diploma would improve my standing in a foreign land in terms of culture and knowledge. I wondered whether my parents would support the cost of my university dream, especially my mother. I had begged her so many times and asked her to help us to leave China. She probably felt she had already done enough for us, rushing around asking for permission to leave China. After receiving an inch, I probably shouldn't ask for a mile.

I had a dream now. I would pursue literature and writing. I felt I had a moral responsibility to let people in the world know what I had experienced, what I had seen and heard. It would enlighten mankind and reveal the tragedy of dictatorship. I wanted to write a book.

Ling and Orchid encouraged me to study science or engineering. They told me that I was so strong in Math, Physics and Chemistry, I would only need a quick review of what I had learned in school, and I would excel again.

After years of a zigzag life, I had been torn apart and felt worn out. I had lost my ambition to pursue scientific work. When I was a child, I had admired those famous scientists, such as Newton and Marie Curie. I hoped that when I grew up, I would contribute my entire life to science, just like them. Now I had become realistic. There was no chance for me to become a scientist or an engineer. I doubted my ability to pick up science subjects and excel again. I sighed. The future was unknown. The only thing left for me was fear of the unknown and a conflicted mind. Let fate guide me through my future. Go with my fate!

A few days ago, at one of the morning political study assemblies, Mrs. Yang had announced a new safety rule. All girls' braids had to be cut off. My braids had been with me through most of my life. My braids were so short that I hadn't thought they were a safety issue. I tucked my resentment of all those hypocritical rules inside me, so I decided to keep my braids and wait and see.

However, Mrs. Yang kept asking me when I was going to have a haircut. Today, she talked to me directly. "Xiao Lee, I announced many days ago that everyone should have their braids cut off. You seem to never listen!"

I smiled. "My braids are so short. I didn't think there is a safety issue."

Mrs. Yang immediately scolded me. "It is the rule."

"Okay, I will cut them right away," I answered promptly.

The next day, we all went to the hair salon to get a haircut. My hair was cut to ear length. We looked at each other and laughed loudly. We were three little boys now. In this world, it seemed that everyone was only allowed to walk in one direction. Independent of whether this direction would get you to your objective or not, you had to follow the crowd. Otherwise, you would be broken into pieces. When people finally realized they were walking in the wrong direction, everyone would turn around, and then you had to follow the people turning back. Following the crowd would take much longer to get to where you wanted to go, but at least you wouldn't be killed. This was the only way of life for everyone in China.

As I came back from the hair salon for my work shift, I heard loud laughing and chatting from the wafer-processing workshop. The female cadres were very thick with each other. There was no rule or law for them to follow. If it was us, we would be in trouble. Mrs. Yang was the loudest. She continuously joked around shamelessly. No one dared say a word to stop them. After all, it was a workshop and a scheduled work period. The female cadres were not afraid of anyone. As the Chinese proverb goes: "Allow only the officials to set a fire, do not allow the citizens to light candles."

Those cadres continued gossiping about Yan and Ling. Now they criticized Ling as being "too cheap"; she had sold herself for too low a price. Yan wasn't good enough for her. It was a poor match. Good match or not, it really wasn't their business. If Ling dumped Yan, they would criticize Ling for deluding the poor and bending to please the rich. People's lips can flip back and forth easily.

Under all the external pressure, Ling started having doubts herself, but she declared, "At this stage, breaking my promise to Yan would be immoral."

She sighed helplessly. "Living is like a dream. Whether it is a good or bad dream, one must keep dreaming. Let it be."

Orchid and I were thinking Ling had begun to lose her senses. If she had any doubt about such an important commitment, she shouldn't continue.

Ling said, "I already considered my future to be dim. If the worst comes, I could always jump into Huangpu River!"

I thought what Ling said was inconceivable. I shouted at her, "Are you really determined to create a tragedy for yourself? Do you intentionally follow Anna Karenina as your life model? Normally, people fall in love to experience eternal happiness together. Yet you are preparing to jump into the Huangpu River. Knowing there are tigers on that mountain, you still climb it."

Ling was burning with all her conflicted emotions. She couldn't stop crying.

The next day, Ling invited me to visit Yan's home. Ling told me that Yan's mom was a simpleminded and kind person and his father was a seventh-grade machinery fitter. Ling wanted me to meet Yan's mom and

295

dad. Yan's parents were extremely nice to us. They were typical workers, a Red class family.

Although Ling had told me that Yan's mom was a simpleminded woman, she held her composure. Even though her supposed future daughter-in-law was from a high official's family and had graduated from Jiangsu Zhongzhou High School, a future mother-in-law surely shouldn't lose her high ground as a family elder. From a spectator's point of view, she was a typical uneducated, traditional woman, yet a shrewd and keen-witted one. She knew Ling was a good catch for her son.

After returning from Yan's home I saw Orchid chatting with the equipment workshop people, and I joined in. I used to get along with the equipment workshop people very well. I sometimes helped them with their documentation work when Ling and Orchid were in Laiyang. Strangely, they suddenly were very cold toward me and totally ignored me. I was bothered. Was it because I had visited Yan's home? They were just a bunch of small-minded people. "Who cares?" I said to myself.

Since I hadn't received permission to leave for America, I continued my work as usual. However, my inborn, forthright temperament, which had long been suppressed, started to crop up. Our rebellion and hatred toward the female cadres became obvious. Mrs. Yang was determined to knock down our "arrogance."

During lunch hour, Mr. Hua came to us and asked us to return the company-owned water thermoses. Someone had reported we were using the company-owned thermoses and electric hot plates. Although we returned the items belonging to the company, we were furious. For Pete's sake, we were living in the company. Why couldn't we use company stuff? We felt we deserved better accommodation from our company. Mr. Hua had promised us that he would give us a better living space after the new building was completed. Yet today, a year later, we were still stuck in this little dim attic. No workers should live under such poor conditions permanently.

We thought to ourselves, *There's no universal love in this place. People are unkind and mean-spirited.*

We felt people should be sympathetic to us, instead of being so hypercritical. We were the true proletariat, owning nothing. We were young and immature. We vowed to dig out the informer and have our revenge. We cursed those female cadres, hoping they would have an ominous future. "One who does not seek revenge against injustice is not a gentleman!" (有仇不报非君子), *Count of Monte Cristo*!

That afternoon Mr. Hua came up to our attic to check whether there were any more company-owned thermoses in our attic! Our attic was a mess. The place was so small. Our bedding and personal stuff were piled up and scattered across the entire attic floor. You could hardly find space to step into our room. Anyone who saw this predicament would have compassion. We were angry. We felt we couldn't be silent any longer. Like a volcanic eruption, we suddenly disgorged our anger and complained about the mistreatment we had endured from the female cadres.

While we were complaining, suddenly Mrs. Sheng started screaming downstairs. She wanted Mr. Hua to sort out a family dispute. Mrs. Sheng was a female cadre, and her husband also worked for our company. She was having a fight with her husband. She looked like she had just been pulled out of muddy water. Her face was covered with tears and mud. Mrs. Sheng wanted Mr. Hua to judge who was to blame, she or her husband. What a show! We sniggered that such a private matter between husband and wife had been brought into the open. Was this the kind of behavior we should follow? Later, we found the name of the informer. As we guessed, it was Mrs. Yang. We swore we would let Mrs. Yang swallow her own poison someday.

The next day we worked on the second shift, so, in the morning, we bought some vegetables from the market and cooked lunch in the kitchen. Mr. Hua had taken away our electric hot plate, so we had lost that convenience. Using the big stove in the kitchen was a hassle. We had to chop the wood and set a fire in the pit under the big wok. The administrative and accounting office people seemed idle. They all gathered in the kitchen, and everyone tried to get a word in. In a short time, the kitchen was seething with excitement. Mr. Hua was there too. They seemed very nice and were concerned about our living conditions. Maybe our complaint to Mr. Hua had aroused their compassion.

Mrs. Yang seemed unable to give up on us. Today she went to Mr. Hua again and suggested that, if we had spare time, we should help other workshops instead of being idle. The problem was she was idle herself. Should we follow her and go to different workshops to gossip and make fun of each other? We didn't understand why Mr. Hua even listened to her. Revenge will follow the trail of evil. During the next evening meeting, Mrs. Yang was more than 10 minutes late.

Mr. Hua asked, "Where is Mrs. Yang?"

We all shouted, "We haven't seen her yet!"

All the "labor in training" were smiling happily. We had mocking smiles and a twinkle in our eyes. We had become mischievous imps.

Good-bye, My Closest Friends

I received a letter from Xiao Mei. She said that the application to America still hadn't been submitted by the Public Security Bureau. They needed information about the exit city and travel plan. During those days, there was no diplomatic relationship between China and the US, and there were no direct flights from China to America. It was the first time for our local government to process a permit for foreign travel. The problem was we also had no answers to their questions. The Public Security Bureau suggested we write to the Shanghai International Travel Agency (a government-run agency) to obtain the necessary information. I wrote a letter to the Shanghai International Travel Agency and felt worrisome.

Finally, I also received a letter from Mother. I didn't realize going to America was so complicated. It appeared there were still plenty of difficulties ahead of us. Mother said that after leaving China, we wouldn't be able to travel directly to America. We had to stay in Hong Kong for a while and apply for an immigration visa to America. The process could take many months. Mother and Father had already arranged a family for us to stay with in Hong Kong. It wasn't Aunt Ermay's home. I wondered why.

From the movies and novels available in Communist China at this time, I thought Hong Kong to be a place of worldly temptation, a Vanity Fair. The idea of living in Hong Kong scared me. There must be differences between real life in Hong Kong and the exaggerated descriptions in novels. Oh, well, let fate decide everything. One can only pray for peace and happiness from heaven, God's will. I comforted myself.

At night, I expressed my concerns to Ling and Orchid. Together, we imagined all possible scenarios and assessed all the difficulties that might lie ahead for me. Yet we had no idea how the people in the world outside of China actually lived. We were young and full of hope. Soon the conversation became more positive. Again, they encouraged me to pursue a university education and have a career in scientific research. They said I should do something good for the world. Scientific research was a highly respected, unsullied contribution to the human race.

I, myself, was more pessimistic. Scientific work must proceed systematically. My golden age had already passed. Six years of my youth had been lost since the start of the Cultural Revolution. During that period, I had never even touched the subjects of Math, Physics, and Chemistry. I thought it was similar to an ignored, uncultivated garden that used to be beautiful. After years of corrosion by destructive chemicals, the evergreen pine trees and beautiful flowers could no longer be grown on this wasteland. Doing scientific research had been my childhood dream. I lamented, "My childhood hopes and dreams had been a delusion. I am not living in utopia anymore."

Summer had returned. Ling and I were working in the testing workshop on the second shift. It was a hot, humid day. I was sweating like a pig, and my shirt was wet. I told Ling that I was going to have a quick wash and change. When I returned, Mr. Hua called me to his office. Why did he call me? Was it because our revenge toward Mrs. Yang had been too obvious, or had someone reported me sneaking out during work hours? I hurried up and went to see Mr. Hua.

The conversation seemed to scatter around randomly and be of no importance. I didn't understand the purpose of the meeting. Finally, Mr. Hua showed me a letter from the Shanghai International Travel Agency. It turned out, instead of replying directly to me, the agency had sent the information to our company. They let our company know that I intended to travel overseas. I didn't realize that the agency spied for our government.

Since my intention had already been revealed, I had to tell Mr. Hua everything. I blamed my parents in America for pushing the Yiyang Public Security Bureau to grant me permission to go to America. The Public Security Bureau was already processing the permission. They asked me to write to the Shanghai International Travel Agency for certain information that they needed for my application. This sudden news shocked Mr. Hua. He had never heard of a Public Security Bureau processing a permit to travel overseas. Since the start of the Cultural Revolution, no one had been allowed to leave China. In a place like Zhongzhou, there was no such thing as travel to America.

After experiencing all the political ups and downs during a life of hardship, I had become toughened. I continued my work calmly. That night I wrote a letter to the Yiyang Public Security Bureau. I let them know that we would exit at Shenzhen to Hong Kong first, and then from Hong Kong to America. I also politely urged them to speed up the process.

Ling was still in misery. These days she got angry very easily. She seemed to hold some sort of resentment against Orchid and me. *Just because you have a boyfriend, you can dump your other friends?* I was bothered by Ling's attitude toward us. *Are Orchid and I too conventional on the issue of their dating?* I blamed Yan. He must have said something that stirred Ling's anger toward us. The three of us had been living happily together. Then after Yan was added, our friendship became complicated. Ling was laden with anxiety, but she seemed to keep her secrets away from us. She was suffering. We seemed to have become an extra burden to avoid. What was wrong with her? Was there a secret she couldn't reveal to us? Did her family find out she was dating Yan? Had her family intervened? I was worried for her.

At the same time, I received a letter from YeYe. As usual, the letter she sent me was within the letter she sent to her parents, and her parents then handed it to me. Since YeYe worked for a weaponry factory in the Da Bie Mountainous region in Anhui Province, she never contacted me directly. A few weeks ago, I told Mr. Yin that I might leave China and go to America. YeYe wrote to congratulate me on my new journey and wish me the best for a beautiful future. She only wrote a few words and seemed very dry. Oh, well, it seemed my friendship with YeYe had ended a long time ago.

Thinking about it, I realized that friendship is driven by our feelings toward each other brewed by frequent contact. If you share a life together, you have a common purpose, common struggle, and common language, you will build feelings toward each other, regardless of whether they are good or bad feelings. When you live in separate corners of the world, you have your own life to pursue, your own likes or dislikes, and you struggle for your own survival. In these circumstances, friendships will end. Your

301

image will fade from your friend's mind. It's just like the death of a friend. The only difference is, in one situation friendship disappears gradually; in the other, there is a sudden loss that makes you sad. The dearest friendship between the three of us in Zhongzhou looked likely to disappear soon. What sadness! Thinking of Ling's recent unfriendliness, I sighed. "Take things philosophically. Nothing in this world is worth my concern."

Our company fell into dire straits again. During the hot testing of diode rectifiers, the leaky current kept increasing. We had failed again. Our cadres were very worried. We were at a critical juncture. Was it time to end the mission of the Red Flag Semi-conductor Company? Was it God's will that allowed the three of us to be together and enjoy an indelible friendship for over a year, and then allow it to dismantle itself following my departure? It was God letting us experience a modern "Prospect Garden" life, and then sending us toward another unknown. Life in the Red Flag Semi-conductor Company flowed slowly. People were busy with their daily trifles. They were still joking, gossiping.

I was quietly waiting — waiting anxiously day and night for my verdict. I was reminiscing yesterday, reluctant to part with today, and longing for a sunny tomorrow. The days passed incredibly slowly and were profoundly dull. Waiting is always hard. Those days I worked the night shift. Most of the time, I was ordered to write the Big Character posters. The political wind never stopped blowing. Summer was so hot and humid. I had lost my appetite and felt exhausted. I no longer wrote in my diary about daily life. I only jotted down some quotes from books that resonated with me, or inked-in a short statement about what I had seen or heard during work.

I wrote, *If you ask me how much my anxiety has increased, just see the over brimming river flowing east!* (问君能有几多愁，恰似一江春水向东流).

On July 27, 1972, I received a telegram asking me to return home immediately. The government had granted us a passport to go to Hong Kong. I went to say good-bye to YeYe's parents. At the same time, I picked up the 200 Yuan that I had asked them to keep for me from my high school days during the Destroy the Four Olds movement. I thought it would be important to have some money while I was in an unfamiliar place like Hong Kong. YeYe's parents asked me to write them once I settled in Hong Kong, so that they didn't need to worry about me. YeYe's parents were always very nice to me. I thanked them for their kindness.

I came back to our little attic and packed up my belongings in a hurry. "Storms could gather without warning" (天有不测风云). Anything could happen. It was an opportunity to escape the tiger's den. While I was packing, I saw my diary under my pillow. I hadn't written anything for almost a month. Sadly, I had to say good-bye to my diary forever. It would be unwise to take this diary with me as I passed through checkpoints. I had once hoped this diary would be a source of enlightenment and inspiration for my future life and work. I once wished it could also be a guide for a book. Especially lately I had used Balzac's hand-notes style. I hoped every sentence in my diary would be a reflection of a whole event or the portrayal of a person, just like a drop of water can reflect the entire sun. It was so regrettable that I couldn't bring it with me.

The next day, Ling and Orchid walked with me to the bus station. Ling gave me a red wallet. She told me that every time I used this wallet, it would remind me of our friendship. We waved good-bye and tears welled up in our eyes.

Farewell

Although the expiration date on my passport was August 31, we decided to leave as soon as possible. I only stayed at home for a few days.

Grandmother knew clearly it would be the last time she would see me and Xiao Mei, the two granddaughters that were spoon-fed by her. She raised and nurtured us for more than 20 years. We, just like my father and Aunt Ermay, would leave her forever. Nothing could be more miserable than to part forever. The entire household seemed immersed in sad thoughts. Aunt Zhen and Grandmother didn't complain about each other. Everybody understood, it would be the last time Xiao Mei and I would be with them. We would never see each other again. Even Little Tiger was quiet. Although America and China were on the same Earth, we would be separated as if it were Earth and heaven, life and death.

Aunt Zhen would accompany us to Guangzhou. We would go to Shanghai first, and then go to Guangzhou by train. We would stop at Hangzhou to retrieve Mother's gold from the local government. From Yiyang to Shanghai, we needed to take a bus to Wuxi, and then take a train ride to Shanghai.

I missed Ling and Orchid so much. I was determined to see them again. Instead of taking a bus to Wuxi, I took a bus to Zhongzhou, then from Zhongzhou I went to Shanghai the next day. I seemed even closer to Ling and Orchid than to Grandmother. I left home one day earlier than Aunt Zhen and Xiao Mei. Aunt Zhen and Little Tiger took me to the bus station.

Grandmother leaned on the door, watching me walk away with tears in her eyes. Grandmother suddenly looked so frail and old with completely white hair and shrinking stature. She was languishing. My vision became murky. My eyes were misty with tears. I turned my head and walked away. It was my lifetime regret that I didn't spend my last night with

Grandmother instead of staying with my friends. I hadn't said a nice word to Grandmother. I took her for granted. I didn't thank her for raising me. We quietly walked to the bus station. Little Tiger cried when I said goodbye to him.

I walked into the Red Flag Semi-conductor Company for the last time, where I was greeted by friendly coworkers. I would no longer be their competitor. I had become irrelevant to them. I would soon be wiped out from their world.

Mrs. Yang was friendly. She said, "Xiao Lee, if you were going to the Soviet Union, we would hold a going-away party for you."

I politely thanked her. She was so ignorant. She didn't realize that Chairman Mao hated the Soviet Union even more than he hated America.

That night, the three of us were very quiet. We were no longer talkative. We were all immersed in deep thoughts. Probably we were all thinking about our own future, our own destiny. Ling and Orchid took me to the train station the next day. This time, there were no tears, not even more words. Words couldn't express our feelings. We stood quietly for a few seconds. Ling suddenly stepped up and held my hands. She said bravely and firmly, "Write to me!"

Does she really mean it? She could be condemned for having a foreign friend, I thought.

I suddenly realized I might never see them again. I burst into tears. I nodded my head, waved my hand, and swiftly walked toward the station gate.

I met Aunt Zhen and Xiao Mei at Aunt Phoenix's place in Shanghai. Wu Nai Nai was back from visiting her niece's village. She remembered the day I walked her to her niece's home in the sweltering heat. She didn't know that, after I returned, I had heat exhaustion and the sickness saved me from "up to the mountains and down to the countryside." She was cheerful and cooked us a nice dinner.

Under Mother's instructions, we should only bring a couple of changing clothes. All the clothes worn in China were not suitable in Hong Kong. Over the last few years, I had gathered quite a few books such as, of course, the *Dream of the Red Chamber*, together with the *Three Hundred Tang Poems*, the *Song Lyrics Collection*, books on Chinese calligraphy, and even a collection of the works of Shakespeare. Grandmother knew I loved my books. Every time my distant cousins from God Pond Valley visited us, Grandmother made sure they did not touch my books. It was regrettable that I couldn't bring them with me.

Xiao Mei and I only carried small, homemade, cotton fabric book bags. At the last minute, I stuck in a thin *Chinese Herbal Medicine Handbook* that had recently been published for the Barefoot Doctors. On the first page, there were many quotations from Mao. I thought this book wouldn't have any trouble passing the checkpoint. Aunt Phoenix thought we looked so countrified, uncouth. She bought us each a more fashionable shoulder bag as a going-away gift to replace the homemade book bag.

The next day we took a train to Hangzhou. We stayed with Mr. Lou for a couple of days and waited for the local government to return Mother's gold. We also met Aunt Wei's husband and her two boys at Hangzhou. One boy was only a toddler, while the older boy was approaching his teenage years. Although no one mentioned Aunt Wei, seeing her two motherless boys was very sad. Aunt Wei's suicide gave me the courage and strength to leave China for America. Aunt Wei's suicide was also a fatal mental blow to her older son, who later killed himself before reaching adulthood. The family was bereaved, ruined.

Finally, the Hangzhou local government processed our request to return Mother's 9 *liang* of gold. When we arrived there, we were told that, by law, no one could own gold. They only gave us 900 Yuan instead of 9 *liang* of gold. They told us that according to our government one *liang* of gold was only worth 100 Yuan. Even though my mother was an American citizen, she still had to obey Chinese law and so could not own gold.

We reached Guangzhou in the middle of the morning. We went to the currency exchange window to convert Chinese Yuan into Hong Kong dollars. Unfortunately, by government law, each exiting passenger was only allowed to carry 50 Hong Kong dollars. With the 900 Yuan from the Hangzhou government, plus my own savings of more than 300 Yuan, I thought this would have provided some sort of cushion to cover any difficulties we might face in Hong Kong. We had to surrender all the extra cash to Aunt Zhen. Xiao Mei had also saved quite an amount of money. Aunt Zhen got a windfall! Since our youth, Xiao Mei and I had always spent money carefully and had never indulged ourselves. We felt we had mistreated ourselves, and so, that night we stayed in a reasonably expensive (by a poor girl's standard) hotel without bed bugs! We also had dinner at a restaurant located in a garden. On the way back to the hotel, we decided to buy a pineapple. We had never seen a pineapple before. We didn't know how to eat it and discovered the pineapple core was hard and inedible.

The next day we took a train to Shenzhen. This train was special; only local peasants and people holding an exit passport were allowed onboard. We said good-bye to Aunt Zhen at Guangzhou train station. I was never very close or tremendously attached to Aunt Zhen, yet for all the times we were on the same sinking ship, it was sad to say farewell. We had spent so many tough times together. Aunt Zhen must have also felt sad after seeing us grow up from babies. Now we would part forever. She must have felt a loss.

I stepped into the train and gazed back at the station. I suddenly felt I was at a loss. I was leaving the world I knew behind. I seemed to be stepping into a cave. Confronting me was a world of darkness and unknown.

Farewell, my grandmother!

Farewell, my friends!

Farewell, my motherland!

Acknowledgments

English is not my native language. When I stepped onto American soil, I was unable to understand or pronounce the simplest of English phrases, such as "How are you?" Writing this book was a tough, almost overwhelming, challenge. Without my husband's help and support, this manuscript would probably still be sitting on my computer. During the writing process, we self-edited this book together to correct typos and improve the overall phrasing, so that the content accurately expressed my thoughts. My husband also designed the book cover. His patience and encouragement during the entire process enabled me to complete this book. Thank you, Tony.

When I finished the first draft, I sent a portion of the book to my daughter Carol. Her encouragement at that time was one of the driving forces behind my completion of this book. Thank you, Carol!

I often used the "Google Translate" App. I thank "Google" for the development of such a useful App. I would also like to acknowledge extensive use of "Wikipedia" - it provided a rich resource for which I am truly grateful.

About the Author

Dr. Ann Lee Peebles was born in Nanjing, Jiangsu Province, China, in 1947. Her father moved to America in 1948 to attend graduate school. Her mother followed her husband in 1950. She and her sister were left in China under the care of their grandmother. In 1951, during the Campaign to Suppress Counter-revolutionaries, her family was condemned as an anti-revolutionary family and came under siege. She lived through a tough childhood as her family endured untold suffering.

She was called an "American daughter" and was discriminated against by the Communist government and society in general. During the Cultural Revolution, she was condemned as a "Black Bastard" (黑崽子).

1972: she was allowed to leave China; 1973: she arrived in America and reunited with her parents. She initially worked as a house-cleaning lady and afterwards as a nurse assistant in various convalescent homes. This allowed her to attend college and independently support herself.

1975: she received a California State scholarship and attended the UCLA School of Engineering. She received her BS, Master's, and PhD degrees in Electrical Engineering from UCLA.

1981: she was named as a UCLA Graduate Woman of the Year. 1982: she was honored as one of the Outstanding Young Women of America; she also received the Outstanding PhD Candidate award at UCLA.

After her PhD graduation in 1982, she worked for the Aerospace and Defense Industry in Southern California. During her tenure, she received many US and European Invention Patent awards.

Made in the USA
Las Vegas, NV
14 November 2020

10893930R10189